MW00713498

THE NEUROSIS OF
PSYCHOLOGY

SPRING JOURNAL BOOKS
STUDIES IN ARCHETYPAL PSYCHOLOGY SERIES

Series Editor
GREG MOGENSON

OTHER TITLES IN THE SERIES

DIALECTICS & ANALYTICAL PSYCHOLOGY:
THE EL CAPITAN CANYON SEMINAR
Wolfgang Giegerich, David L. Miller, Greg Mogenson

RAIDS ON THE UNTHINKABLE:
FREUDIAN *AND* JUNGIAN PSYCHOANALYSES
Paul Kugler

NORTHERN GNOSIS: THOR, BALDR, AND THE VOLSUNGS IN THE
THOUGHT OF JUNG AND FREUD
Greg Mogenson

THE NEUROSIS OF PSYCHOLOGY

PRIMARY PAPERS TOWARDS A CRITICAL PSYCHOLOGY

COLLECTED ENGLISH PAPERS
VOLUME ONE

WOLFGANG GIEGERICH

Spring Journal Books
New Orleans, Louisiana

© 2005 by Wolfgang Giegerich.
All rights reserved.

Published by
Spring Journal, Inc.;
627 Ursulines Street #7
New Orleans, Louisiana 70116
Tel.: (504) 524-5117
Fax: (504) 558-0088
Website: www.springjournalandbooks.com

Cover design by
Michael Mendis

Printed in Canada.
Text printed on acidfree paper.

Library in Congress Cataloging in Publication Data
Pending

Contents

Acknowledgments vii

Sources and Abbreviations ix

Foreword xi

Introduction 1

CHAPTER ONE: Ontology vs. Phylogeny? A Fundamental
Critique of Erich Neumann's Analytical Psychology 19

CHAPTER TWO: On the Neurosis of Psychology or
the Third of the Two 41

CHAPTER THREE: The Leap After the Throw: On
'Catching up With' Projections and on the Origin
of Psychology 69

CHAPTER FOUR: No Alibi! Comments on "The
Autonomous Psyche. A Communication to Goodheart
from the Bi-Personal Field of Paul Kugler and James
Hillman" 97

CHAPTER FIVE: The Present as Dimension of the Soul:
'Actual Conflict' and Archetypal Psychology 103

CHAPTER SIX: The Provenance of C. G. Jung's
Psychological Findings 119

CHAPTER SEVEN: Jungian Psychology: A Baseless
Enterprise. Reflections on Our Identity as
Jungians 153

CHAPTER EIGHT: Jung's *Thought* of the Self in the Light
of Its Underlying Experiences 171

CHAPTER NINE: The Question of Jung's 'Anti-Semitism':
Postscript to Cocks 191

CHAPTER TEN: Hospitality Toward the Gods in an
Ungodly Age: Philemon – Faust – Jung 197

CHAPTER ELEVEN: Rupture, or: Psychology and
Religion 219

CHAPTER TWELVE: Deliverance from the Stream of
Events: Okeanos and the Circulation of the Blood 233

CHAPTER THIRTEEN: The Lesson of the Mask 257

Index 263

Acknowledgments

Earlier versions of the following chapters have been published previously:

Chapter 1 as "Ontogeny = Phylogeny? A Fundamental Critique of E. Neumann's Analytical Psychology" in *Spring 1975*, pp. 110-129.

Chapter 2 in a slightly shorter version as "On the Neurosis of Psychology or The Third of the Two" in *Spring 1977*, pp. 153-174.

Chapter 4 as "Comments on 'The Autonomous Psyche. A Communication to Goodheart from the Bi-Personal Field of Paul Kugler and James Hillman'" in *Spring 1985*, pp. 172-174.

Chapter 7 as "Jungian Psychology: A Baseless Enterprise. Reflections on Our Identity as Jungians" in *Harvest 33, 1987-88*, pp. 91-103.

Chapter 9 as "The Question of Jung's 'Anti-Semitism': Postscript to Cocks" in *Spring 1979*, pp. 228-231.

Chapter 10 as "Hospitality Toward the Gods in an Ungodly Age: Philemon – Faust – Jung" in *Spring 1984*, pp. 61-75.

Chapter 11 as "Rupture, or: Psychology and Religion" in *Zen Buddhism Today*, Annual Report of the Kyoto Zen Symposium, No. 6, November 1988, Kyoto, Japan (The Kyoto Seminar for Religious Philosophy), pp. 39-49.

Chapter 12 as "Deliverance from the Stream of Events: Okeanos and the Circulation of the Blood" in *Sulfur (A Literary Bi-Annual of the Whole Art) 21* (Winter 1988), pp. 118-140; Chapter 13 as "The Lesson of the Mask" in *Sulfur 45/46*, Spring 2000, pp. 109–113.

The following chapters were newly translated from German for this volume:

Chapter 3, "The Leap After the Throw: On 'Catching up With' Projections and on the Origin of Psychology," first published in 1979 as "Der Sprung nach dem Wurf. Über das Einholen der Projektion und den Ursprung der Psychologie" in GORGO 1/1979, pp. 49-71.

Chapter 5, "The Present as Dimension of the Soul: 'Actual Conflict' and Archetypal Psychology," first published in 1978 as "Die Gegenwart als Dimension der Seele— Aktualkonflikt und archetypische Psychotherapie" in *Analyt. Psychol. 9* (1978), pp. 99-110.

Chapter 6, "The Provenance of C. G. Jung's Psychological Findings," first published in 1984 as "Die Herkunft der wissenschaftlichen Erkenntnisse C. G. Jungs" in GORGO 7/JG. 4 (1984), pp. 1-31.

Chapter 8, "Jung's Thought of the Self in the Light of Its Underlying Experiences," first appeared in a Japanese translation (2001) in W. Giegerich, "Shinwa to Ishiki" (Yungu Shinrigaku no Tenkai [Gîgerihhi Ronshû], 3) translated and edited by Toshio Kawai, Tokyo (Nihon Hyôron-sha) 2001.

I would like to take this opportunity to express my gratitude for James Hillman's great support of my work during my early years as a writer in the field of Jungian studies. I also wish to thank him and Clayton Eshleman for providing space for my articles in their respective journals (*Spring; Sulfur*). And a special thank you to Greg Mogenson as editor and Nancy Cater as publisher for intelligent, smooth, and productive collaboration.

W.G.

Sources and Abbreviations

For the most frequently cited sources, the following abbreviations have been used:

Briefe: Jung, C. G. *Briefe*. 3 vols. Ed. Aniela Jaffé. Olten and Freiburg im Breisgau: Walter-Verlag, 1972-73.

CW: Jung, C. G. *Collected Works*. 20 vols. Ed. Herbert Read, Michael Fordham, Gerhard Adler, and William McGuire. Trans. R. F. C. Hull. Princeton: Princeton University Press, 1957-1979. Cited by volume and, unless otherwise noted, by paragraph number.

GW: Jung, C. G. *Gesammelte Werke*. Zürich and Stuttgart (Rascher) now Olten and Freiburg i:Br: Walter-Verlag, 1958 ff.

Letters: Jung, C. G. *Letters*. 2 vols. Ed. Gerhard Adler. Bollingen Series XCV: 2. Princeton: Princeton University Press, 1975.

MDR: Jung, C. G. *Memories, Dreams, Reflections*. Rev. ed. Ed. Aniela Jaffé. Trans. Richard and Clara Winston. New York: Vintage Books, 1965. Cited by page number.

O&H: Neumann, Erich. *The Origins and History of Consciousness*. Trans. R. F. C. Hull. Bollingen Series. New York: Pantheon Books, 1954.

Foreword

The critical thinker, dedicated in his commitment to a particular school of thought, will be heartened, perhaps even inspired and guided, by the felicitous phrase, traditionally attributed to Aristotle, "I love Plato, but I love the truth more." This certainly can be said of the author of the papers collected in these volumes. Once lauded by James Hillman as the person doing "the most important Jungian *thought* now going on,"[1] Wolfgang Giegerich has for more than three decades dedicated himself to what he has called "thinking the Jungian myth onwards."[2] A lover of Jung's psychology, especially on account of what he has praised as its authentic notion of soul,[3] Giegerich has at the same time been compelled by an even greater regard for truth to become its most exacting critic. Sometimes, as Giegerich has told me, this task has proven as difficult as "cutting into [his] own flesh."[4] Seminal thoughts of Jung's, in which he as a Jungian analyst has had a personal stake, have had to be rigorously interrogated. But this is as it must be, for only as Jung's psychology is reflected into itself in the light of its internal contradictions can its vaporized essence be alchemically distilled and the elixir within it found.

Now it is important to emphasis that the truth that is to be loved more than Plato, Jung, or any other thinker is not a truth imported from outside. As what Giegerich calls "the discipline of interiority," psychology works strictly by means of the application of the theory in question or matter at hand *to itself*. Eschewing external touchstones (i.e., the validity standards of other disciplines), a psychology that is

---

[1] James Hillman, "Once More into the Fray: A Response to Wolfgang Giegerich's 'Killings'," *Spring 56* (1994), p. 1.
[2] Wolfgang Giegerich, "The 'Patriarchal Neglect of the Feminine Principle': A Psychological Fallacy in Jungian Theory," *Harvest: Journal for Jungian Studies* 45.1 (1999), p. 7.
[3] Wolfgang Giegerich, *The Soul's Logical Life: Towards a Rigorous Notion of Psychology* (Frankfurt am Main: Peter Lang, 1998), pp. 39-43.
[4] Personal communication, October 20, 2000.

truly psychological in its form and approach proceeds by means of *internal* reflection, *immanent* critique, reading Plato in terms of Plato, Jung in terms of Jung—dreams, symptoms, and other phenomena in terms of themselves as well.

Clearly, the contrast that sets off psychology as just described from scientifically-conceived approaches that operate in terms of the idea of objectivity and external verification could not be stronger. And further to this it could be said that from the former's point of view, scientific psychology is to be adjudged as having been set up from the outset in terms of a fallacy. Committed to an external form of reflection, scientific approaches assign the epithet "inner" to such phenomena as images, emotions, and memories, while continuing naively to view these as if they were simply out there in front of consciousness, unadulterated and pure.

But how then, if not by science, are we to proceed? How can psychology get to interiority or "the soul" from within itself, right from the start?

Working by means of what is known in philosophy as transcendental deduction, Kant launched his critical philosophy by asking how the mind must be constituted for it to be possible for us to have the kinds of experience that we do. Psychology, working with a more colloquial form of the same style of argumentation, asks similar questions with respect to its ideas, its theories.

Examples are legion, there being no particular kind of phenomenon that psychology has to be about. As we have already indicated, all that is required is that the subject matter, whatever that may be, is taken subjectively or hermeneutically in terms of itself.

Humming a few bars of this music brings a fanciful series of colloquially expressed, transcendental-deduction-type questions to mind.

What does psychology's having formulated the ideas that it has say about its conception of itself? And how do the scales stand in their balance when each is weighed against itself as against a feather? Is there a remainder left over when the math is done? Something extra that must now be accounted for through subsequent acts of reflection? The review in the journal, we may ask more specifically, has it a hefty enough handle for the blade that it wields? The procedure we have invented, the operation we have performed, can these still to be rated a success given that the patient died? And the smoke of this cigar even, is it as weighty in its own new way as the Havana that first gave it off?

"Never forget," advised Jung, "that in psychology the *means* by which you judge the psyche is the *psyche* itself."[5]

A few sentences from Hegel, the philosopher most referenced by Giegerich, may be cited here. The first of these merely expresses the logical form of the questions we have just asked: "... in what consciousness within its own self designates as the *An sich* or the true, [in this] we have the standard by which consciousness itself proposes to measure its knowledge."[6] The second helps us to understand, with Hegel and Giegerich, that reflection, far from needing to be rejected when it does not measure up to itself, must think its contradictions on a whole new level, transforming itself thereby: "... [T]he Absolute [as the sublated form of the contradictions that have given rise to it] is ... the identity of identity and non-identity, opposition and unity are both in it."[7]

In the papers that follow, topics as diverse as Neumann's fanciful history of consciousness, analytical psychology's theory of projection, Jung's thought of the self, and the question of a Jungian identity are reflexively applied to themselves in the manner just described. The upshot of this is that in each case the topic under consideration ceases to be a mere subject matter *of* psychology. While certainly remaining this on one level, each becomes, by virtue of its having been reflected into itself, an illuminating commentary with respect to the greater question of how a psychology that can think on its own authority, out of the depth of its own notion, constitutes itself. As Giegerich has expressed this, "What at first appears as a content of consciousness [e.g., the aforementioned topics *of* psychology] is in truth the seed of what wants to be a new form of consciousness at large."[8]

The account that I have just given of the reflexive movement that is at play in this first volume of Giegerich's *Collected English Papers* applies as well across all four. Indeed, as the reader will discover as he

---

[5] *CW* 18, § 277.

[6] Cited in Charles Taylor, *Hegel* (Cambridge: Cambridge University Press, 1975), p. 135.

[7] Cited in Taylor, *Hegel*, p. 67.

[8] Wolfgang Giegerich, "Is the Soul 'Deep?'—Entering and Following the Logical Movement in Heraclitus' 'Fragment 45'" *Spring 64* (Fall/Winter, 1998), p. 19.

or she takes up *Technology and the Soul* (Vol. 2), *Soul-Violence* (Vol. 3), and *The Soul Always Thinks* (Vol. 4) in their turn, the new form of psychological consciousness that began as a seed with the title paper of the present volume, "The Neurosis of Psychology," comes increasingly to the fore.

We started with an adage from Aristotle about his love of truth being greater than his love of Plato. This we then extended to Jung. Turning now to Giegerich's papers, we may restate this adage again, this time with psychology as the subject. Usually, psychology is taken to be identical with the things to which it is applied, that is, to psychic phenomena of various kinds. The difference between such phenomena in their *positivity* and the logic of psychology as *negativity* (or reflection into itself) is not recognized, not drawn. Instead, we have a proliferation of different psychologies. The problem here, as Giegerich has pointed out, is that each of these so-called psychologies proceeds as if psychology could simply be found out there in the objects it empirically observes. Such naiveté, however, drastically shortchanges Jung's crucial insight that all experience is psychically mediated such that no phenomenon, whether "inner" or "outer," is immediately observable apart from the constitution of consciousness itself. Returning to this insight (even hoisting Jung upon it at times, as upon his own petard), Giegerich has shown that it is precisely because all phenomena are reflected from the outset that the question of their logic, the question of their truth, arises. We cannot, as Giegerich has argued, simply have psychology— "*just like that*"—in the form of the phenomenal topics that interest us, but only as, in the case of each of these, and through critique of each one's seeming immediacy, we come to love truth more.

If there is a thread through the labyrinthine turns of Giegerich's *Collected English Papers*, it is to be found in our recognition that Giegerich's most important contribution to psychology resides in his having rigorously thought psychology through in terms of the "psychological difference" that I have just described. Taking this thread up now in our turn, may we, as lovers of this phenomenon or that psychology, yet learn with Giegerich that a truly *psychological* psychology can be founded only through our loving the truth more.

Greg Mogenson

Introduction

There have been many designations for the psychology established by C. G. Jung and continued, in one form or another, by the so-called Jungians: "Jungian psychology," "analytical psychology," "complex psychology," "archetypal psychology." Jung also sometimes referred to his psychology, without giving this phrase the status of an official name and without explicitly indicating that he meant his own psychology, as "the modern psychology of the unconscious." But he could also speak of "my critical psychology."[1] Again, this is more a description than a name. But for reasons that I will briefly expound here, "critical psychology" might be a good candidate.

The last phrase I quoted is from the year 1957. But "critical psychology" occurs in Jung's writings already much earlier, at least in the early thirties, e.g., in his "Foreword to the Argentine Edition" (1934) of *Psychological Types*[2] and in a letter to Wolfgang Kranefeldt from 1933.[3] In the earlier use of the phrase it refers to a rather straightforward idea, as Jung's explanation shows: "a critical psychology dealing with the organization and delimitation of psychic processes that can be shown to be typical,"[4] "a critical apparatus for the sifting of the empirical material."[5] The straightforwardness of the thinking prevailing in these quotations lies in the fact that there is here a clear distinction between the typology as a tool ("apparatus") on the one hand, and the material or object to which this tool can be applied, on the other. The fact that Jung here rejects, or reduces to secondary importance, the "characterological diagnosis of the patient" in favor

---

[1] C. G. Jung, *Letters 2*, p. 378, to Bernhard Lang, June 1957.
[2] *CW* 6, page xv.
[3] Letter to Kranefeldt of October 24, 1933 (Jung Papers, Wissenschaftshistorische Sammlungen, ETH Zürich), cited in Sonu Shamdasani, *Jung and the Making of Modern Psychology: The Dream of a Science* (Cambridge: Cambridge University Press, 2003), p. 86.
[4] *CW* 6, page xv.
[5] See note 3 above.

of the typification "of psychological occurrences" does not really change the clear separation of instrument here, and material critically "sifted," "organized," and "delimited" by means of it there.

Jung's earliest reflections that led into his later typology had served, however, the purpose of making conscious the problem of the "personal equation." The origin of his typology around 1913 and earlier had been the wish to explain *psychologically* the basic theoretical differences between the Freudian "eros" perspective and the Adlerian "power" perspective on psychological processes, which for Jung could not be resolved by declaring the one to be true and the other false. The idea of basic attitudinal types, types of psychic movement (extraversion versus introversion), seemed to offer an explanation. What is interesting in this context is that this idea broke through the linear opposition of psychologist (student of the psychic processes) vis-à-vis the psychic processes and began to approach a circular conception of the relation between psychologist and psychological reality: the psychic movement of the libido was not only at work out there in the patient, but also in the analyst, and not separately (or the one after the other), but rather in such a way that precisely while the psychologist observed the psychic processes in the patient, he was himself subject to psychic processes, so that his explanations were just as much a psychic phenomenon as that which they were supposed to explain. It is one and the same psychological life that appears on both sides.

In the early days Jung did not yet fully realize the momentous consequences of this seminal insight of his for the basic constitution of psychology. But over the years the decisive difference between psychology and the natural sciences impressed itself upon him. It dawned on him that in psychology it was the soul itself that had to recognize the soul. This insight found its clearest and most systematic expression in Jung's late essay, "On the Nature of the Psyche" (1954, earlier version 1946). There we read,

> [Psychology] lacks the immense advantage of an Archimedean point such as physics enjoys. … The psyche … observes itself and can only translate the psychic back into the psychic. … There is no medium for psychology to reflect itself in: it can only portray itself in itself, and describe itself. … [In describing psychic occurrences] [w]e have not removed ourselves in scientific regards to a plane in any way above or besides the

psychic process, let alone translated it into another medium. (*CW* 8 § 421, transl. modif.)

... [P]sychology inevitably merges with the psychic process itself. It can no longer be distinguished from the latter, and so turns into it. ... [I]t is not, in the deeper sense, an explanation of this process, for no explanation of the psychic can be anything other than the living process of the psyche itself. Psychology has to sublate itself as a science and therein precisely it reaches its scientific goal. Every other science has a point outside of itself; not so psychology, whose object is the very subject that produces all science. (§ 429, transl. modif.)

Soul is self-reflection, self-relation, and psychology (psychological explanations or descriptions) is one of the ways in which the soul reflects itself. The opposition basic to the sciences of subject and object, theory and nature, does not exist in and for psychology. Psychology cannot be a science. It *is* in itself and from the outset *sublated* science, in itself *sublated* 'scientific' psychology. The clear distinction between psychology and its subject-matter, the soul, cannot be maintained: psychology is itself soul and soul is interpretation of itself (psychology). Both soul and psychology follow a "uroboric" logic.

While it is one of the greatest merits of Jung's psychology to have advanced to this insight, it is deplorable that Jung viewed the situation of psychology, which he analyzed correctly, negatively as a "tragic thing" (§ 421) and felt that psychology therefore finds itself "in an unfortunate situation" (§ 429, transl. modif.). This negative assessment is what is in my view "the tragic thing" about Jung himself.[6] As far as I can see, his unspoken and express ideal remained the idea of a psychology as an objective science and of the psychologist as the neutral observer of the psyche as a fact of nature (for even in the very passage that contains his amazing insight it is explicitly "in comparison with the other natural sciences" that psychology finds itself in the said unfortunate situation).

So he had only the resigned realization that—sadly—this ideal could on principle not become real. He did not measure up to his

---

[6] Cf. however *Letters 2*, p. 567 (to Bennet, 23 June 1960), where Jung says concerning the fact that "in contradistiction to all others" [sc. other sciences] psychology "tries to understand itself by itself": "a great disadvantage in one way and an equally great prerogative in the other!"

own insight. He saw it correctly, he presented us with those statements that truly overcome what we might call the prevailing positivism of the conventional scientific mind, but he perceived and evaluated them from below, from the old positivistic standpoint as his standard and measure. He did not let go of the very expectations and that value system that his own insights surpassed and shattered. His perspective, or better, the logical form of his consciousness, did not accommodate to the semantic content that his consciousness entertained. The revolutionary insight was restricted to the "semantics" of consciousness, while consciousness's "syntax" remained unaffected. Jung envisioned a grand conception from afar, but did not take the additional step of entering it, of applying it to his own mind-set or to the logical constitution of psychology. His was and remained an external reflection (*äußere* or *äußerliche Reflektion*) about psychology, while the message of this external reflection was that psychology *is* internal or immanent reflection.

More than that, Jung was also not able to hail this situation of psychology (the way he described it) as the distinction and privilege of psychology, and as its singular opportunity. Far from being psychology's tragic handicap, the inevitable self-reflective character of psychology is actually something like its Promised Land. Only if its character would have been consciously embraced by psychology would it have come home to itself, would it have logically been united with the soul and in this way, and only in this way, become truly psychological. Its alienation or exile from its home, the land of the soul, and from its subject-matter, the life of the soul, would have ended. But Jung did not rise to the level required by his own insight, on which he could have appreciated that this complex, involved structure of self-reflection both betrays and requires a *higher* status of consciousness; that it is indicative of the conquest of a higher degree of logical refinement of the mind and a significant cultural advance beyond the naive innocence of the *stance of immediacy* for which there is an unambiguous separation of theory here and fact there.

Incredible as it is, as late as in 1954 he even openly declared the nonpsychic as the standard and measure for the psychic. "If we are to engage in fundamental reflections about the nature of the psychic, we need [!] an Archimedean point which alone makes a judgment possible. This can only be the nonpsychic ..." (*CW* 8 § 437). A clear confession on his part to external reflection as the basis of psychology in all fundamental matters and to an ultimately "positivistic" stance. When it is a question of the nature of the psychic itself, then all of a sudden the psychic does no longer have "everything it needs within itself."[7] Rather, Jung suggests that you have to have left psychology and taken your position outside the psyche—become unpsychological—to become able to understand the nature of the psyche. He gives a reason for his view in the continuation of the quoted sentence: "... for, as a living phenomenon, the psychic lies embedded in something that appears to be of a nonpsychic nature. Although we perceive the latter as a psychic datum only, there are sufficient reasons for believing in its objective reality." The ordinary, everyday world-experience of the ego is assumed to be decisive. This experience is what Jung here makes his basis. While *empirically* and *semantically* the whole world is, as Jung stresses again and again, embedded in the psyche and we are inescapably surrounded by the psyche on *all* sides (which is even confirmed once more also in this very quote: "a psychic datum only"), *logically, epistemically,* and *syntactically* it is the other way around for him. Jung (at least here) does not want psychology to take its own medicine, that medicine which is, e.g., expressed in his warning (concerning the individual psychological *phenomenon*), "Above all, don't let anything from outside, that does not belong, get into it ..."[8] He does not want psychology *to go under* in its own interiority in order to find the deepest "truth" about itself *exclusively* within itself and through its own *self*-reflection.

However, he is able to rescue it from its own interiority only by means of a dissociation. The (alchemical) "Immersion in the Bath" is, as it were, reserved for the experiencing individual in the practice of psychology (analysis), but refused when it comes to "fundamental reflections" on the part of psychological theory, i.e., when it is a question of the logical form of psychology itself.

This inability of Jung's to see the basic situation of psychology described and lamented by him, namely that it does *not* have an Archimedean point, as a fundamental step forward on the part of the

---

[7] *CW* 14, § 740.
[8] *Ibid.*

soul is, by the way, one of the reasons why he needed vehemently and, as it were, "instinctively"[9] to reject Hegel.[10]

But be that as it may, despite these shortcomings, Jung did bequeath to us the precious insight into the mutual entwinement of psychological observation and observed psychic phenomenology and the inextricable immersion of psychology as a theoretical discipline in that which this discipline is about, namely the soul's life. Psychology does not have the soul's life neatly in front of itself as a positivity, a natural given. It is from the outset *itself* an expression of this life, so that it has the life of the soul at once in front of itself and behind its back, as its *a posteriori* and its *a priori*. This is what it means to say that the soul is self-reflection. The self-reflective character of the soul has the consequence that the soul's life on principle cannot be a self-same (thing-like) object for psychology, a 'fact.' The soul is in this sense not to be comprehended as a piece of nature, nor in ontological terms (in terms of being: as an entity, a substance). It is essentially mental, noetic, logical.[11] It is not an immediate, but in itself an already reflected reality. There is not first a soul as an existing entity that then also happens to reflect itself as one of its activities. "The soul" *is* self-reflection and nothing else: it *is* interpretation *and* what it is the interpretation of is itself interpretation. We could express it this way: the real occurrence of such self-reflection, the event that a "uroboric" logic has become explicit, is what we call, with a still mythologizing and substantiating name, "the soul." And because "soul" and "psychology" are only two different moments of the same in the sense of the unity of the unity and difference of psychology and soul, psychology is likewise not a theory about or interpretation of certain straightforward (immediate) natural facts or events. Having a self-reflective structure, it is the interpretation of *interpretations* (views, theories) of reality. When I said that psychology cannot be a science,

---

[9] Out of a strong affect and without any sufficient knowledge of Hegel, as he himself explicitly confessed.

[10] On Jung and Hegel see my article "Jung's Betrayal of his Truth: The Adoption of a Kant-based Empiricism and the Rejection of Hegel's Speculative Thought," in *Harvest: Journal for Jungian Studies,* vol. 44, no.1, 1998, pp. 46-64.

[11] 'Logical' in this discourse means 'of logos-nature.' It does of course in no way want to suggest that the soul always conforms to the formal laws of *correct reasoning* (logic in the instrumental, technical sense). It is not a reference to the special philosophical discipline called formal logic. It is much closer to the (however imaginal) alchemical concept 'mercurial.'

I meant that it cannot operate with the fiction that it has its object directly vis-à-vis itself and that this object is what it is, independent of its (psychology's) interpretations.

Through these considerations based on Jung's later insights our notion of "critical psychology" has become much more complex and deeper. A critical psychology in this sense implies a psychology that tries to get to and hold itself on the level of the uroboric logic briefly described. It remains of course to us to draw from Jung's insight the necessary consequences that he could not fully draw for himself. What was and remained for him an envisioned content of his thinking *in front of* consciousness has to become for us the very basis as well as the intrinsic logical form of our psychological thinking itself. And the papers collected in this volume have for the most part the purpose of preparing the ground for such a conception of psychology or even showing it in action.

But if these papers are on the way to a "critical psychology," 'critical' can also entail the more ordinary meaning, in our case a caustic criticism in the sense of "trying the spirits," whether they are in accordance with the developed constitution of psychology or not. There is such a tremendous simplification at work in Jungian psychology as practiced by Jungians. Far from having drawn the consequences from the significant insight gained by Jung about the self-reflective character of soul and psychology, it has usually even fallen behind this insight and operates naively with the idea of a psychological reality as an immediate given, with its belief in the soul as a natural fact, with symbols and archetypes as objective entities, etc. (A marked exception is Archetypal Psychology, established by James Hillman, with, for example, its ideas of psychology as soul-making, of the fiction of case histories, of the poetic basis of mind, and of the archetypal perspectives governing our viewing of and thinking about psychological material. Here one sees a self-reflective structure at work.) What generally rules is a stance characterized by immediacy and positivity, by objectivistic, naturalistic, and personalistic thinking, which is absolutely incompatible with a psychology that has become aware of itself. Even where those insights of Jung's are quoted, they are usually only paid lip-service to and have no feedback effect whatsoever on the constitution of psychology and the actual mentality of the psychologist, which stay immune.

A "critical psychology" must push off from this type of simple psychology. For this reason we need an equivalent in psychology to what Nietzsche, in the subtitle and preface to his *Götzendämmerung,* called "philosophizing with a hammer." What Nietzsche had in mind with the hammer was not a tool for smashing. He even compared the hammer to a tuning fork (!), because what he was trying to discern with the help of the soft touch of a hammer was whether that to which it was applied gave "that famous hollow sound" or not. There is no need for smashing, because for psychology, as for philosophy, the hollow sound, if it is made audible, *is* the self-destruction of that which is hollow. Nevertheless, this type of critique is still external reflection because the hammer or tuning fork is brought to bear upon the text or doctrine under investigation from outside. We need to be clear about this and distinguish it from the actual "critical psychology" which is self-reflective. In this "Introduction" I already tried the hammer on Jung's scientistic stance. Jung's revolutionary insight about the self-reflective nature of psychology proved to sound hollow because it was not self-applied to psychology.

The papers in this volume were all written as separate pieces, and often for particular occasions such as conferences. But although this was not intended at the time of writing, they not only "circumambulate around the same center," but at least in part can be shown to follow a consistent, even if unintended, line of thought. Each paper contributes an exploration of one essential aspect or component of a psychology that would deserve its name. In the following comments I will, in retrospect, attempt to clarify the inner coherence of the different topics and different thrusts of the individual papers.

The first paper in this collection, on Erich Neumann, is, as the subtitle indicates, devoted to a "Fundamental Critique" of his psychology, a critique obviously only in the sense of external reflection, as explained above. Neumann's work and the essential claim it entails are taken as objective 'givens' and are then subjected to a critical examination. Despite this external nature of the critique, the issue is decisive for Jungian psychology. What is at stake in Neumann's conception is the relation between the empirical-historical and the archetypal or mythic (transcendence), the personal or individual and the human race. The main critique in my paper is that in each case, the way the two poles are set up in his scheme amounts to a mystification. This mystification is the result of the fact that an essential psychological complication that is alluded to in the subtitle of Jung's *Mysterium Coniunctionis*, namely, the "separation and synthesis of the psychic opposites," is not heeded. Neumann, it is shown, "synthesizes" (amalgamates, even equates) the opposites just like that, without their prior unrelenting separation. The unity that should actually be the *result* of a mediation in the sense of the unity *of* the separation *and* unity *of* the opposites thus turns into a flat, immediate (however *inflated*) unity. ("Ontogeny = Phylogeny? A Fundamental Critique of E. Neumann's Analytical Psychology.")

But the papers that follow operate already in the spirit of a "critical psychology" in the higher sense of a self-reflective psychology (although the psychologizing "with the hammer" still plays a role here, too). Thus, what emerges in "On the Neurosis of Psychology or The Third of the Two" is that what practical therapeutic psychology tries to deal with 'out there' in the patients, neurosis, is already, although unbeknownst, inherent in the theory of psychology itself. The innocent tendency to focus on cases and on psychological material before consciousness keeps psychology unconscious about the fact that the theory (or theories, in the plural) that guide its consciousness are always in on it, from the outset. But how strong the tendency to avoid the self-reflective *structure* of psychology is reveals itself especially in two facts. First, the very idea of self-reflection exists *only* in its literalized and acted out form as a *separate* activity and as *personal* behavior, namely, in the form of training analysis preceding one's own practice of analysis. Secondly, even the inseparably uroboric character itself of the psychological appears to the conventional psychological consciousness only as stuffed into the literal social sphere, where it is positivized as those phenomena that are called transference and counter-transference. What should actually be the intrinsic *form of the constitution* of psychology is reduced to *empirical events* occurring in the course of the practice of psychology. The empirical persons have to carry the load that psychology as theory or the logical constitution of psychology does not want to shoulder. It is systematically kept free from the uroboric logic that would turn it into true psychology, while at the same time psychology can live with the feeling of constantly giving this logic its due since, after all, it does attend with great effort to the personalistic transference.

The true locus of the soul is not the empirical individual in its positivity. Its true locus is psychology, psychology not as it is abstractly conceived as a science, but as that concrete living thought to which the individual can rise up.

After psychology has come home to *itself* from its outward fixation upon the empirical persons and events it studies, the opposition of inwardness and outwardness as such needs to be reflected. This is the task of the paper on projection ("The Leap After the Throw: On 'Catching up With' Projections and on the Origin of Psychology"). It turns out that in the sense of the uroboric entwinement of the opposites true interiority is not reached by retracting the outward movement inherent in the phenomenon of projection, in order to turn inside (to what is *in* ourselves). On the contrary, this outward movement needs to be followed, even surpassed, and only thereby is interiority as "the land of the soul" reached. Or rather, it is not reached, inasmuch as "the inner" is not a literal existing place that one can go to, but is originally *produced* as the result of the interiorizing movement *into* the "pro-jection" (into the ideas or fictions produced by the soul) or of the self-abandonment on the part of the subject to the soul's productions. "The soul" *is* not, it must be *made*, however in such a self-contradictory (dialectical) way that what is only the produced result is nevertheless at once the origin of the whole movement. It goes without saying that with this psychological attitude the conventional positivistic and abstract notion of truth as something strictly 'objective' is dissolved, too. For psychology, appearance, fiction, subjective views are no longer the abstract opposite of truth.

Once we have arrived in the interiority of the soul through our relentless surrender to the soul's outward movement, another step is necessary: a radical *closure* of the created interior space. The dedication to the soul's movement now continues in the form of an unreserved commitment to the psychological phenomenon (the "projected" content) so as to *exclude* anything from outside that does not belong. This is the way to establish the psychological equivalent to the hermetically sealed alchemical vessel and to conceive of the psychological phenomenon, the phenomenon in its eachness, *psychologically* as a true *prima materia*. For psychology at large this means that it has to proceed systematically from the presupposition of the autonomy of the psyche. It must not have an "alibi": no elsewhere outside, no external causes. Precisely not a wish, as Jung still had it, for a translation of the psychic process into *another* medium. ("No Alibi! Comments on "The Autonomous Psyche. A Communication to Goodheart from the Bi-Personal Field of Paul Kugler and James Hillman.")

A similar closure is constitutive for psychology in a temporal sense. In "The Present as Dimension of the Soul: 'Actual Conflict' and Archetypal Psychology" I explore this aspect: unreserved dedication to the psychic phenomenon at hand in its present reality (even if it is a pathology), without any toying with the idea of any causes lying in the past nor with the idea of a future developmental goal for the person. (The attack in this paper on the developmentalism in psychology is characteristic of the early days of "archetypal psychology.") The psychological aim must not be to free the person suffering from it of the pathology, but to listen to what this pathology has to say and to learn to see the world through its eyes. In this paper, first presented in 1977, I first introduced the concept of the "psychological difference," the difference between man and soul. With this emphasis on the present we see that the "eachness" mentioned in the previous paragraph needs to be complemented by "nowness" and, I might add here, by "my-ness," as the three characters of psychological truth.

If "closure" in the sense indicated is constitutive for psychology, this has consequences for the particular nature and status of the concepts and basic insights of psychology itself. In "The Provenance of C. G. Jung's Psychological Findings" an attempt is made to explore, by way of example, the question of how Jung arrived, and why he had to arrive, at the concept of archetypes so central to him. The goal is, however, not to trace the factual historical development of Jung's thinking that led him to his theory of archetypes. Rather, this paper is concerned with the psychological and logical "source" and inner necessity of that concept. It becomes very clear how and why Jung's psychology is incompatible with the empirical natural sciences. The concept of archetypes can, by contrast, be shown to be the necessary result of that particular methodological stance that can be called truly "phenomenological" because of its commitment to the eachness of each phenomenon. This methodological stance opens up for us the "soul" (the inner depth and truth) of the phenomenon at hand, and this inner depth and truth is what Jung calls "archetype." The phenomenological approach is only capable of opening up for us the archetypal depth of a phenomenon because it stays faithful to how it, the phenomenon, *appears*. Psychological truth is the truth of the *appearance*, a truth irrespective of the difference between 'fact' and 'illusion' (or 'delusion')—and in this sense *absolute* truth: truth *absolved* from the difference between fact and illusion. The appearance (*Schein*) has its truth within itself, it *is* the archetypal truth of the phenomenon. Just as in the paper about the present as dimension of the soul the betrayal of the phenomenon at hand by going back behind it to its causes in the past was rejected, so here the attempt to desert the appearance ("phainomenon"!) by seeking a factual truth behind the appearance and precisely in contrast to the appearance (because *this* truth would expose the appearance to have been mere semblance).

By unreservedly giving itself over to the soul's movement and the infinite depth of the phenomenon at hand, psychology no longer has a solid ground to stand on. As Jung had stated, psychology merges with the psychic process itself. It is not any sort of scientific ('positive') theory or doctrine, a sum-total of empirical findings and axiomatic assumptions on which, as a secure base, all further work can rely; no, even *as* theorizing it is nevertheless just movement, process, fluidity. This has consequences for the question of what constitutes the identity of a Jungian. There cannot be an identity in the positivistic sense of that word. Psychology proves to be a "baseless enterprise." In this sense the movement that was previously described as an outward movement can now be seen as simultaneously a fall, a drop into the bottomlessness and infinity of the soul. But precisely and exclusively in its bottomlessness psychology finds *its* solid base. ("Jungian Psychology: A Baseless Enterprise. Reflections on Our Identity as Jungians.")

Once it has been comprehended that psychology merges with the psychic process itself, the very notion of a 'subject' doing psychology is affected, too. It cannot hold its ground as the ego that is conceived as the self-identical and neutral observer of the course of events. It is not only that it does not have a solid ground to stand on, as was pointed out in the previous paragraph. Even its *internal* identity as a positivity or stable substance dissolves. What emerges in the discussion of "Jung's *Thought* of the Self in the Light of Its Underlying Experiences" is that the subject, who is the "second creator" of what it sees, is in itself a union of opposites; it is its own opposite and thus self-contradictory.

But if it is both itself (its own identity) and at once in itself its own other, then it can no longer be imagined in ontological terms as a being, some sort of entity, but has to be comprehended as negativity, as logical life, as the play of the opposites.

The thought of the Self as conceived by Jung would not have been possible in ancient times, although the idea of a union of opposites, of the unity of unity and difference of man and his Other (God), was certainly a familiar thought pattern in ancient times. The "Self" is something new. What emerges here is a sense of history, of history as a radical difference. The difference in psychological terms can be spelled out as that between a thinking in terms of myth or ontology versus one in terms of *logos*, between the sphere of "semantics" and that of "logical form" or "syntax." History is, as it were, the soul's alchemical laboratory in which, among other things, "the Self" can be formed.

It was inevitable that the historicity of the soul would surface once it has been understood that psychology merges with the psychic process itself. For what does it mean that with psychology we have not removed ourselves to "a plane in any way above or besides the psychic process," that psychology "can no longer be distinguished from the latter"? If the soul is in itself movement or process it must be *fundamentally* historical, in other words, precisely not *immersed* in history and *subject to* time like everything on earth, because then the psyche would be imagined as a logically aloof substance that is merely secondarily, empirically exposed to historical change; soul and history would be imagined as two distinct realities. But no: soul *is* itself history, and history *is* the soul's self-unfolding. There is not a soul behind, above, or beside the historical course of events. We must not imagine it as an atemporal substance, as a set of anthropological constants "above the psychic process." Jung once wrote, "I have to be everywhere *beneath* and not *above*."[12] What Jung expressed here as his subjective attitude needs to be applied to psychology itself, to the "objective," theoretical stance of the psychologist. Psychology needs logically to go under into the psychic process itself, and it does so only to the full extent if it no longer resists its merging with the historical process in such a way that nothing is left behind. This is why a volume about a "critical psychology" must necessarily include a historical perspective.

---

[12] *Letters 2*, p. 34, to Erich Neumann, 5 Jan. 1952.

A short paper looking at the results of strictly historical research by a historian, although it is not primarily concerned with the question of the constitution of psychology, is included here because it tries to discriminate between a literal historical approach to history and a psychological one ("The Question of Jung's 'Anti-Semitism': Postscript to Cocks").

In "Hospitality Toward the Gods in an Ungodly Age. Philemon—Faust—Jung," the historical difference mentioned, the difference between the ages of myth and modernity, is explored. It reveals itself as a complete reversal. The stances toward the world in the two ages are diametrically opposed. The age of myth is characterized by a fundamental openness, a receptivity or "hospitality" to the nonpositivistic (the logically negative) dimension of the world: to the gods, the imaginal—the inner infinite radiance of the concrete phenomenon or situation in its eachness. It is the same inner radiance of the *phainomenon* ("appearance") that, according to the paper on "The Provenance of C. G. Jung's Psychological Findings," led Jung to develop the concept of archetypes. The age of modernity, by contrast, systematically closes itself to this depth dimension of the phenomenal world and instead insists on positive facts and results. But this modern closure to the infinity of the world is of course the precondition for psychology. As long as a "mythic" mode of being-in-the-world existed, psychology in our sense was neither necessary nor possible. In C. G. Jung we can see that and how *on the basis and in the style of the modern stance,* which expresses itself also in the existence of psychology, the equivalent to the ancient "hospitality" toward the inner divine depth of phenomenal life re-emerged.

Because the historical difference amounts to a complete turnabout, it can also be experienced as a fundamental rupture, and, if one looks at the characteristic contents on each side, as a watershed that separates "religion" from "psychology." Because this rupture puts religion on one side of this gulf and psychology on the other, the two are incompatible. Not, however, because they are simple, undialectical opposites, like fire and water or yes and no, but because psychology has to be comprehended in a comprehensive sense as the successor configuration to religion. The successor renders that which it succeeds obsolete. He or it takes the place, the office, that was formerly held by his or its predecessor. So it is precisely their identity in their difference that renders psychology and religion incompatible. Psychology is not a specialty field in the concert of the sciences (as Ulrich Mann imagined). It is *sublated* religion (just as much as it is sublated science and sublated immediate, personalistic psychology). Once consciousness has gone beyond that stage in which its deepest essence and highest values articulated themselves in the form of religion and entered the stage in which it has a psychological stance toward the world and life, it stands, religiously and metaphysically, with empty hands. But it is precisely this emptiness that has the potential of turning into a new openness and receptivity. ("Rupture. Or: Psychology and Religion.")

The dialectic of openness and closure in the context of the radical historical reversal is the topic of "Deliverance from the Stream of Events: Okeanos and the Circulation of the Blood." The fundamental closure that was expressed in the age of myth in the image of world-encircling Okeanos as absolute border turns out to be the condition of the possibility of the mind's infinite openness to the infinite, to the gods in the world. Okeanos as the river whose waters constantly flow back into itself is the imaginal form in which the uroboric logic articulated itself on the consciousness level of mythology. The ultimate closure of the human world that turns the world or life into the hermetically sealed vessel on the one hand and the uroboric logic on the other are two sides of the same coin. The early modern world, by contrast, burst open this "ontological" closure and lived in a fundamentally endless world extending into infinity. But along with this opening of the definition of the world, the closure did not disappear altogether. It reappears in the constitution of the human being (the "symptom" of which for a psychological understanding is Harvey's discovery (or rather, psychologically speaking, "invention") of the circulation of the blood). The human being can now *ipso facto* be the modern subject ("ego") and as such the subject of a modern personalistic psychology with its introspection and the individual's narcissistic concentration upon himself. We arrive here at a point where we see the imaginal background and the historical coming-to-be of that psychology that was critiqued in the paper "On the Neurosis of Psychology or The Third of the Two," so that in a way a circle closes itself.

The last piece, "The Lesson of the Mask," on a primary level is an exploration of what psycho-logically occurs in the masked dances in archaic societies. But implicitly this discussion serves as an imaginal portrayal—or should I say allegory?—of the soul's life, as an exemplification of a nonsubstantiating conception of soul *as* movement, of a deliberate self-abandonment to and allowing oneself to go under in this movement. As such *deliberate* wholehearted dedication (in the realm of empirical behavior) to an *autonomous* process, it can be an abbreviated sensual model for the (logical) movement that is required for psychology to come into being, for a psychology that has come home to itself. This would be a psychology that *knows* that it exists not at all or only uroborically, dialectically, self-contradictorily, *as* the ever new headlong plunge into the movement towards its *finis* or *telos* or *teleté* in order *there* to arrive at its first beginning or origin. At the same time, this last paper can also be considered an indirect answer to the first paper in this volume: a resolution of the serious problem that was discovered in Erich Neumann's psychology. For here, in "The Lesson of the Mask," we see how the psychic opposites, the empirical and transcendence, the (logically) positive and negativity, the finite and infinity, can in fact be mediated in the sense of the union *of* the separation *and* union *of* the opposites.

*   *   *

All the papers in this volume were written during the 1970s and 80s of the previous century, except for two which were written later. Naturally my thinking has evolved since then, and if I were to write on the same topics now, I would probably do so in a somewhat different way. But I can still today stand by the basic ideas and positions presented in these papers; the changes would not only, but mainly concern certain shifts of accent and the style of articulation (one most notable difference would be the transition from the sometimes "ontological" language inspired by Heidegger to a "logical" phrasing indebted to Hegelian thinking, which is much more appropriate for psychology; another, the shift from the belief that with the notion of "the imaginal" psychological thought had arrived at the deepest essence of the soul to the insight that we have to go beyond "the imaginal" to the comprehension of soul as "logical life"; the attentive reader might, however, sense that the later standpoint is already implicitly present at many points in the papers antedating this explicit shift). I did not make any attempt to adjust the texts to reflect how I would see and formulate things at present. However, they do not appear here in exactly the same form as they were originally printed. Apart from minor changes such as corrections of printing errors, in a few instances I re-inserted from the manuscripts some passages that for space or other reasons were omitted in the printed journal versions (especially in the "On the Neurosis of Psychology" and the "Hospitality Toward the Gods" papers). Also, in the two cases of comments on articles by others, I expanded the titles to give some indication of the theme.

Wolfgang Giegerich
May 2005

CHAPTER ONE

Ontogeny = Phylogeny?
A Fundamental Critique of Erich Neumann's Analytical Psychology

A mong analytical psychologists and even among representatives of other fields, Erich Neumann's work enjoys the highest recognition. This is not only attested to by phrases referring to him, such as "the one truly creative spirit among the second generation of Jung's pupils, the only one who seemed destined to build on Jung's work and to continue it,"[1] but even much more so by the fact that for many Jungians his terminology and orientation seem to have become second nature. Neumann indeed presented us with a grand and captivating scheme of psychic development, both of mankind and of the individual, a scheme that promised to give Analytical Psychology a firm footing and a systematic structure, and at the same time to serve as a tool by means of which one could hope to make comprehensible the entire range of psychic phenomena in the group as well as in the individual, in past and present, in the healthy and the ill. But as about 25 years have passed since his main work first appeared and we can regard it from some distance, the question of whether Neumann really based *his* Analytical Psychology on Jung's work, and above all of whether his entire outlook withstands a critical examination, forces itself upon us.

---

[1] Gerhard Adler, "Erich Neumann: 1905—1960", *Spring 1961,* p. 7.

We start with our astonishment at the fact that in *The Origins and History of Consciousness*, a work clearly conceived as a historical study, Neumann hardly ever refers to dated or dateable events. Of course, in a history of first beginnings we cannot expect datings precise to the very year, but without some organization of the material presented in terms of time, even if very approximate, a "history" is inconceivable, even a depth-psychological one. Jung, e.g., in *Answer to Job*, based *his* '*Entwicklungsgeschichte*' on clearly historical events (the composition of certain biblical passages, the declaration of dogmas, etc.). Neumann, by contrast, bases his history exclusively on mythical motifs and shows himself to be completely oblivious to the historical when, instead of asking when and where certain myths appeared for the first time, and by which other myths they were preceded and followed, he compiles examples for a mytheme from various ages and illustrates, e.g., the idea of 'upper' castration with the Oedipus myth as well as with a modern drama (Ernst Barlach)—not by way of amplification in order to elucidate the *meaning* of a motif, which would be legitimate, but in order to establish *stages* in the development of consciousness. We cannot help but ascertain a fundamental contradiction between Neumann's declared historiographic intention and what he actually offers; whatever Neumann's work may be, it is not a history.

But perhaps Neumann was mistaken about his own intention and therefore also inadvertently misled his readers in his title and introductory comments. Perhaps he was not concerned with history but, in actuality, had an entirely different aim, which he succeeded in carrying out. When Neumann speaks of mythological (not cultural-historical) stages of development and stresses that "stage" here does not refer to "any historical epoch,"[2] we might suppose that his actual intention was the representation of "stages" within myth itself (as opposed to cultural history), of a sequence of mythical images in the sense of a background process to be located somehow 'above' history. Then it would have to be shown that one motif presupposes another and is itself the basis for still others, that is to say, that there is a *genetic law inherent in myth*.

But here, too, we are deserted. Neumann does not show that the creation myth precedes the hero myth or that the latter is followed

---

[2] *O&H*, p. 41.

by the transformation myth. Just as, historically speaking, any mytheme may occur at any time, so myth itself does not contain any evidence for a genetic sequence of the individual myths. Every myth, by its very nature, has its origin and meaning in itself and is therefore a completely independent tale.

We now can see what Neumann does: he does not present stages of myth itself, but rather his own organization of the available mythological material, a genetic schema not derived from myth but preconceived and projected upon it. Though logical and in itself satisfactory, this schema is nonetheless 'fictitious', a speculative construction without empirical foundation.

We have seen that the book in question is not an Ursprungs*geschichte* of consciousness. But if it attempts to organize the multitude of mythological motifs, it follows that we must also doubt whether it is a history of *consciousness*. For mythological or archetypal images by definition belong to the so-called collective unconscious. Consequently, the emergence of the hero, as an archetypal motif, does not represent the rise of ego-consciousness *out of* the "collective unconscious," or the origin of consciousness in general, but an event *in* the collective unconscious. As long as we separate the collective unconscious and consciousness as two systems in opposition to each other, a study of mythemes naturally cannot inform us about the origin and history of ego-consciousness. Indeed, we cannot derive consciousness at all out of unconsciousness, but must conceive of it as a principle in its own right. *Mythology can inform us only about the various patterns of consciousness.*

It follows that the student of the development of consciousness must turn to the realm of empirical history and not to that of myth and archetypes. Where the *Ursprungsgeschichte* of consciousness ceases to be a history, it also no longer treats of actual consciousness. Neumann seems to have felt this. Why else the emphasis on history? Although *de facto* he only moves in the realm of myths, he after all also aims for an understanding of cultural history in his work. Neumann's systematization of mythological images could serve this purpose only if the speculative pattern of mythological stages could be shown to correspond to an actual (historical) cultural development in the sense of phylogeny.

Is there in cultural history a "regular sequence"[3] of developmental stages of consciousness? Did history necessarily and unambiguously lead from matriarchy to patriarchy, from the uroboros via the separation of the primal parents and the struggle of the hero to the transformation? This question can be answered in the negative with some degree of certainty. For how then would it be possible to find, even among primitives (among whom according to Neumann "the earliest stages of man's psychology"[4] prevail), full-fledged hero-myths, that is to say, myths presupposing a considerably developed consciousness, according to the system in question? If early and primitive cultures were indeed to be understood primarily in terms of the so-called earliest stages, they could not at all have developed a mature myth of the sun-hero, fully integrated into their cultic life. There must be even greater doubts with respect to the myth of transformation, which is supposed to be an indication of the highest stage of development and yet belongs to the oldest accessible cultural store of mankind. Cannibalism, human and animal sacrifices, the cults of the dead, shamanism—to name only a few of the most marked phenomena—occur with modern primitives as well as with the early cultures of the past as far back as the Stone Age, where our cultural-historical knowledge ends (or begins, if you wish) and bear witness to the decisive presence of the transformation myth.[5] Conversely, all late periods in the cultural development both of individual civilizations and of mankind naturally have their creation myths, which allegedly correspond to early ages.

So, too, matriarchal and patriarchal consciousness cannot be shown to ensue in history with the regularity of a law. The medieval world of Islam was, e.g., clearly characterized by a masculine consciousness, while in simultaneous and likewise decidedly medieval Catholicism the mother archetype exerted a strong influence in the shape of the Mater Ecclesia and her priests as well as in the Mother of God. As far as the masculine mentality is concerned, medieval Islam, on the other hand, corresponds, rather, to Protestantism, which is characteristic of modern times. Furthermore, medieval scholasticism, with its spiritual character (father archetype), was replaced, as it were, by the natural sciences of our time, which by virtue of their subject matter (Mother

---

[3] Cf. *O&H*, p. xxi.
[4] *Ibid.*, p. xix.
[5] Cf. Heino Gehrts, *Das Märchen und das Opfer* (Bonn: Bouvier, 1967).

Nature) and their 'materialistic' mode of thinking (concretism, empiricism, quantification, search for elements) prove to be in the service of the Great Mother (and are not, as is commonly held, evidence of a "patriarchal" consciousness).

In a similar way, one could produce examples of additional deviations from the postulated sequence from other ages of cultural history. Of course, Neumann offers an explanation for such discrepancies. "In individual development and perhaps also in that of the collective, these layers do not lie on top of one another in an orderly arrangement, but, as in the geological stratification of the earth, early layers may be pushed to the top and late layers to the bottom."[6]

Here he overlooks the fundamental difference between geological stratification and development in stages. For in the case of geology, one is dealing with material, concrete layers in space, where transposition is possible, whereas cultural development is subject to the law of irreversible time. A transposition of temporal stages is a contradiction in itself; if the "stages" are irregularly and randomly arranged in historical time, this must refute the concept of stages. For we also do not say that the earlier geological layer can be displaced in time towards a later geological age, but only that it can be transposed upwards in space.

Such deliberations force us to the conclusion that the application of the idea of development to cultural history is unfruitful; it does not work. There are changes in history, but there is no evolution. This is a conclusion also arrived at by most historians of religion after the attempt of decades or more to force some evolutionary pattern onto history, such as the sequence of belief in souls, in spirits and in gods (Tylor) or of prereligion, polydemonism, polytheism, monotheism (R. Otto). Mensching remarks on this subject that "there can be no doubt that these forms of religion cannot be subordinated to a historical evolutionary schema."[7] According to Jensen also, such stages are mere speculation.[8] Hillman made the same point for psychology with reference to a relevant monograph by Radin.[9]

---

[6] *O&H*, p. 41f.
[7] Gustav Mensching, *Die Religion* (München: Goldmann Taschenbuch, n. d.), p. 277 (my translation).
[8] Adolf Jensen, *Mythos und Kult bei Naturvölkern*, 1951, p. 335, cited by Mensching, *op. cit.*, p. 273.
[9] James Hillman, "Psychology: Monotheistic or Polytheistic," *Spring 1971*, pp. 193ff.

In our context, the contributions of anthropology to the topic of cultural development are more momentous by far than the question of the evolution of forms of religion. When, e.g., we read in Eliade that "we do not know whether the matriarchate ever existed as an independent cycle of culture" and that "ethnologists are in agreement upon one specific point—that matriarchy cannot have been a primordial phenomenon,"[10] then this strikes a mortal blow at *The Origins and History of Consciousness,* as does the statement that "there is no proof that secret societies, as a general phenomenon, were a consequence of the matriarchate." Eliade, on the contrary, considers irresistible the conclusion that the men's secret societies derive from the mysteries of tribal initiation (independently of a particular type of culture).[11]

To speak at all of a phylogeny in the psychic realm is even more fundamentally denied to us. For if we should take the term phylogeny to refer to cultural history as far as it is known to us, this would be the same as if we wanted to base a representation of ontogeny solely on our knowledge of the mental development of adults of advanced age. Cultural development, as far as it is accessible to us, is not phylogeny any more. The latter precedes cultural history by hundreds of millennia. Just as the mental development of a philosopher or artist by no means follows fixed laws of sequence in the sense of ontogeny, but is, in every individual case, different and new, so also must the intellectual history of mankind not be confused with a phylogeny. If, however, we realize that the cultural history known to us is a late history, then any speculation as to the course of phylogeny becomes impossible in view of our total ignorance concerning the psychic situation of early mankind.

Neumann makes the following objection to Freud's idea of the castration threat by the primal fathers in the primal horde: "Science has discovered nothing that could possibly support such a theory ...."[12] The same objection could be raised to Neumann's own theory of the *Ursprungsgeschichte.* But perhaps he invalidated such an objection in advance, for he also writes:

---

[10] Mircea Eliade, *Myths, Dreams, and Mysteries,* trans. Ph. Mairet (New York: Harper Torchbooks, 1967), p. 177.

[11] *Ibid.,* p. 201.

[12] *O&H,* p. xxi.

> A reduction ... to historical and personalistic data ... is
> scientifically impossible. ... It is one of the tasks of this book to
> show that, in regard to these and similar 'complexes,' we are really
> dealing with symbols, ideal forms, psychic categories, and basic
> structural patterns. ... When we say masculine or feminine
> dominants obtrude themselves at certain stages, or in certain
> cultures or types of person, this is a psychological statement
> which must not be reduced to biological or sociological terms.[13]

Such utterances, although limited to the castration complex and
other such "symbols," may by implication suggest that in the last
analysis, Neumann wants everything he says understood as "symbolic
facts" which then could not be located in empirical ("personalistic")
history. Quite apart from any endeavors to derive myths from
historical events, the mere attempt to search history for
correspondences to the mythological patterns Neumann establishes
might already be considered reductive. If he indeed means all his
concepts to be exclusively symbols, then the book in question is in
fact not a history and does not aim to be one. It moves solely in the
realm of archetypal images and waives any claim to its possible
relevance for the facts of empirical reality. Moreover, if the uroboric
phase, matriarchy, the separation of the world parents, etc., are meant
as strictly symbolic, this would also mean that the phases and stages
themselves, indeed the entire notion of evolution and phylogeny in
general, are likewise to be taken symbolically and not as in any way
referring to historical processes.

Thus, we return to our earlier characterization of *The Origins and
History* as fictitious or as a speculative construction, but *we are* now in
a position to see this fact in a new light, in its positive aspect: *The
Origins and History of Consciousness* is, on the whole, purely symbolic,
that is to say, a myth, an archetypal fantasy. Neumann's work does
not belong to the area of science: neither to the study of history
(because it is oblivious to empirical facts), nor to a science of myth
(because it is not concerned with laws inherent in myth itself), nor to
an archetypal psychology (because it does not investigate the
phenomenology of an archetype at the same time recognizing that the
investigation itself expresses the archetype). In science one enters into

---

[13] *Ibid.*, p. xxif.

a cognitive relationship with some object. The *Ursprungsgeschichte,* on the other hand, rests as a purely symbolic idea in itself, and as a myth it most nearly belongs to the realm of literary fiction. The fantasy of phylogeny is, as it were, a self-representation of an archetype. This by no means makes the value of the book questionable—its worth merely lies on a different level: instead of directly enriching our knowledge *about* the soul, it is itself one of the "timeless documents of the soul" (to quote a book title), and one could write a psychological study about it with the heading, "A Modern Myth—On Things That Are Seen in (or into?) History."

To prevent a possible misconception—the *Ursprungsgeschichte* is not to be considered a myth because so many motifs from various mythologies occur in it. Even without mention of any such motif it would remain a myth. These motifs are merely used by way of illustration and as a means of expression for the actual myth of the *Ursprungsgeschichte*, as building blocks and carriers of meaning. They function as the letters with which the myth of genetic development is written. What makes the book a mythos is the archetypal fantasy of genetic development itself, the idea of phylogeny and of the progressive differentiation from the uroboric One to the radiant sun-hero.

The regrettable thing about this mythos, as about most other modern myths too (Freud, Marx!), is that it is *not presented as myth, but as science*. It is an involuntary myth. Just as Freud derives, reductively and literalistically, the family romance of the neurotic from actual childhood experiences and the family situation, so the "hero myth of the neurotic" and the idea of evolution are here, too, taken as factual and historical despite the insistence on the archetypal and symbolic. Because of this amalgamation of the archetypal with the empirical-factual, the mythic fantasy of genesis is deprived of its true nature and cannot be what it is. This amalgamation is responsible for the scintillating character of the book, for the oscillation between the historiographic and the purely symbolic.

It is not the projection upon the dark beginnings of history which perverts the myth. Even in the mythological age, creation myths were most likely projected into the historical past without losing their true nature. No, it is the fact that in our secularized and positivistic age the projection falls upon a history no longer open to metaphorical and mythic understanding, a history frozen into hard scientific-empirical fact. Likewise, concerning the involuntary character of the myth, it cannot be demanded that one's confinement therein be dissolved, in other words, that Neumann step out of the myth of genesis and write a truly scientific account of *Ursprungsgeschichte.* For this would be a demand for de-mythologizing. On the contrary, it is to be regretted that the confinement in this myth is not openly acknowledged and accepted, but that it is, rather, converted into supposed scientific knowledge and thus smothered. And indeed, it is this lack of acceptance and insight, and this conversion, which make the confinement all the more absolute, and yet at the same time paradoxically amount to an attempt to step out of the myth.

When at this point we pause to reflect, we realize that it should have been clear from the outset that, as regards phylogeny, we are dealing with an archetypal or mythical idea. How was it possible for this myth to be confused with empirical history in the first place? Of course, genesis is a theory, a point of view, a fantasy, and not a fact! Even in biology, where this fantasy is at home and where there are many more facts supporting it, this remains a truism. Thus, Adolf Portmann, speaking as a biologist, frequently describes the concept of evolution as what it is: not a scientific truth, but a matter of *faith.*[14] As a myth it is indeed a religious idea, and that is why it exerts such a tremendous fascination and captivates not only Neumann but also those who follow him. Because it is an archetypal and religious system, it forces itself upon consciousness as having absolute, unquestionable truth and therefore remains unreflected, even unseen, so that, like the repressed, it must return "outside" in history, as an "observed" empirical fact.

Not only Neumann's followers, but also we ourselves (despite, or rather in, our very criticism) were blindly contained in the same myth when, at the beginning of this paper, we tried to corroborate or refute Neumann on the basis of empirical argumentation, such as when we asked whether there is in fact a regular sequence of stages of consciousness in history—as if such questions were not entirely irrelevant from a psychological point of view. It is not our business as psychologists to base our insights on historical or biological facts. For if this were so, psychology would be a branch or offshoot of biology and history. We are not historians, and we are not (or ought not to

---

[14] E.g., Adolf Portmann, "Die werdende Menschheit. Das Ursprungsproblem der Menschheit", *Historia mundi,* ed. Fr. Valjavec, vol. I (Bern: Francke, 1952), p. 28.

be) concerned with empirical, but with *psychological* truth, that is to say with the imaginal. And it is therefore from the imagination that we should derive our knowledge. The historian or biologist may be concerned with a possible factual evolution, but even then it would be the task of the psychologist to remind him (if he should forget what Portmann realized) that "evolution" is an archetypal idea and is not grounded in empirical nature. It seems, however, that at present we psychologists have to be told by the biologist (Portmann) what should have been a basic insight for us. Something (some "factor") obviously keeps us from the truly psychological orientation and makes our thinking unpsychological by making us wish for, or even need, empirical verification, scientific truth, and systematizations. This "factor" is our containment in the Great Mother/Hero myth, whose nature it is to create the (mythic!) fantasy of the possibility of heroically breaking out of myth, into "fact," "truth," "science."

The amalgamation of the imaginal with the empirical is not without consequences. Thus, the archetype is said to have a historical aspect (in addition to its "eternal" significance).[15] Philosophically speaking, this is a fallacy for which there can be no support. How can an *arche-typon*, a primordial image, have a genetic or historical aspect? Jung terms the archetypes "categories of the imagination," or also "divine figures." That a category could in itself have a historical aspect is a *contradictio in se*. 'Quantity', 'time', 'causality' as categories remain forever what they are. *They* do not develop, even if our knowledge and ideas about them might change. The Gods too are, in principle, timeless; they live "in eternal youth." The divine child is always a child, the old wise man was never a youth. To be sure, there is an archetype of development, just as there also is a God of history, but there is no development, no regular sequence of the archetypes, and thus there are no archetypal phases. One could never succeed in establishing a consistent chronology of events reported in the various myths because mythic "events" do not, in principle, follow one upon the other as in empirical time, but are, as images, juxtaposed and contaminated with each other. To put the cause of development into the archetypal realm, into the world of the Gods, is to reduce the archetypes; although one may still conceive of them as transpersonal and place them in the

---

[15] *O&H*, p. xvi.

"beyond" of the collective unconscious, nevertheless, they would now be limited to empirical-temporal conditions. It would mean that one brought the Gods down from Olympus and deprived the categories of their *a priori* character, as conversely history would be freed of its earthly weight. For there would then be only the "stories above" (Thomas Mann), and no longer history below, but the myths (the stories above) would have to take over the character of history too.

The postulate of an historical aspect of the archetype demands that we imagine the archetypes as programmed or, figuratively speaking, equipped with a kind of clockwork triggering them at the right moment, i.e., causing them to constellate like an automaton. To what extent such a mechanistic or biological fantasy shaped Neumann's consciousness can be illustrated by the following statement: "As organs of the psyche's structure the archetypes just as autonomously become active [*schalten sich ein!*] as do physical organs and determine the maturation of the personality in a manner analogous, e.g., to the biological-hormonal components of the constitution"![16] The categories of biology are applied to the spiritual, and the latter is thereby reduced to the "biological."

Although actually self-evident, it nevertheless must still be stressed that evolution, if it should exist, belongs to the phenomenal realm, and thus can be explained only *a posteriori*, from empirical conditions, not from the archetypes. To be sure, in the course of history different archetypes have been constellated, now this one, now that. But why and how this was, and whether or not there has been a regular sequence, can be learned only from the facts of history, not from myth. *Entwicklungsgeschichte* is an area to be examined by biology, history, or related empirical sciences. An archetypal psychology, however, cannot contribute to it. Neumann and we who believe him do not notice (or, at least, we disregard) the fact that archetypes, as *mundus imaginalis,* possess an entirely different ontological modality from the events of the historical world of man to which the genetic belongs. With the fantasy of genesis (which is in itself true because it is archetypal) nothing has been determined as to the genetic character of history, neither one way nor the other.

---

[16] Erich Neumann, *Ursprungsgeschichte des Bewußtseins* (Zürich: Rascher, 1949), p. 4 (my translation).

The amalgamation of the empirical and archetypal is also obvious in the concept of "*Ursprungsgeschichte*" which, within an archetypal psychology, is self-contradictory in that two heterogeneous elements, the archetypal origin and empirical-factual history, are joined together and thus placed on the same level. But the origin must not be sought for at the beginning of history, but is correlated to every present moment. *Ursprung und Gegenwart,* as Jean Gebser entitled his book, belong inseparably together by virtue of their polar separation. The origin is (at least for an archetypal view) never in history, or temporally before it, but "above" it, in a "place above the heavens" (Plato), or *in illo tempore*, as Eliade likes to stress. Conversely, history must not be merged into the archetypal origin. The concept of an *Ursprungsgeschichte* is not fundamentally different from Freud's postulate of a (historical) primal horde except that in Neumann the mythic origin swallows up history, while Freud allows the mythic fantasy to merge with history. This may be the reason for Neumann's frequent and sharp attacks on Freud, because his view is not so fundamentally different from Freud's after all. Neumann is able at one and the same time to locate the origin in transpersonal myth and yet to understand it as actual (pre-)history. Thus, neither the factual nor the imaginal can be true to its own nature.

*   *   *

Whereas in *The Origins and History* the archetypal phases were, so to speak, suspended in the air because they lacked an empirical foundation, the relationship between the factual and the archetypal seems to be the opposite in Neumann's *The Child: Structure and Dynamics of the Nascent Personality*: there the discussion of ontogeny is indeed based on empirical facts, and there can be no doubt that as far as children are concerned there is development, growth, and maturation. But that this development proceeds in *archetypal* stages seems to me extremely questionable. Is it not possible that in *The Child* a physiologically determined growth is merely "dressed up" as archetypal? Remarkably enough, academic psychology and psychoanalysis were able to set up psychologies of development sufficiently describing the known facts without needing to have recourse to the notion of archetypes. What does "uroboric stage" add to the "symbiotic or dyadic relationship of mother and child" in psychoanalysis? Is this not merely a different formulation for the same idea? We must not forget that even instinct-oriented psychoanalysis has long gone beyond Freud's personalistic attitude. I cannot help having the impression that *The Child* is at bottom an instinct-psychological study only 'secondarily' 'translated' into the archetypal. And such must be the case, for we have already seen that an actual development cannot be explained by having recourse to archetypes. Genetic growth, where it is not a perspective (an archetypal idea), is a natural process, and even in the case of mental development it is biological or quasi-biological, not archetypal or spiritual.

Neumann has not shown that the archetype of the uroboros governs early childhood; he merely *uses* this image to describe the initial psychic condition—or rather his view of this condition. That is to say, it is his consciousness that is structured by the archetype of the uroboros, *he* has an uroboric fantasy and projects it upon the child, just as Freud placed his theory of penis envy into the minds of girls: "Freud's fantasy *of* the little girl's mind becomes a Freudian fantasy *in* the little girl's mind," as Hillman[17] puts it. The fact that the uroboros is taken from mythology does not make it a description of actual childhood in any way more—or less—archetypal or mythic than Freud's concept of orality. On the contrary, whereas a concept does not claim to give archetypal insight, the use of a mythic image for the description of empirical facts identifies the archetypes with, and reduces them to, empirical reality, while at the same time degrading what could be a fantasy in its own right to a mere figure of speech.

A psychology of development concerned with actual ages and occurrences cannot be an archetypal psychology because it literalizes the imaginal. Not even the frequent use of the word archetype and of myths can alter this. Whether one projects the Oedipus complex *or* the uroboros into actual childhood, one betrays a reductive thinking. Jung, in writing about the child, was not concerned with actual childhood, but with the archetypal child motif and specifically warned against confusing it with the empirical child (*CW* 9.i, p. 161n.). A psychology is archetypal only if it takes to heart the basic insights contained in the following statement:

---

[17] James Hillman, *The Myth of Analysis* (Evanston: Northwestern UP, 1972), p. 243.

> The child, like the 'primal horde' of the prehistorical past, is an unknown *tabula rasa* or *prima materia*, upon the ground of whose emptiness one may freely propound one's fantasies without contradiction or even response. When we parade forth the child, the primitive, the animal, or the archaeological past—and, I would add, the patient—as observational basis for psychology in order to support a theory by grounding it in 'origins,' nowhere could we better reveal the archetypal fantasy of the theory we are in this manner justifying. The true origin is the archetypal fantasy itself, not the objective scene where the fantasy is 'observed' as 'fact.'[18]

Opposing the concept of an archetypal ontogeny does not mean rejecting the idea that the child's mind, too, is structured by archetypes. Of course it is. But a simple schema does not help us here, any more than it does in the case of adults. What I want to object to is the unfortunate amalgamation of the archetypal and the genetic, which brings with it a kind of mechanistic automation and which nails down both the child to only a few, rigidly defined archetypal possibilities and the archetypes to a limited number of stages. Furthermore, it literalistically confines the imaginal in the factual, whereas the archetypes should conversely enable us to amplify, in the direction of soul, the merely natural, the instincts, and factual reality, and to proceed beyond the monotony and factuality, i.e., beyond the 'mono'-interpretation, of what is given. ... Also, a psychology with a genetic orientation cannot be interested in a differentiated understanding of archetypal images. It prefers to recognize the uroboros in paradise, in the womb, the grave, the mandala, the cohabitation of Heaven and Earth, in Okeanos and Purusha, and thus to diagnose a certain phase of consciousness, using a mythic image as an abstract concept, rather than to work out the *specific meaning of each individual image*.

Now, as far as the equals sign between ontogeny and phylogeny is concerned—the view that "ontogenetic development" is "a modified recapitulation of phylogenetic development"[19]—we can again refer to Portmann, according to whom even the "biogenetic law" originates in a creed,[20] or we can say all that is needed with the following

---

[18] *Ibid.*
[19] *O&H*, p. xx.
[20] Adolf Portmann, *Zoologie und das neue Bild des Menschen* (Rowohlts Deutsche Enzyklopädie), no date, p. 78.

statement: It is nowhere established (despite E. Neumann) that the phylogenetic stages (if there are such things) necessarily parallel stages of individual consciousness (if there are such things).[21]

*   *   *

We have herewith answered in the narrower sense the question posed by our topic. Now we shall trace out more broadly the background of the amalgamation of the archetypal and the factual by examining Neumann's work for its immanent intention. We see the thrust of all his scholarly endeavors directed towards one single center, towards one highest idea: the *Einheitswirklichkeit*. Interestingly enough, Jung also introduced a concept with the same literal meaning: *unus mundus*. But as Marie-Louise von Franz pointed out, there is a fundamental difference between the two concepts.[22] Whereas the *unus mundus* exists only *in potentia* or could perhaps be said to have only an ideal existence, so that the antinomial character of this world, especially the separation of physis and psyche, remains untouched, the *Einheitswirklichkeit* posits an actual unity in our world, from which we originate in a historical sense and from which we are separated merely through the development of consciousness. It is an immanent unity that even becomes almost concretely visible to our consciousness (which normally must resolve everything into opposites) in some zoological phenomena,[23] e.g., and above all in the uroboric relationship of mother and child. For Neumann, even the milk of the mother—in its physical factualness!—is a part of the archetype, and "among all functions of motherliness which to our consciousness appear as physical or psychic" there exists a "contamination and participation"[24] in other words, the opposites actually do not exist; nature and spirit, archetypal image and factual reality, are contaminated with each other or are one and the same. It is "only" our consciousness which divides what in literal reality is One. The place of the *mysterium coniunctionis*, in which the opposites, without losing their peculiar character, can unite in, and by virtue of, a Third,

---

[21] Hillman, "Psychology: Monotheistic or Polytheistic", pp. 195f (modif.).

[22] Marie-Louise von Franz, *Zahl und Zeit* (Stuttgart: Klett, 1970), p. 16n.

[23] Erich Neumann, "Die Erfahrung der Einheitswirklichkeit", *Der schöpferische Mensch* (Darmstadt: Wiss. Buchges., 1965), p. 62ff.

[24] Erich Neumann, *Das Kind,* ed. J. Neumann (Zürich: Rhein-Verlag, 1963), p. 93f (my translation).

is taken by a factual unity containing the opposites in a state of amalgamation comparable to a compromise.

A remark of Neumann's clearly shows with how great a force the archetype of oneness must have driven him: "Analytical psychology, contrary to psychoanalysis, has a primarily monistic orientation. Its libido theory does not assume a speculative opposition of eros and thanatos, but replaces it with the secondary polarization of the primarily uniform libido ....."[25] This is by no means true for analytical psychology as such. Here the libido is not only hypostasized, in contradiction to Jung—for Jung, libido is not a *dynamis*, a something, but as energy it is rather a mere (theoretical) concept of quantity, so that the question of uniform vs. polar structure does not apply in the first place—but it is also obvious that such views are in strongest contrast to the basic principles of Jungian psychology.

The problem of opposites holds so prominent a place in Jung's psychology that Leonhard Schlegel[26] was able to base his discussion of it on the idea of the polarity of the psyche. Also, according to this psychology the dynamics of the psyche exclusively exist by virtue of the tension of opposites. And Jung himself expressly rejected any kind of monism:

> So far as I myself can pass judgement on my own point of view, it differs from the psychologies discussed above in this respect, that it is not monistic but, if anything, dualistic, being based on the principle of opposites, and possibly pluralistic, since it recognizes a multiplicity of relatively autonomous psychic complexes (*CW* 4 § 758).

How fundamental this dualism was for Jung can be seen from the fact that he conceived of even the ultimate principle, God, as an internal antinomy or paradox. "God himself", he wrote to Neumann on 5. 1. 1952, "is a *contradictio in adiecto* ...."[27]

It is now very important to realize that the faith in *Einheitswirklichkeit* is not a genuine monism such as materialism or

---

[25] *Ibid.*, p. 55 (my translation).
[26] Leonhard Schlegel, *Die Polarität der Psyche und ihre Integration. Eine kritische Darstellung der Psychologie von C. G. Jung* (vol. 4 of his *Grundriß der Tiefenpsychologie*) (München: Uni-Taschenbücher, Francke, 1973).
[27] C. G. Jung, *Briefe*, ed. A. Jaffé, vol. 2 (Olten/Freiburg: Walter, 1972), p. 241 (my translation).

idealism, where only one pole is accepted and the other one is explained reductively in terms of the first. We already said that the *Einheitswirklichkeit* contains the opposites in a state of amalgamation, and indeed the very word unity implies, or presupposes, a fantasy of opposites. Paradoxically, the fantasies of unity and of opposites seem to belong to the same archetypal configuration, the one being the answer (almost inherent) to the problem presented by the other. This problem is the same as the one Schiller expressed in the following lines:

> *Ach, kein Steg will dahin führen,*
> *Ach der Himmel über mir*
> *Will die Erde nie berühren …*

(Alas, no footbridge will lead thither / Alas, Heaven above me / Will never touch the Earth ….) It is the vision of a world rent into two halves, an 'upper' one which as 'Idea' contains all spiritual meaning, but volatilizes, and a 'lower' one, which, being 'phenomenal,' is heavy and concrete, but utterly without meaning.

Of course, in psychology we are not wont to use these terms, but in our language the same old pair of opposites reappears, e.g., under the names Ego/Self. It is, however, not sufficient to characterize the Ego-Self fantasy as one of opposites, for there are different types of opposition. We are here specifically dealing with a dualism in the sense of the Law of Contradiction, i.e., the mutual exclusion of the opposites. Schiller's image beautifully reveals which archetype is at work here producing such a hopeless ontology. This image is the motif of the separation of the world parents, only too well known to us from the *Ursprungsgeschichte*.

Thus, we again see that one and the same archetype, the hero myth, both creates the problem of polarity and provides the answer to it (i.e., the content of Neumann's psychology)—at once and *a priori* so that we cannot say which is first, problem or solution. But there is no solution to this problem. The question, as it is posed under the dominance of the hero archetype, excludes an answer from the beginning. Nothing can unite Heaven and Earth once they are defined as separated. We here encounter the tragedy of the heroic ego, which can only continue to separate, dissolve, analyze, and kill, but never again find connectedness, not because such connectedness is altogether impossible, but because it has no place within a myth aiming for separation and violence. The "premise" of the vision structured by the hero archetype is war, opposition, severing; the "conclusion," therefore, cannot be oneness and monism. Within the hero mythology, the One can only occur as 'origin' in the past: as something from which one is again fundamentally separated by time.

It is not necessary for us here to enter into the question of to what extent this vision is responsible for the problems of the modern West (alienation, fragmentation, pollution, etc.) and specifically shapes the scientific mind. Our fate, however, may well depend on whether we are able to move out from our confinement in the ultimately deadly hero myth. As we said, there are other visions of the opposites, such as Goethe's symbolic *Weltanschauung*, and the "as above, so below" of magic, astrology, and also alchemy, visions in which the question and the answer are "formulated" entirely differently: Heaven must not touch the Earth because there is a connection despite and even by virtue of the separation. The principle of unity must not be literally fantasied as factual *Einheitswirklichkeit* negating the polarities, but can also be envisioned as a *complexio oppositorum* which at one and the same time ultimately acknowledges the opposition and represents the paradox of their oneness ....[28]

Schiller was aware of and expressed the dilemma of his ontology, and probably also knew about its hopelessness. Hence his lamentation. In Neumann, however, the problem seems to have been "solved" through the device of amalgamation. The footbridge that Schiller lacked was provided by the fantasy of genesis, which made it possible to simply get rid of the problem by identifying the dualistic idea of "Heaven above—Earth below," i.e., a spatial fantasy, with a temporal-linear one. Thus, the archetypal origin ("above") was amalgamated with the temporal origin ("in the beginning"), and the collective unconscious as *mundus imaginalis* was identified with that unconscious out of which consciousness differentiates itself. And vice versa. Likewise, the libido was hypostasized. Whereas in the last analysis the genetic theory tries to present the problem of opposites as an apparent problem, it, instead, itself proves to be an apparent solution. By placing time and the line of development, which begins at a pointlike origin, into the archetypal realm, the "above-below"

---

[28] Cf. Andrew Jaszi, *Entzweiung und Vereinigung. Goethes symbolische Weltanschauung* (Heidelberg: Stiehm, 1973).

problem is of course avoided, but, therefore, also not solved. Instead, the Whence, which Jung says is less essential than the Whither (*CW* 4 § 759) (Whither also to be understood in the sense of Where), again determines the orientation. For within a genetic fantasy, the *aim* of monistic oneness can only be imagined as *origin* and in the past. Thus, origin and goal, forwards and backwards, reconnect in a uroboric circle, showing that even linear thinking ultimately returns to a circular type of thinking.

In a late letter to Jung (18. II. 1959) Neumann seems, however, to have detached himself from linear thinking.

> As far as I for my part am concerned, it is so that the Jewish historical secular 'evolution' [*historische Diesseits'entwicklung'*] becomes ever more problematic to me, as do all evolutionary theories, and the 'actualisation of messianism' in individuation ever more decisive. ... What is valid are the developmental phases of consciousness in individual development; everything else 'historical' belongs to the constellation of the ego as 'time', as do family and physical constitution. The realization of the ego-self-unity is vertical.[29]

Though somewhat cryptic, as Jung also felt the entire letter to be, these sentences amount to an unmistakable renunciation of history, phylogeny, *Ursprungsgeschichte*, and the genetic theory. Here the historical, empirical world (ego) and the archetypal or mythic realm (self) are kept apart, and linear evolution in "horizontal" time (beginning–end) is likewise distinguished from the "vertical" relation ("above–below", ego–self, archetypal realm–empirical reality, *Ursprung–Gegenwart*).

However, it would be a mistake to assume that Neumann here wanted to revoke his earlier work. Instead of resolving the amalgamation, these statements in fact reveal its background. For in the *Ursprungsgeschichte* the amalgamation came about, as we have seen, because the historical was depreciated, but nevertheless stole into the archetypal itself as a genetic aspect of the archetypes. By dethroning the Gods, man becomes identical with them, according to Jung; so the depreciated empirical-temporal (of the "isolated

---

[29] Printed in Aniela Jaffé, *Der Mythos vom Sinn im Werk von C. G. Jung* (Zürich/Stuttgart: Rascher, 1967), p. 180f.

unique historical ego"[30]) must conversely burden the archetypal realm or the self with this very same temporal aspect. To the same degree that horizontal time is made light of, the vertical ego-self axis must take it over and carry it, so that the evolution is now thought to proceed along this vertical axis instead of in historical time. Then the imaginal itself receives a literal and factual character which is to be distinguished from the reverse process of projecting fantasy onto fact or into the empirical realm. Even when projected, myth lives and can move the soul, as the myth of the primal horde probably did for Freud although he did not see that it was a myth. But it is disastrous if the archetypal is seen for what it is and is yet simultaneously forced to become factual, for then myth is stifled on its own ground. Nevertheless, even this stifling of myth is the doing of archetypal persons, the doing of the Great Mother/Hero myth, as we pointed out. Therefore, here, too, a myth is alive and is, though blindly, being enacted.

It would seem to be this Hero/Great Mother constellation that is responsible for the one-sided emphasis on the vertical ego-self axis and for the depreciation of historical time; that furthermore promises meaning by creating the fantasy of an "absolute and extraneous knowledge" and of a "fixed order," i.e., that kind of meaning Mother Nature can provide; and that finally helps sustain a fundamental ideological optimism[31] by making light of all the trials of history, of all suffering and imperfection, because it conceives of them as belonging merely "to the constellation of the ego as 'time'." Thus Neumann denied that today we are experiencing a "*Verlust der Mitte*" (a loss of the center, Hans Sedlmayr) and he believed that the morbidity of a person was voided if, in addition, he possessed creativity.[32] By promising redemption from history and fate, and by making us strive for the certainty and safety of a deductive system[33] corresponding to the "fixed order" in nature, the Hero/Great Mother myth (= the ego-

---

[30] *Ibid.*, p. 181.
[31] Cf. C. G. Jung, *op.cit.*, Vol. 3, 1973, p. 99, editor's note 8; cf. also E. Neumann, *Krise und Erneuerung* (Zürich: Rhein-Verlag, 1961).
[32] Erich Neumann, "Georg Trakl – Person und Mythos", *Der schöpferische Mensch*, pp.247ff.
[33] Cf. *O&H*, p. xvii: "The deductive and systematic method of exposition here adopted."

self-axis psychology) lures us away from the anima, the soul, keeping us from being moved by the unknown.[34]

Notwithstanding his other important achievements, Neumann[35] did not render analytical psychology a service in introducing the genetic approach. By following him, that is to say, by taking his system, his phases and stages literally instead of symbolically, we base psychology on an unfitting ontology within which a truly archetypal psychology cannot thrive, while empirical reality is at the same time deprived of its concreteness; we, at bottom, reaffirm—despite our anti-positivistic concern with the symbolical and transpersonal—the Darwinian prejudice according to which we like to ascribe unconsciousness to the primitive and a highly developed consciousness to ourselves; and above all, we fall into the Hero/Great Mother myth and thus become unpsychological.

---

[34] On the anima as mediatrix to the unknown see James Hillman, "'Anima' (II)", *Spring 1974,* pp. 124ff.

[35] We should not overlook the fact that Jung had some words of praise for Neumann's work, e.g., *CW* 5 § 3. But it is not our task here to discuss Jung's position regarding Neumann's thought.

CHAPTER TWO

On the Neurosis of Psychology or the Third of the Two

From the very beginning, depth psychology has been exposed to attacks. Nowadays, it is especially the political Left that criticizes it, accusing it of tinkering with individuals while neglecting the real causes of psychic disorders which are inherent in the societal system. On the one hand, we must not shrug such a criticism off; but on the other hand, we must realize that in the last analysis it cannot truly affect our discipline because political-social categories are, in principle, not applicable to the nature of psychology. We must insist that psychology be assessed from psychological points of view, just as physics or medicine or politics are assessed according to physical or medicinal or political criteria, respectively. We must not ourselves succumb to the temptation (despite the obvious fascination it holds today) to use in psychology a sociological or political thinking. In this sense I wish, to be sure, to do justice to the critical concern in this paper, but I want to develop and make plausible the criticism strictly from within psychological thought itself and from within depth psychology's own tradition. For both in Freud (especially in his piece on the interminable analysis) and above all in Jung we already find crucial beginnings of an immanent (psychological) critique of depth psychology, and our task is merely to take them up and develop them, whereas so far they have, for the most part, been ignored.

1. THE THIRD PERSON OF PSYCHOTHERAPY

In contrast to 'group therapy,' we speak of 'individual therapy,' *'Einzeltherapie.'* A strange formulation, for does it not imply a one-person affair? This formulation evokes reminiscences of the early "talking cure," the monologue of the patient, in which the therapist functioned only as an observing audience, an outsider. Through this term a conventional medical thought pattern seems to intrude into our psychological thinking, or rather, cling to it, although we believe we overcame it long ago. Surely, we know and accept that psychotherapy is a two-person affair, a dialogue, that the analyst is inevitably drawn in, and that Jung even went far beyond the acknowledgement of a duality based on transference by demanding that the doctor step out of his role altogether and enter fully into the process on an equal footing with the patient. Just as the patient is to lift his mask in analysis, so is the analyst supposed to give up his anonymity. Mutuality takes the place of asymmetry. We know and affirm this—but the term "individual therapy" (let alone our practice) shows what a powerful hold conventional thinking has over us. We obviously still think of psychotherapy as a one-way process in which everything revolves about the patient. *He* has to be cured. *Psychotherapy is fixated on the patient.*

Jung even went beyond the dialogue idea to a dialectic understanding of psychotherapy. Whereas a dialogue is an interaction or communication between *two* persons, dialectics involves a Third. A dialectic understanding of therapy thus implies that doctor and patient are not alone. There always is a third factor, a third "person" present. This idea of the Third characterizes Jung's view of psychotherapy throughout. We read, e.g., in "Psychology of Transference" (*CW* 16 § 399), "Psychological induction inevitably causes the two parties to get involved in the transformation of the third and to be themselves transformed in the process." It is this third "person" on which the therapy ultimately depends. The psychological induction is here not thought of as running from the patient to the analyst or vice versa, but rather as an embeddedness of both persons in the Third, in "mutual unconsciousness" (*CW* 16 § 364). Instead of asymmetrically concentrating on the patient, both persons now focus their attention on this objective third factor.

What is this factor, who is the third person of psychotherapy? It is, of course, the soul, which is no longer to be imagined as the individual property of each of the two other persons, but must be given independent reality. It is the world of complexes and archetypal images, of views and styles of consciousness, and thus it is also psychology itself, in the widest sense of the word, including all our ideas about the soul, its pathology and therapy, as well as our *Weltanschauung*. "As the most complex of psychic structures," writes Jung (*CW* 16 § 180), "a man's philosophy of life forms the counterpole to the physiologically conditioned psyche, and, as the highest psychic dominant, it ultimately determines the latter's fate. It guides the life of the therapist and shapes the spirit of his therapy." The third person unfolds into two aspects or counterparts, which can be distinguished, but ultimately belong together: the soul itself and the theory about it (psychology), and, if we follow Jung, it is the latter on which the fate of the former depends.

Our psychological theories are thus of highest importance to the outcome of therapy (cf.: *CW* 10 § 340). They are present from the beginning, and they guide and shape the spirit of therapy. If psychology is in this sense the third autonomous person with a living and decisive presence in psychotherapy, it may also be suspected of having its own unconsciousness—and possibly even its own neurosis.

2. THE NEUROSIS OF PSYCHOLOGY

It was again Jung who formulated this suspicion and elaborated on it. In a paper written in 1934, he comes to the conclusion that "[t]here is no way, it seems to me, how the psychotherapy of today can get around doing a great deal of unlearning and relearning, ... until it may succeed in no longer thinking neurotically itself." (*CW* 10 § 369, transl. modif.). To begin with, psychology itself thinks in a neurotic fashion, according to Jung. In the same paper we find a number of different formulations for this idea, mainly in reference to Freud's psychoanalysis. Thus, Jung argues that precisely that which happens to the neurotic has been raised to the level of a 'theory' by the psychoanalyst, so that patient and doctor ride "the same hobbyhorse" (*CW* 10 § 362). "It is positively grotesque that the doctor should himself fall into a way of thinking which in others he rightly censures ... and wants to cure ..." (*CW* 10 § 356). Or, "Freud, in other words, took the neurotic conjectures seriously and thus fell into the same trap as the neurotic ..." (*CW* 10 § 365, modif.).

These sentences contain a scandalous thesis. Neurosis is not what the patient has and for what psychology provides the remedy, but is already inherent in therapeutic psychology itself. Patient and doctor— a case of *folie à deux*! Instead of being the healing answer to neurosis, instead of overcoming it and bringing an end to it, therapeutic psychology is the continuation of neurosis by other means. Or, in the words of the cynical joke attributed to Karl Kraus, psychoanalysis is that disease of which it purports to be the cure.

Because Jung exemplified this thesis mainly by psychoanalysis, it was usually taken as an expression of his alleged anti-Freudian resentment and thus it was not felt necessary to take it seriously. We do not want to follow this train of thought and place Jung's idea within a fantasy of the battle among the schools of depth psychology. We, rather, take it seriously, as containing an important principle, a critical tool with which to examine *our own* psychological assumptions. Our critical question is: where do we, in and with our theories, ride the same hobbyhorse as the patient?

The question is not directed at us as persons. Our purpose here is not to analyse the neurotic features of the therapist as a private individual, but rather those of psychology itself, which we are here regarding as an autonomous "person." We want to find out whether our psychological theory has taken over neurotic thought patterns and mechanisms into the structure of its own "consciousness" and whether it tries to fight or cure those very same mechanisms in the patient in order to defend itself against becoming aware of its own neurosis. Does psychology "act out" (on the level of theory) instead of "remembering," *erinnern*? Of course, it is impossible to review the sum total of our psychological ideas in this paper. We must content ourselves with a number of characteristic examples that show the principle indicated by Jung at work in central areas of our psychology.

3. THE 'NEGATION OF THE NEGATIVE'

I take this phrase and idea from Erich Neumann's *Depth Psychology and a New Ethic*, where it is revealed as being at the core of the scapegoat mentality of old ethics, whereas depth psychology in its entirety has meant the confrontation of modern man with all those factors that he wanted to close his eyes to. This was true from the very beginning of psychoanalysis with Freud, who brought about the recognition of sexuality within a Victorian world, to Jung's emphasis on the shadow and his attempt to integrate the idea of evil even into the image of God. *The* principle of depth psychology is the *lifting of the repressions,* and there can be no doubt that this principle guides the practice of analytical psychotherapists, who do not want to talk the patient out of his symptoms, but allow him (or her) to 'regress,' that is, to follow the path of his pathology. So much for analytical practice. But how about psychological theory?

It seems to me, what our theory thinks about regression can be summarized in the oft-quoted saying *"reculer pour mieux sauter"*: regression for the purpose of an even better progression. We affirm pathology and regression, but only because a reward is in the offing. Psychological theory holds out a carrot, much as in Christian theology the promise of Heaven makes the vale of tears palatable. It is only a token acceptance, necessitated by the circumstances, but not a wholehearted affirmation. Just as the neurotic, if it turns out that his fantasy cannot be realized, is ready to put up with all kinds of disagreeable symptoms and to accept all sorts of concessions—so long as he does not have to give up his fantasy altogether—so is psychology willing to make concessions to the id, the infantile fantasies, and pathology, if it can thereby avoid having to change its innermost attitude of hostility towards the pathological. Even if in analytical practice the symptoms and the regressive tendencies are accepted, our thinking retains the habitual attitude that we call negation of the negative. *Reculer pour mieux sauter* means a return, not of the repressed, but of repression! The repression that we fight in the consulting-room returns as a repressive spirit in our very own theory. Here our psychological ideas clearly follow the neurotic mind.

Likewise, when psychotherapy as a whole is conceived after the model of medicine and thinks of itself mainly as a healing and curing profession, it inherits the hostile position that medicine holds towards illness. A standpoint which continues the hostility of the patient toward his disturbance is of course not in accordance with the principle of depth psychology. Both Freud and Jung were aware of this. Freud clearly stated that psychoanalysis was not a department of medicine, not a chapter in a psychiatry textbook, not even medical psychology, but psychology purely and simply.[1] And Jung went so far as to reject altogether the will to heal and change, or at least to query it. "But when a patient realizes that cure through change would mean too great a sacrifice, then the doctor can, indeed he should, *give up any wish to change or cure*" (*CW* 16 § 11, my italics), for what we call healing actually amounts to an amputation (*CW* 10 § 355). Instead of the usual hostile attitude, Jung envisions a gratefulness toward the neurotic symptoms (*CW* 16 § 11) and demands, "We should even learn to be thankful for it [the neurosis], otherwise we pass it by and miss the opportunity ..." (*CW* 10 § 361). "In the neurosis is hidden one's worst enemy and best friend. One cannot rate him too highly [!] ..." (*CW* 10 § 359). "We should not try to 'get rid' of a neurosis, but rather to experience what it means, what it has to teach, what its purpose is. ... A neurosis is truly removed only when it has removed the false attitude of the ego. We do not cure it—it cures us" (*ibid.* § 361). Here Jung's thinking has fully given up the *reculer pour mieux sauter* attitude. This is true depth psychology, because the negative is no longer negated, not even secretly, but unconditionally "*erinnert*" and affirmed—without leaving open an escape hatch.

Jungian theory distinguishes a positive from a negative aspect of the archetypes, and when we find the negative aspect at work in a patient, we think it necessary to 'constellate' the corresponding positive one. Here our "panic fear" (*CW* 10 § 530) of psychopathology expresses itself, as well as does our attempt to combat it through apotropaic measures. We use the good mother to drive out the bad mother. The negative must not be. But we do not simply fight it through activities (constellating the positive aspect), but also theoretically through the "neurotic trick of euphemistic disparagement" (*CW* 10 § 365): we conceive all "negative" images as merely temporary, as an expression of an intermediate stage that hopefully will be followed by 'positive,' 'prospective' images. Thus we devalue the negative. Darkness is 'nothing but' a night-sea-journey upon which there will be a new sunrise, and it is for the sunrise that we are willing to go into the dark. Even worse—"death" becomes the road to rebirth. If this is how we

---

[1] "Nachwort zur 'Frage der Laienanalyse'," in Sigmund Freud, *Studienausgabe*, Ergänzungsband, Frankfurt 1975, p. 343f.

see death, as a mere passage, it does not have a full reality of its own. It is degraded to a means to an end.

Thus, psychology takes sides for life and for light and against darkness and death; it belittles the negative, and through such thinking tries to overcome it, to leave it behind or below. Here we have in our own theory what Jung terms the denial of the left hand. The acceptance of darkness is, so to speak, acted out. We want the patient (or ourselves as persons) to accept it; we project the task of accepting it onto persons and into the consulting-room, and thereby save our theory from having to admit darkness and death into its innermost structure. By the same token, we like to use the formula 'not yet,' this variety of the 'nothing but,' and thus place the negative or imperfect into an *eschatological* fantasy of development or growth. The patient is 'still' in the oral or uroboric phase, he has 'not yet' reached the genital level or the solar-rational stage. With such formulations we implicitly cast out the condition in which he is now; the present condition is not accepted as what it is, but only for what may come out of it. Inherent in the positive hope for a better future is a condemnation of the present. We only *seem* to accept the shadow; in actuality we still repress it, only in a more subtle and less obvious way. The very distinction between the positive and the negative means a dissociation. Moreover, as a *moralistic* value judgment, it necessarily involves a devaluation and repudiation. Speaking about symbols, Jung takes a stand against such thinking. "The moralistic and hygienic temper of our days must always know whether such and such a thing is harmful or useful, right or wrong. A real psychology cannot concern itself with such queries; to recognize how things are in themselves is enough" (*CW* 6 § 203). Positive (prospective) and negative are not psychological categories but instruments of moralistic repression.

Our theory is full of ego; ego-psychology, ego-functions, ego development and stages of the ego, ego-consciousness, and ego-strengthening. What does this mean if not that our theory is dominated by, or fixated upon, the very same ego that ought to be "removed" by the neurosis, as we heard from Jung? "'To hell with the Ego-world!...'" (*Letters 2*, 9 January 1960, to Hugo Charteris). Psychology has again incorporated a neurotic aberration into its very theory. The archetype of the hero, who in some ways can be considered a paramount model of neurotic behavior, has even been made the quasi-official prototype of 'healthy development.' It is the hero who makes the fateful cut that splits the left hand from the right, the precious elements from the waste, and thereby produces the neurotic fantasy, i.e., the condition of dissociation, where "before" there had been wholeness.

When such a heroic ego is confronted with the consequences of its violence and tires of its show of strength, it may long to abandon itself to the "Great Experience," the *Urerfahrung* (Neumann), the "Peak Experience" (Maslow), or the "Creative Moment," something quite out of the ordinary, which, therefore, can also not be attained within ordinary life. This ego will wait for an oversized numinous experience, for the very special Archetypal dream, or practice all sorts of meditative techniques, or even make use of drugs to go on its special trip. A term like Great Experience implies a betrayal of the small events of everyday life and the hero's impotence to experience them. The thinking behind such terms alienates us even more from ourselves and from simple things by depreciating them and inflating us. The place of authentic feeling experiences is then taken by the attempt, requiring great effort, "to repeat a spontaneous, irrational event by a deliberate, imitative arrangement of the analogous circumstances ..." and "through the application of a method, to attain the effects of the primordial experience ...." "Curiously enough, one does not realize that this was a state of spontaneous, natural emotion or *ekstasis*, and thus the complete opposite of a methodically construed imitation" (*Letters 2*, 19 October 1960, to Melvin J. Lasky). If we make clear to ourselves the zeal that psychotherapy applies to the purpose of inventing methods to enable patients to feel again and to develop their emotional life, their body sensitivity and their relationships, the zeal to teach them how to practice meditation and to let out primal screams, one recognizes in this zeal the same heroic ego-mentality that is actually supposed to be overcome through these efforts for an ability to surrender oneself and to practice meditation.

Another type of negation of the negative can be found in the attitude that characterizes conventional depth psychology. Whereas therapy aims for flexibility, spontaneity, free association and active imagination and wants to provide a temenos of warmth and understanding, psychology as theory is interested in hard facts, in a systematic body of experientially based knowledge about the psyche in well-defined concepts, and tries to give itself a scientific air by using a technical jargon, typology, clinical expressions, even 'cases,' by designing tests and employing various other methods for the validation of its findings.

In our practice we take heed of Jung's advice to steer clear of any rigid technique and to be open to the individuality of the patient and to the requirements of the moment. But our theoretical thinking is dominated by practical and technical questions: group therapy or not? Is one allowed to touch the patient? What to do if the patient ...? How to deal with transference reactions? Could "other" techniques, such as gestalt or primal scream, enrich our repertoire? Such are the questions that really interest us, which shows that the technological mind is firmly rooted in the thought of psychology itself. The attitude prevailing in psychological theory is one of control, of "directed thinking," of grasping. If we raise such questions, if the method of how to deal with technical problems is so close to our hearts, does this not mean that we then permit ourselves to entertain the very recipe mentality that we want to dissuade our patients from, for example when they ask us for the ready-made solution for getting rid of this or that problem? "'Technique' is incommensurable. The personality of the patient demands all the resources of the doctor's personality and not technical tricks" (*CW* 10 § 338, transl. modif.). It cannot be that this applies only to the consulting room. It must also be valid for our own theoretical thinking. But obviously our theory uses the very same defense mechanisms of rationalisation and intellectualisation that it fights in the patient; imaginative theorizing, so-called speculation, is banned from theoretical psychology as is a feeling-toned personal involvement and mode of rhetoric. Psychological theory excludes from itself, from its own attitude, the very modes that as psychotherapy it practices and aims at in the consulting room. Symbolic thinking is something that the patient (or modern man in general) is supposed to develop, but our theory balks at it as at "inferior thinking."

Even our idea of wholeness partakes of neurotic thinking. For we expect to achieve completeness through adding previously neglected functions to the number of well-developed ones or by compensating a one-sidedness through supplying the lacking side. In this manner we will get only an aggregate of functions, which *in themselves* are one-sided and split off, but we will never get wholeness.

"Just as the addition of however many zeros will never make 'one'" (*CW* 10 § 516), the addition of functions or personality aspects will never bring about oneness. Even after their combination, they will remain one-sided.

Jung ridiculed the mistaken idea of completeness in a letter of 9. I. 1960 (to Hugo Charteris), discussing the topic of "Socrates and his flute." He states that "[t]he story starts with his *daimonion*, whispering into his ear: 'Thou shouldst make more music, Socrates!' Whereupon dear old well-meaning Socrates went to buy a flute and began lamentable exercises. He obviously misunderstood the advice, but in a characteristic way," by taking the inner voice "literally and technically as if he were a modern man"—or, I would add, as if he were a modern Jungian psychotherapist. What was his misunderstanding? That he thought he could achieve wholeness through compensating his one-sided philosophical activities (thinking) with the 'opposite' activity (music). The equation "philosophy + flute = wholeness" is obviously wrong according to Jung. Compensation does not mean a *behavior* (in the widest sense of this word: all directly or indirectly observable actions of the organism) that is added to the one-sided activity, but it means a change of *attitude*. Instead of thinking on the level of behavior (= literalizing), Socrates should have understood the counsel psychologically. Then he would not have played the flute by way of counterbalance; he would and could have stayed with philosophy—but he would then have philosophized in a less rationalistic, more "musical" fashion. The one-sidedness was not one of behavior (his specialization in philosophy), but one of the attitude with which he practiced this true and only profession of his (cf. Berry, "On Reduction" on this[2]). Thus ,Socrates acted out the compensation on the level of *behavior* when he should have accomplished it on the level of *psychology*, that is, in the "*Erinnerung*" (recollection/interiorization), by an inner change of mind.

Now, returning to ourselves and to psychology, we can say that we too try to act out the idea of wholeness by projecting it onto the patient as a task to be accomplished and by understanding it on the level of behavior in terms of balancing the various functions or activities. But for Jung, wholeness is a matter of the "*Blick fürs Ganze*," having

---

[2] Patricia Berry, "On Reduction," *Spring 1973*, p. 80f. and *passim*.

"an *eye* for the psyche as a whole" (*CW* 10 § 370, transl. modif.), not of becoming a psychological Jack-of-all-trades. It is not our specialization that has to change, but the narrow-mindedness with which we see. The place where wholeness has to be achieved, where the inferior function has to be developed and where the shortcomings that we call "shadow" have to be integrated is not mortal man as person—to think so would be hubris—but it is psychology, the psychology of each of us, as it was the place for Jung himself when he wrote his *book* on types. With these comments we are already touching upon the topic of the following section.

4. PERSONALISM AND REDUCTIONISM

In the same paper that gave us our touchstone with which to examine psychology for a possible neurosis, Jung describes "the prime evil of neurosis" as the loss of the "great relationship." He "who denies the great must blame the petty." Thus did Freud want to "put an end once and for all to the larger aspect of the psychic phenomenon," says Jung with reference to *The Future of an Illusion*, "and in the attempt he continues the baleful work that is going on in every neurotic: destruction of the bond between men and the gods ..." (*CW* 10 § 367). Psychology again perpetuates the very principle behind the patient's neurosis.

What Jung attacks here could be called the empiricism of psychology, that view which, because it denies "the great," looks for the causes in "the petty," i.e., tries to "explain" the neurosis causally from all kinds of "empirical" factors: sexuality or any biological instinct, the bad mother, family structure, social conditions, an organic deficiency, experiences during infancy, the trauma of birth, etc., etc. In all such theories the defense mechanisms of displacement and projection are at work; not only is our interest then directed outside our own field and psychology rooted heteronomously in other branches of knowledge (biology, sociology, behaviorism, medicine, and so on), but the neurosis itself is displaced far away from ourselves, from the soul, into some extrinsic factor. The neuroses must under no circumstances—such theories proclaim—be located within the soul. The external source of the neurosis may of course have to be sought relatively close to us, such as in our body (sexuality) or in some "inferior function"—it will be acceptable as long as it can be experienced (imagined) as something external and objective, in other words, as long as it does not involve our innermost subjectivity, the soul.

Jung, by contrast, advocated the idea that the neurosis *originates*, not from any empirical factor, but "from the soul of the sufferer. Nor does it come from some obscure corner of the unconscious, as many psychotherapists still struggle to believe ..." (*CW* 10 § 337, transl. modif.). Scientific psychology, which aims for knowledge of objective facts, avoids the use of the word "soul" in favor of "behavior"—and this for no small reason. It is not a matter of 'mere words,' but one of intensest reality: scientific objectivity helps us to 'get out of it,' it helps us to defend ourselves against the neurosis and to keep it at bay, outside.[3] We are wrong to believe that word-magic occurs only in the primitive and in some patients; it happens now and on our home ground of psychology. The avoidance of the word soul and the "euphemistic disparagement" of the word behavior is an all-too-anxious attempt to seal off our most intimate subjectivity against any 'evil' influences. Little wonder that such an isolated (autistic) psychology acts out the idea of relationship to excess.

Paradoxically, the carefully avoided subjectivity unwittingly returns within the objective scientific world of facts, in more than one way. I do not here want to go into the topic of the "subjective conjectures" (*CW* 10 § 356) that underlie the allegedly objective 'explanations' and 'laws' of scientific psychology, but will restrict myself to the discussion of personalism. Empirical psychology knows only of psychological phenomena that belong to persons, that is, it can conceive of them only in terms of personal property, of 'mine' or 'his' or 'yours' (cf.: *CW* 12 § 562). The root metaphor of psychology is atomism. First come all the individual persons and only then the soul (each person's soul, instincts, feelings, and thoughts). If the soul exists for psychology as countless individual, separated souls, how can there be wholeness? Likewise, the psyche itself is thought to be made up of self-identical units (called agencies, functions, and the like), units, that is, that are originally and primarily conceived as separated and which make a whole only on account of their being combined within one system (aggregate). We already talked about the fact that the very structure

---

[3] (Note added December 2004) i.e., to *logically* defend ourselves..., to keep neurosis *logically* at bay.

of our theoretical thought establishes the isolation and separateness that it wants to overcome through striving for wholeness. We also know that addition (combination) cannot create a whole out of what is defined as split off, but that a change of our *theoria* in the direction of a "*Blick fürs Ganze*" is indispensable.

Now we add that psychology must *start* from the "whole," from "the great," from the "bond between men and the gods," if it wants to arrive at wholeness and heal the neurotic splits. This is why Jung thought very little of basing our insights on case studies, on clinical observation within the consulting-room. "The scope must be widened to reveal ... the meaningful whole" (*CW* 10 § 354). For this reason, Jung turned to such seemingly remote and odd fields as mythology, gnosticism, and alchemy when it was a question of seeing "the full range of the human psyche" (*CW* 10 § 369) at work. And instead of explaining the "larger aspect of the psychic phenomenon" from the consulting-room experience, he conversely tried to see the patient and personal behavior in the light of the insights gained from such eccentric studies.

Why Jung turned to such odd fields and what is meant by "the great" and "the petty" can become clearer from an analogy that E. Wind uses in a similar connection. He talks about an iconographer who on account of his reductive approach discovered that "the symbolic creations of geniuses are unfortunately harder to nail down to a definite subject than the allegorical inventions of minor artists" and adds:

> If this be so, there is something wrong with the manner of nailing down. A method that fits the small work but not the great has obviously started at the wrong end. In geometry, if I may use a remote comparison, it is possible to arrive at Euclidean parallels by reducing the curvature of a non-Euclidean space to zero, but it is impossible to arrive at a non-Euclidean space by starting out with Euclidean parallels. In the same way, it seems to be a lesson of history that the commonplace may be understood as a reduction of the exceptional, but that the exceptional cannot be understood by amplifying the commonplace. Both logically and causally the exceptional is crucial, because it introduces ... the more comprehensive category.[4]

---

[4] Edgar Wind, *Pagan Mysteries in the Renaissance* (New York: Norton, 1968), p. 238.

But are we Jungians not making use of the more comprehensive category, are not we too starting with the "whole" and the "great"? For after all, the concepts of the collective unconscious and of the archetypes are in the center of Analytical Psychology. Yet, when we look at what we actually do, then I think it is an illusion to assume that Analytical Psychology is any less personalistic than, say, psychoanalysis. The difference is merely that the latter openly admits its personalistic and reductive approach whereas our theory disguises it.

We talk of the concrete mother and the other women in the family and entitle this "the *matriarchal* sphere"! We describe a mother as negative and then say she evoked the negative aspect of the mother archetype through her nature. What are we doing here? If a bad mother evokes the bad aspect of the mother archetype and a good mother the good aspect, then this means that the concrete person is the actual and decisive reality. The archetype is then no *primordial* image any more at all, it is not originary, but a derived and dependent factor— if not merely a big, inflated, but empty word behind which there is no other reality but the personal mother. It is a mere duplication of this mother, in the same way as Freud describes the imaginary parents in the family romance of the neurotic[5]: these new and ennobled parents show characteristics that derive from the recollection of the real parents, so that the child actually does not remove the father, but only magnifies him. This euhemeristic analysis fits perfectly to our personalistic use of the term archetype: even if we rightly frown on personalistic reduction where it is used to disparage archetypal fantasy material—there *are* things which legitimately can be, even ought to be, subjected to a reductive interpretation: our inflated concepts.

The origin and root of the archetypal images (the way Analytical Psychology *comprehends* them) are the empirical persons. It is for this reason, too, that in Analytical Psychology we almost exclusively find the mother (+ anima), father (+ animus) and the self archetypes: the richness and multitude of archetypal figures that we find in mythology has dwindled to these three or five (showing that *our* "archetypes" derive from, and depict, the (aggrandized) real family. This means that the old sensationalist fallacy is still at work and is only disguised in Analytical Psychology. How honest and relieving is Freud's language!

---

[5] "Der Familienroman der Neurotiker," in Sigmund Freud, *Studienausgabe*, vol. 4, p. 226.

He means mother and he says mother. We mean the very same mother, but blow her up to an archetype. Thus we destroy what the term archetype actually and 'originally' refers to; we cancel that imaginal 'substance' from our thinking, but succeed in concealing this loss because with a kind of 'immunization strategy' (H. Albert) we retain the *word* archetype as well as the numinous aura adhering to it. This aura, however, is now attributed to persons or to parts of the empirical personality. By thus undermining the concept of archetype from within and pressing the transpersonal into the narrow confines of the personal and empirical (understood personalistically) we even more definitely put an end to the larger aspect of the psychological phenomenon than Freud was able to do by denying it altogether. Our conventional use of archetypes therefore is the very opposite of "starting out with the more comprehensive category": it amounts to nothing less than an apotheosis of the personal(istic) and thus absolutely and unquestionably moors the "prime evil of neurosis" in our theory because it provides divine authentication for it.

5. The Effect of Psychology

Psychology has fallen into the very mode of thinking that it objects to in the neurotic. But if psychology itself is neurotic, how can it have a healing effect (which it obviously does have)? This is a very curious dilemma, since we cannot rightly deny either the neurosis or the healing effect. There seems to be only one possible answer: psychology does not heal *despite* its neurosis, but *because* of it. This would also fit in with the insight that *'healing' is itself a neurotic concept.* Could it not be that the patient is freed of his (personal) neurosis because in therapy it is transferred to psychology, so that the latter carries it for him? In Freud's view, the neurosis changes into a transference neurosis. But what happens to this new neurosis, where does it go when the transference is "dissolved"? Are we to think that the transpersonal objective realities called "transference" merely dissolve into thin air?

I would say they are again transferred, but this time not onto a person, but onto an objective structure. It is psychology that receives the neurosis into itself, as into a container, and thus relieves the patient. The instrument of this transference is the endless number of interpretations ("working through") during analysis, by which the neurosis is deepened and widened ("amplified") and the patient's mentality raised to the objective level of psychology. What is sometimes called the "objectivation of the neurosis" could mean precisely this process. The patient is cured through his new connection with the impersonal theory which claims universal validity (e.g., overcoming of the Oedipus complex; individuation). Thus, he gains a more objective, transpersonal attitude towards himself. What cures is the impersonal character of theory, which appears in psychology as it does in any body of hermeneutics, in science, philosophy, or religion. This is the reason why *any* psychology works in therapeutic practice. That our psychology happens to be personalistic in its *content* does not alter the fact that *as a system of meaning* it remains objective and transpersonal. Indeed, from an archetypal view, it is itself of archetypal substance, although it is the very point of this psychology to deny anything archetypal (Freud) or to abuse the archetypal concepts reductively (Analytical Psychology). (In other words, personalistic reductivism is itself an archetypal mode).

If this be so, the principle of *epistrophé* (the reversion or return of our personal idiosyncracies to the appropriate archetypal dominants)[6] would be confirmed once more; it would be the principle even behind conventional, often anti-archetypal psychotherapy, and analysis would work with theory *as* an autonomous factor even while denying it to be such. Inasmuch as such a revision is not a matter of intellectual comprehension, but requires, in order to have psychic reality, a ritual, we can understand why the tedious process of therapy has to be repeated with every patient anew. Therapy does not overcome, but on the contrary fully *initiates* into, that (archetypal) world that is called neurosis (and which is embodied in psychology). It is this initiation that relieves the individual person. Our psychology serves the same purpose as, e.g., the Mithraic cult or its successor, Christianity, did for the man of late antiquity. As redemptive religions they proclaimed the victory of light over darkness (what we would now call The Successful Repression) and thereby enabled the individual to reflect his personal neurosis against a transpersonal background and to give it a home there. Psychology with its eschatology of development is not merely

---

[6] On "epistrophé" see James Hillman, *Loose Ends* (Zürich: Spring Publications, 1975), p. 50.

a parallel to, and successor of, Christianity, but it is a true redemptive religion with a very severe cult—only in disguise.

Our psychology *can* be successful in therapy. But of course, the neurosis as such remains, and each successful analysis helps to neuroticize psychology once again or, at least, to keep it neurotic. Psychology as a whole does not heal the split; it, rather, perpetuates the neurosis and firmly moors it. And the cure of the patient is only one part of the effect of our therapeutic psychology. The other side is that over 80 years of psychotherapy have by no means been able to reduce the number of psychic disorders on a collective level. Psychology at large is abortive; it miscarries. Neurosis and medical psychology are fruits off the same tree. *Together* they seem to be one of the "games people play," such as cops and robbers.

The displacement or transference from the personal level to objective psychology means that this psychology, as a cultural phenomenon and as a general way of looking (neurotically) at oneself and the psyche, carries the seeds of ever new neuroses in itself; what disturbances it takes from the patient, it somehow returns to the population at large ("*Zeitgeist*"). Our psychology has built repetition-compulsion into therapy; for every patient who completed his analysis there are several others waiting to begin one. With these findings we add a further aspect to Freud's pessimistic idea of the interminability of analysis. He discussed the unending duration of the analysis of the individual patient and the possibility that an analysis may be terminated with momentary, but not with definitive (prophylactic) success. Our different point of view additionally takes into account the effect of analysis for the un-analysed population at large, i.e., the *epidemic character of the disease called analysis*. Our result confirms the conclusions of Hillman, who approached this same topic, also with reference to Freud, from his chosen perspective of hysteria and mysogyny.[7]

6. THE THERAPY OF PSYCHOLOGY

In the past, we have been able to practice psychotherapy in good faith, in the knowledge that even if we personally have our share in the neurosis, we at least served a cause that was above

---

[7] James Hillman, *The Myth of Analysis* (Evanston: Northwestern UP, 1972), pp. 291ff.

board; the shortcomings and failures in therapy were due to (all-too-) human frailty, not to the very method of psychotherapy. Now we have, in addition to the humiliating insight of the possible neurosis of the therapist, to live with the much more hurtful discovery that even our cause, psychology, is thoroughly neurotic. Should we, therefore, abandon it? Of course not. For if we did so, we would once more react to *neurosis with defenses and repression.* No, as therapists we must also accept the neurosis of our own discipline. Jung says that one should be grateful to the neurosis and learn not how to get rid of it, but how to bear it. It is above all psychology that has to learn this lesson, not only the patient. The false ego-centeredness of our theory has to be disposed of. So psychology itself must be its own *first* patient. We now have to realize that the analysis of the persons involved (patient and analyst) will not suffice; theory needs analysis just as badly. Not all is done if I as analyst have subjected my personal neurotic mess to analysis; my impersonal mess, the neurosis of my psychology, remains untouched. (And yet, it is the *impersonal neurosis that is closest and most intimate to us,* since it is rooted in the transpersonal core of the personality.) This is why Jung spoke of the necessity for psychology to "unlearn and relearn," of the need for a "radical revision" (cf. Hillman's title: *Re-Visioning Psychology*) and for a "liberation from outworn ideas which have seriously restricted our view of the psyche as a whole" (*CW* 10 § 369f.). Above all, he demanded a critique of the premises and presuppositions underlying our thinking, indeed, a *"critical psychology."*

Freud, in his paper on "Analysis Terminable and Interminable," realized that the attempt to shorten the duration of analysis shows a remainder of medicine's impatient disdain for the neuroses and himself opted for "setting oneself the goal, not of abbreviating, but of deepening analysis."[8] This necessary deepening, however, must not be understood in terms of duration or thoroughness in detail, nor as penetration to ever 'earlier' disorders (primary narcissism or prenatal traumas) or more basic causes (Freud's biological bedrock). These are the wrong categories, which necessarily make analysis interminable (infinite) since one can always find something more basic or earlier. This thinking

---

[8] "Die endliche und die unendliche Analyse" in Sigmund Freud, *Studienausgabe,* Ergänzungsband, Frankfurt, 1975, p. 387 (my translation).

amounts to the futile attempt to come to an end by following the Euclidean parallels to infinity.

The deepening of analysis must rather be taken as a progression to a fundamentally new level, to Edgar Wind's "more comprehensive category," to the "curvature of non-Euclidean space." Psychology must be curved (*intentio obliqua*), bend backwards, reflect on itself. The same analytical principles with which it hitherto turned to the patient (with the empiricist *intentio recta*) it may now apply to itself and thus complete and fulfill the analysis by taking itself, as third person, seriously. This is what "critical psychology" means.

So far we psychotherapists have acted (and researched!) just as unconsciously in our profession as did Jung's Kenya natives when they performed the ritual of greeting the rising sun. We have, of course, a rich knowledge of what to do and to say and how to interpret, but if we were asked (as the Africans were by Jung) why we behave and think that way, we could, as those natives, put forward no other ground than "because it is the truth, that's the way the facts are, just look at all this case material" and would, with this dogmatism, betray our unconsciousness. (That our facts are to some extent empirically validated, whereas the Kenya ones were not, obviously makes no difference as regards consciousness. Valid empirical evidence *may establish true knowledge, but does not make more conscious.* Superstition and science, despite their fundamental difference, are thus on the same level in this respect because they share the same blind(ing) belief in facts. "The collaboration of the psyche—an indispensable factor—remains invisible" [*CW* 10 § 498].)

The principle of depth psychology is the lifting of the repressions, and the psychoanalytic "fundamental rule" was established to serve this principle. Freud states about the application of this rule, "It is a most remarkable thing that the whole undertaking becomes lost labour if a single concession is made to secrecy. If at any spot in a town the right of sanctuary existed, one can well imagine that it would not be long before all the riff-raff of the town would gather there."[9] I think that our much neglected psychological theory is such a sanctuary. There, as we have seen, all the neurotic ideas gather. Psychology acts out its insights in its 'behavior' (i.e. psychotherapy), but the theory, as the

---

[9] "Further Recommendations in the Technique of Psycho-analysis," in Sigmund Freud, *Collected Papers*, vol. II (London, 1953), p. 356n.

'consciousness' and 'attitude' of psychology, is protected and defended against any such insight. I have given a number of illustrations for this. By way of a reminder. I want to point out the effect or inherent purpose of the genetic approach: the uroboros, primary narcissism, the *Einheitswirklichkeit*, magical thinking and the like are (via projection) placed as far away as possible from ourselves by our theory, either into what we *are* not (prehistoric man, the infant, or the creative genius) or what we by no means *want* to be (the neurotic patient), in order to avoid that our own thinking and way of viewing—our innermost subjectivity—become affected by these realities. We do not want to give up this last resort and refuge and change fundamentally, without reserve (what Jung termed to radically "unlearn and relearn"). The last and most secret, most interior stronghold of the old ego-centered attitude is psychological theory, whose involvement in therapy and transference is not subjected to analysis the way that of the other two persons is. Now we see why analysis miscarries despite its tremendous effort: the entire undertaking becomes lost labour because a concession has been made, even if only at a single spot.

There is an iron curtain between therapy and theory. The practitioner, stressing feeling-experiences, depreciates theory as an intellectualism; for the psychological scientist theory is something sacred that must be kept clean from emotions, imagination, and neurosis. Through this dissociation we get both a neurotic practice and a neurotic theory. That intellectualizing one's affects is a defense mechanism is generally accepted, but that the reverse, ignoring theory for personalistic introspection, etc., is also used as a defense, is not seen. It would of course not help if theory were made more practically relevant and the practitioner occupied himself more with theory. This would bring the two extremes closer, but no matter how close they come, the neurotic split of psychology would remain. What is needed is their oneness, "wholeness." This is what Freud was driving at when he spoke of the "*Junktim zwischen Heilen und Forschen*" (the package of curing and research).[10] Therapy *is* theoretical and theory works therapy. We cannot actually restrict therapy to the consulting room and theorizing to books. Jung writing his theoretical and psycho-

---

[10] "Nachwort zur 'Frage der Laienanalyse'," in Sigmund Freud, *Studienausgabe*, Ergänzungsband (Frankfurt, 1975), p. 347 (my translation).

historical studies did not merely provide theoretical tools for analysis. His written work is in itself therapy, full-fledged therapy, inasmuch as it aims at affecting our attitudes of consciousness. By thinking otherwise, *we* would split off theory.

Conversely, we are subject to a self-deception if we believe an ever deeper introspection or the abandonment to feeling experiences à la primal scream would bring a genuine initiation into the 'inner world.' Introspection means that we look *into* ourselves and thus obviously *from* outside. Initiation by contrast means to enter, but when this happens we are in "it" and part of it and therefore can no longer look into it. Abandonment to feeling experiences implies, to be sure, to enter. But as the term abandonment suggests, something was left out and behind which therefore does not participate in the transformation process and thus can serve as anchor and firm ground. The experiences may be as intensive as they come, yet nothing truly essential in the sense of initiation will have happened because of the *reservatio mentalis*, of the prior exclusion of our mind, which remains as rationalistic and egotistic as before. Only one half enters and feels. Or it is the whole ego that enters, but then the *reservatio mentalis* would mean that despite being whirled around as a unit by the emotions, the inside structure of the ego would stay intact. In the so-called feeling experience it is the old ego that experiences and feels. It remains the self-identical subject even when it 'relates.' It is true that psychology must be subjective. But its subjectivity cannot be the ego's, 'my' personal property—it, rather, must be an impersonal and objective subjectivity, one that first gives me my sense of 'my-ness.'

As we said, psychotherapy is fixated on the patient or at best on patient and doctor (on *their* personal experiences and reactions), in short, on the personal. Thus, personalistic psychotherapy is truly a *folie à deux*, a Buberian I-Thou encounter, because only two persons are accepted, *tertium non datur*. The "grammar" of psychology is faulty, we cannot conjugate properly: I, thou—that is where we stop. But the proper "conjugation" (Greek: *syzygía*!) knows of a third person, of the objective and impersonal It (the objective psyche, the "great," *Psychologia*) which is present along with the two other persons because it is their impersonal and larger aspect. Freud came so close to it with his id, but unfortunately placed the id *within* the individual as a *part* of the personality. Where psychotherapy is seen in terms of the dialogue between two persons, an I and a Thou, there is no syzygy and no conjugation, but an absolute "*disiunctio*" (cf. *CW* 16 § 397); (Jung's usual word is dissociation): doctor – patient, sane – neurotic, conscious – unconscious, thinking – feeling, etc. The eros of transference may then try as hard as possible to bind the two together, it will never get beyond a "transference *neurosis*." Where the framework of psychology is personalistic because the third of the two is not seen, there *can* be no *coniunctio*. The "soul's child," which according to Jung (*CW* 16 § 465) is the goal of transference (and of psychotherapy), will not be born: such a psychology *must* be abortive; it must miscarry; soul-making cannot take place. Psychotherapy will instead have to devote itself to "practical" purposes (curing, ego-strengthening, behavior modification, sensitivity training, emotional experiences, development of all functions, etc.) and turn technological, as Faust did after the *coniunctio*, which had almost been achieved, finally failed. In his case, too, it had to fail since the "objective process of the union" was disturbed by "Faust's personal intervention," his identification with the mythological (= transpersonal) figure Paris (*CW* 12 § 558f.).

Jung always insisted: the origin of the neurosis lies, not in the past, but in the present, that is, close to home. In this spirit we would need to concentrate on what is closest to home: our attitude of consciousness, our theories. In order to make psychology we must "*erinnern,*" to make soul, come home. Instead of looking for the archetypes out there and thus reifying them, we need develop an archetypal *approach*; instead of locating the psyche in persons we must learn to see *psychologically*; instead of talking about the uroboros in the child or in the patient, our psychology must advance to a *uroboric consciousness*. If psychology has become its own first patient and if its "space" is curved, so that all "straight" lines return into themselves as with the *draco caudam suam devorans* (the dragon devouring his tail), it will no longer be fixated on the patient, on behavior, and on the practical.

Both founders of depth psychology, Freud and Jung, looked at the analytical cure with a certain detachment, Freud confessing that he had never been a therapeutic enthusiast, no true physician and had never had a strong desire to help the suffering, Jung admitting to a rather meagre interest in people and the external facts of life. This does not mean that they encountered the patient with indifference, but it might throw light on why they were destined to be psychologists. The interest of the psychologist is not directed at the factual person and his behavior, but at things psychological. The curved line which the psychological glance follows meets the patient and the facts—it does not avoid them and instead turn merely inwards (introspection)—but it goes on and returns to where it came from. Not the patient, but its own origin is its goal. Psychology does not speak about the patient, about the external object, but always about *itself*, and psychology proper begins only where it *follows* the uroboros, the dragon of imagination,[11] that is to say, where it merges with the imaginal itself. But in this circular motion the patient is encompassed, not as a fixed point and an end in himself, but as something that is taken along and 'seen through.' The same, however, applies to the seeing subject (ego); it, too, ceases to be a fixed point and enters into the alchemical *rotatio*, so that there will be nothing fixed and 'factual' left, no reserve, the circling motion of imagination itself now becoming the only fact (and 'factor'!). And this dissolving of the two factual persons and their self-identical egos into the circular motion is the actual purpose of therapy. This is what the goal of 'changing the patient' should be taken to mean, whereas the modification of his behavior and what other practical purposes and factual problems classical psychology concerns itself with now appear not to be truly psychological at all, since only the entrance into the *circulatio* is an authentic initiation.

Jung tried very hard to communicate this idea. Already his typological approach of 1913 had the purpose of removing the dispute among the various schools (Freud—Adler—Jung) from the empirical level of fact to a psychological one of viewpoint: instead of empirically proving or disproving the various theories, he reflected on the entirely different question of what made Freud or Adler see things the way they did. His typology was certainly not sufficient for this task (for which reason Jung later let it lie in favor of the much more comprehensive and subtle archetypal theory), but already this early attempt left the scientific fixation on the object and on the factual behind, returning the psychological inquiry into itself and thus recognizing the autonomy of psychology.

---

[11] On the dragon as imagination see James Hillman, "The Great Mother, her Son, her Hero, and the Puer," in *Fathers and Mothers* (Zürich, 1973), p. 112.

With respect to therapy, Jung expressed the same ideas, e.g., by demanding a "counter-application to the doctor himself of whatever system is believed in" (*CW* 16 § 168), since the doctor is just as much 'in analysis' as is the patient, just as much a "part of the psychic process" (§ 166). Both are *within* the process, not the other way around. The "step from education to self-education" (§ 170) is required, and with "this revolution [*Wendung*]" "analytical psychology has burst the bonds which till then had bound it to the consulting-room of the doctor. It goes beyond itself ..." and "can claim to become a property of the culture as a whole [*Allgemeingut zu werden*]" (§ 174, modif.). A totally different view of the soul from the previous biological one is needed, for the soul is "far more than a mere object of scientific interest. It is not only the sufferer but the doctor as well, not only the object but also the subject ... the absolute condition of consciousness itself" (§ 173).

Although certain elements of Jung's *language* here still seem to have a personalistic cast—"self-education," e.g., could be mistaken in the sense of a personal (autoerotic) endeavor on the part of the doctor— the quoted text as a whole nevertheless expresses Jung's vision of what one might call a *transcendental-dialectical psychology*. It goes beyond all empiricism and personalism, beyond the practical and concrete, beyond the consulting room (even *while* it might be there) and views psychology (and the analytical session) from the perspective of *Vermittlung*, mediation. Jung's "revolution" (*Wendung*) is reminiscent of Kant's *Kopernikanische Wendung* (Copernican revolution), just as a formulation such as "the absolute condition of consciousness itself" is analogous to the concern of *Transzendentalphilosophie* for the "conditions of the possibility of *a priori*" of, say, synthetic judgments. The soul is mediation, a "between." But this between (e.g., of transference) is not to be imagined as a (one-way or two-way) arrow, a rope strung between[12] analyst and patient, but rather as something which surrounds and encompasses, as well as transcends, both persons. Even if it is also *in* each of us and as such has an empirical aspect, it is nevertheless in actuality "a single, all-embracing soul" (*CW* 10 § 175, modif.), the "*very* soul of humanity" (*CW* 16 § 65), mirroring Being as such (*GW* 16 § 203), a world of cosmic dimensions (*CW* 10 § 366).

---

[12] Cf. Martin Heidegger, *Die Frage nach dem Ding* (Tübingen, 1962), p. 188.

For this reason psychology can never be a special branch of science, as it must become *Allgemeingut* and start out from an all-encompassing perspective that alone can do justice to a soul of "cosmic" dimensions. The following diagram, adapted from Erich Heintel,[13] may illustrate Jung's vision of the analytical session (and psychology in general).

The soul as mediation occurs twice: as periphery (transpersonal psyche) and as the analyst's personal consciousness (including his psychology), which is governed by the objective dominants and sees the patient accordingly. Our psychological theories are

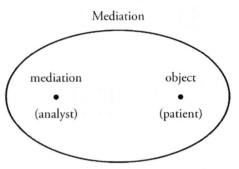

larger than we and prior to ourselves. They surround and encompass both ourselves and what we perceive (e.g., the patient). This vision starts out with wholeness and "the great" and is therefore no longer confronted with the self-defeating task of trying to unite two individual souls that are separated by definition.

In this way we should also conceive the ego-self paradox. The self is not so much in me, not "my" true nature, though it may shine through me. ... Individuation thus does not mean a process of empirical-personal self-actualization, but is a "transcendental purpose" (*CW* 14 § 790)! It is something intangible and undefinable; empirically speaking it is *nothing at all*: "merely" imaginal. From a practical point of view psychology's business is "vain" and "useless"— but therein lies its distinction. In the same vein, Jung states, "To concern ourselves with dreams is a way of reflecting on ourselves— a way of self-reflection. It is not our ego-consciousness reflecting itself .... It reflects not on the ego ... but recollects that strange self, alien to the ego ... "(*CW* 10 § 318). And the dream is not so much "my" dream, but a message from the unconscious, unitary soul of humanity" (*ibid.*). I would add here, however, that it can also not be the ego (ego-consciousness) that is the subject of this

---

[13] Erich Heintel, *Einführung in die Sprachphilosophie* (Darmstadt, 1972), p. 92.
[14] Freidrich Nietzsche, *Der Wille zur Macht*, Aphorism 585.

contemplation. Nietzsche speaks of a "*Ungeheure Selbstbesinnung*: *nicht als Individuum, sondern als Menschheit sich bewußt werden*" (Tremendous *self-contemplation*: not as an individual, but as mankind becoming conscious of oneself).[14] Not only *of* what but also *as* what I become conscious is important: who the subject in me is. I as subject must already, to begin with, be tuned in to the "soul of humanity," to the viewpoint of mediation and the imaginal, in order to contemplate "that *alien* self." *Similia similibus*: it must be the self that contemplates itself in and through me. This is why true psychology presupposes an initiation. It cannot be learned or taught. One must be seized, such as by the grip of pathology.

We have seen that psychology becomes neurotic by defending itself against its own pathology. It thus tries to avoid having to suffer an initiation and to become conscious of itself. In order to bring an end to neurosis, psychology must "*erinnern*" it, take it into itself and return it to its origin, the soul. Then the repression is lifted. We can understand why this usually does not happen and why Nietzsche spoke of a tremendous or dreadful self-contemplation. For from the point of view of the habitual ego this task of psychology is nothing less than to saw off the branch one is sitting on, so that one loses one's firm hold and plunges into the bottomless depth of the "between" space where there are no straight lines and no fixed points. But then the *rotatio* would begin, psychology would be the soul 'recollected' (*erinnert*); therapy and theory, fantasy and fact, analyst and patient could no longer be neatly kept apart. The realm of mediation would be opened up and the "soul's child" be born.

I would like to repeat: the place where psychotherapy has to happen and where alone it would not have to be abortive is the objective, impersonal and yet also most subjective, third person: psychology. Integrating, developing, compensating, healing, "recollecting" (*erinnern*, interiorizing), imagining, introspection, initiation, analysis, expanding one's consciousness and what else psychotherapy aims for are tasks to be accomplished not by the person, but by psychology. Only on this level, on the "higher plane of psychological and philosophical dialectic" (*CW* 10 § 333), can psychology become psychological, because it alone opens the third alternative to the deadlock of opposites: the imaginal realm of the soul's child. Anything truly important cannot happen in *us* unless it happens in our *psychology*. For we are in it—even if we think it is in us. Instead of needing psychological methods for obtaining more intensive personal experiences, we might find out that psychology itself can be our richest and most personal experience: the experience of soul-making.

CHAPTER THREE

The Leap After the Throw
On 'Catching Up With' Projections and the Origin of Psychology

But it is far harder to bring fixed thoughts into a
fluid state than to do so with sensuous existence.
—G. W. F. Hegel

"It is the fateful misfortune of medical psychotherapy to have been born in an age of enlightenment, when the old cultural values became inaccessible through people's own fault (*durch Selbstverschulden*) ...." We could reflect in a number of directions about this memorable sentence of C. G. Jung (*CW* 10 § 370, transl. modif.), which, by the way, is an indirect, but obvious, attack on, and reversal of, Kant's definition of the "Enlightenment" as man's stepping out of his *selbstverschuldete Unmündigkeit* (self-caused state of minority [or mental immaturity; self-caused rather than imposed upon him]). But here I want to take up only one aspect. Jung does not speak about any individual unfortunate features that cling to psychology, but about the *fateful* misfortune of its *origin*, i.e., about a birth defect, as it were, a congenital disease, which fundamentally casts a shadow over everything that psychology does, however correct and good it may be in itself. A congenital defect can possibly be compensated for or covered up by special measures or artificial limbs, but it cannot be undone. In the same way psychology, if it indeed suffers from a birth defect, is incapable of getting rid of its origin by later corrective measures—unless its birth from out of the spirit of the "Enlightenment" be taken back altogether, so that a different origin, from out of a different spirit, out of a different blueprint, might be bestowed upon it.

It is not our interest here to discuss what precisely Jung himself may have viewed as psychology's congenital defect. All we want is to learn something, and take it along, from his idea for our own topic. Obviously, there are two different species of statements in the area of psychology: one can make statements about individual psychic phenomena (or, respectively, verify, disprove, supplement or correct already existing statements); but one can also focus on the whole of psychology, that element in which all psychological statements "fatefully" float on account of their descent, the general spirit that permeates them and gives them their significance. Inasmuch as we proceed here from a specialized theme, projection, one could get the impression that we are concerned with an individual psychological phenomenon: the elaboration of an adequate theory, and method of therapy, of projection. But this is not the case. Our true theme is the origin of psychology in general, i.e., that through which psychology truly turns into psychology. We therefore do not examine the event of projection in its own right, but rather projection as an idea produced by psychology through which, by way of an example, something can dawn on us about the general medium in which psychology moves. One could speak here of a meta-level of reflection (in analogy to what for science is a critical theory of science)—if in the case of psychology this supposed meta-level did not lead into the very heart of psychology itself, in other words, not merely to a point of view external to and above it, but precisely deeper into it, into its interiority, into its own unconscious. For psychology's individual ideas such as "projection" are living impulses stirring within it, impulses that can guide us and set the whole of psychology into motion *from within itself.*

The following comments, thus, do not have the character of scientific statements (assertions, descriptions, explanations of facts), but rather of psychoanalytic "interpretations" through which what is secretly behind or inherently in the apparent "facts" is "exposed." The nature of "(psychoanalytic) interpretations" is such that they often sound like imputations, because they do not correspond to the conscious intentions and opinions of the person concerned. A mother whose unconscious death wishes for her child have been interpreted by her analyst has every right to point out that she honestly loves her child. But the psychoanalytical interpretation does not dispute this; it does not, on the same level as her own description of her situation, want to replace her view with the other thesis, but instead *go behind her view*. Instead of suggesting that the mother does not love her child, but rather hates it, it states that in addition to and behind her conscious love, which is in no way disputed, there is an unconscious hatred, or that her loving care is, precisely, a defence against her unconscious hostile impulses. Jesus called the Pharisees hypocrites. This, too, is an interpretation, for Jesus does not, in the sense of an evaluation of manifest behavior, contest the Pharisees' objective faithfulness to the law and their subjective honesty. He wants to present this very honesty and this undoubted faithfulness to the law as ways of turning away from God. Thus, rather than declaring the Pharisees to be not truly pious in the conventional sense, Jesus explodes the conventional *concept* of piety. For this reason the interpretation must have appeared to the Pharisees as totally unjust and incomprehensible, since they were caught up precisely in the conventional concept of piety and since they did not perform the leap into that other dimension from which Jesus viewed and argued and into which he wanted to drive them. This example reveals that (psychoanalytical) interpretations have, on principle, a "therapeutic," not a scientific character, because instead of "statically" describing or explaining the real, they *propel* our conception of it into a deeper, more comprehensive dimension by radicalizing it (going *back* behind it).

An interpretation may be false, but if it is false, this is not simply due to the fact that it contradicts the conscious self-view as well as the manifest behavior. The same applies to the following discussion of the conventional concept of projection. In it, it will not be a question of the manifest behavior of psychology and the explicit opinions that individual therapists have about projection. The purpose of this discussion is rather to propel psychology beyond the limits set for it by the conventional thought structures, limits which have in advance rendered ineffectual even the greatest range of *content* as well as all subsequent expansion that they doubtless permit.

A genuine interpretation is not our personal opinion about a phenomenon; rather, it merely states what the latter shows. For this reason it cannot rely on the personal declarations of individuals concerning how they *meant* what they said (for then we would remain on the level of "consciousness"). It must base itself on what the very things that they did or said in turn objectively *say* and *entail*: on "objective" features inherent in what has been said, features through which the "unconscious" mind, as it were, betrays itself. In this sense, we shall here, too, stick to the style of psychology's formulations, the substantial content of the terms and concepts it uses, because they reveal what, beyond all explicit intentions, is *really* thought and which fantasy implicitly rules over (and in) the diverse views; not what psychologists think, but what psychology thinks. What we have to start with when proceeding in this way is psychology's most common conceptions, the answers that psychology would naturally and immediately come up with when surprised by the question about projection, because such answers come closest to spur-of-the-moment statements prior to conscious control.

*   *   *

We shall examine the four constituent parts that together make up "projection": (1) the throwing, (2) that which receives what is thrown (the screen or carrier of the projection), (3) the content that is thrown and (4) the thrower.

(1) When asking what "projection" in the most general terms is, the answer might be: When it is a case of a projection, I ascribe something that belongs to me to some other. Images stemming from the psyche of man are seen out there, for example, in the sky as the zodiac. This means, psychology conceives of the throw as a throwing *out*, an ejection. In the case of negative projections, the throwing out takes on the additional character of a throwing away, a getting rid of, since the projection is, after all, explicitly seen as a defense mechanism: something of one's own, something internal is inflicted upon something alien, external, so that the ego may be free of it. Accordingly, the response to projection viewed this way is the therapeutic demand "to withdraw the projection" (as it is usually worded), a demand that of course applies also to positive projections: The projected content must be returned to (into) the subject and acknowledged by the subject as his or her own trait.

(2) As regards the carrier of the projection, the conventional view sees here a distortion of the carrier's reality. Generally speaking, projections lead to misjudgments, to a supposed recognition of the real which, however, is in truth a misapprehension. The therapeutic aim has consequently to be a correction of this misjudgment, producing a correct view of the world.

(3) For that which is thrown, psychological terminology likes to use the name "psychic content." This label is just one, but a clear indication of a whole mentality. The concept of a "content" presupposes the idea of a container.

(4) If that which is projected is a content, then the thrower, regardless of whether this word is seen as referring to the individual or to the psyche, to consciousness or the unconscious, is imagined as a kind of pot or sack in which the said psychic contents had originally been contained and from which they have been ejected through this projection. Since the contents are properties or parts of the personality, but truly belong to the personality only if they are enclosed by it (as the container of the contents) and "possessed" by it, projection amounts, as is said, to a loss of personality, a loss of soul. For this reason therapy has to aim for a taking back of the projection, and furthermore for a firm, lasting integration of the respective content into the container.

*   *   *

What archetypal fantasy is at the root of the conceptions about projection just outlined? In which dimension does psychology move about here? Concerning the first constituent element, one is struck by the opposition of inside versus outside, of "one's own" versus "alien," of "subject" versus "object." How is this opposition, which can be construed in very different ways, apperceived in psychology? We can see it, for example, in the concepts of "subject level" and "object level" for dream interpretation. On the object level, dream images refer to objects existing in physical reality (e.g., one's literal father, one's geographically real home town). On the subject level, they refer to personality aspects or development potentials belonging to the (physically existing) dreamer (e.g., the inner father, the self, one's shadow). The same dream can, to be sure, be interpreted on the subject as well as on the object level, but if so, the inner and the external father are not seen as one and the same, but rather, each of the two interpretations refers to a fundamentally different ontological realm. The inner and the outer are mutually exclusive. The starting point of this thinking is the physical universe, in which there is the planet Earth, upon which in turn there are human beings, all of whom have an interior, a psyche, within themselves. The inner is *within* the human being, the psychical is behavior *of* the human organism. This implies that the physical world is the basis, the bedrock, in this thinking. It is taken as the existent *per se*, the primary, the truly real. The "inner" is merely a tiny "piece" of this world, a special case, which happens to be present only in the cosmically insignificant number of exemplars of *homo sapiens*. It is *not the inner essence of the world* (not even only of man), *but something that occurs in the world as a special phenomenon among and beside others* (and in or on man).

Psychology thus takes the world as it is presented to us by "physics"[1] for granted, without questions asked. It operates within "physics" and the physical worldview as the universal arena within which the psychical occurs as a particular element. Thus, even for psychology, "physics" is the fundamental science upon which it bases itself (as biology did before): the carrier and basis of the inner is the living organism, which in turn is based upon a "stratum" of physical-chemical processes and substances. The inner has here inevitably a lesser degree of realness. The true real is the physical world, which includes the human being as body. The soul is a mere accident, a secondary attribute, which is reflected in the fact that at most psychology deals with ("subjective") *ideas about* and emotional reactions to the ("objective") world; not with knowing and being, but with beliefs and feelings.

The (subjective) ideas about the world here have the world outside of themselves, whereas the world exists *per se*, unconcerned about any ideas about it; this means that the world has likewise the ideas outside of itself, precisely because the ideas themselves are something that

---

[1] I use "physics" here as a handy label for an entire mentality. Rather than basing myself on physics as a specialized science in the narrow sense, I have in mind physics as fundamental science and model for all modern sciences. I also have in mind that physics that is at the center of the "modern world view (*Weltanschauung*)," that has its roots in Western metaphysics and that has, as physics, an essential relation to meta-physics.— My subsequent remarks are not an attack on physics itself, but are exclusively aimed at our physicalized psychology.

occurs in the world. Generally speaking, the inner has the outer and the outer has the inner outside of itself, much as in a house the inner is inside and is kept separated from the outer by the walls of the house. (This separation is what makes, e.g., the technology of air conditioning possible.) In this thinking the terms inner and outer are not merely contradictory conceptions, but appear in addition to be negatively potentiated; they are taken at their word: *the inner is, on top of it, itself inside*, the outer in addition outside. This seems to be a matter of course, but only because we are captives of this thinking to such a degree that we cannot think any more of an inner that is not taken at its word, an inner as, e.g., the one that Goethe, in accordance with the hermetic or alchemical tradition, was still able to conceive: what is inside is outside, what is outside is inside. Here, too, inner and outer remain opposites, we do not get a uniform blend. But the inner is not— negatively raised to the power of two—narrowed down to what is literally inside. Here, too, both remain spatial conceptions, but they are not ascribed to fixed sections of space. We call a thinking in which an image or concept is negatively raised to the power of two and taken at its word, literalistic. The conception of space that rules over this thinking is the special physical space that receives the definition of its nature from geometry. According to the geometric fantasy, space is pure extension. This entails divisibility into fixed spatial pieces or sub-spaces, just like a line can in geometry be infinitely divided into partial lines so that each separate and independently existing part has the others outside of itself. *The fantasy of space conceived as pure extension and therefore divisible into fixed parts is the archetypal root* not only of physics, but also of literalism, of reification in general, the atomization of Being. But it is inherent in psychology, too, as we have seen. The inner is viewed in geometric terms.

This is unmistakably reflected in the fact that in psychotherapy the inner has become visibly materialized in the form of a special interior room reserved for subjective experiences and closed off from the objective world around: the consulting room. Or that it was logically shoved into and locked in the nursery (likewise cut off from the world of adults), in which also the fairy tales (the brothers Grimm: *Kinder- und Hausmärchen*) have been shelved. The distinction between psychology as scientific theory and psychotherapy as the practical *application* of the former also corresponds to the geometric fantasy.

The problem is not that psychology uses spatial conceptions like inner and outer at all, although the psychical, as is repeatedly stated, is actually irrepresentable and non-spatial. No, the problem is that psychology blindly adopts the abstract space provided by physics and construed by geometry; that instead of thinking space imaginally (poetically), it thinks literalistically in *analogies* to physics which it, however, takes for images; that it does not penetrate to *authentically psychological space conceptions* of its own, to the primary space, the space of the soul and the imagination, in which, after all, the derivative space conception of physics, too, has its origin as merely *one* possible view. In my opinion, it is by no means a foregone conclusion that the soul has to be non-spatial and irrepresentable. The idea of the non-spatial and irrepresentable soul is probably only the "geometric" prejudice taken as a dogma. Maybe soul is space and visibility pure and simple? "Image is soul," Jung has said.

The strange thing about the "geometric" view is that it conceives the inner (which is, after all, its own postulate) *as* not to be found, i.e., at bottom *as unreal*. If one looks, for example, at a piece of chalk,[2] it becomes, for this conception, clear that it has an inner, which is hidden beneath its outer surface. But if one breaks the piece of chalk apart, one does not, as expected, discover this inner, but only receives new surfaces, behind which another inner is postulated, which, however, is in turn inaccessible. We see that this type of inner exists only as long as it can hide behind a surface, and it ceases to *be* the moment one tries to look at it directly. This is inherent in the definition of the "geometric" inner and outer. For if the inner has the outer and the outer the inner outside of itself, both of them are under the rule of the outer, an outer which is the scope encompassing both inner and outer, just as conversely in the fantasy of what is inside as being outside and of what is outside as being inside the latter is the ruling element that overarches both outer and inner. We run here into the phenomenon of a *duplication*. There is not only one opposition of inner and outer; there are two: one that as a whole has the constitution of the inner, and one that with both its poles (inner *and* outer) is contained in a fundamental outer, so that in this case the inner (precisely *as* an inner!) is only a variety of the outer.

---

[2] Martin Heidegger demonstrated this theme by means of the example of a piece of chalk, see *idem, Die Frage nach dem Ding* (Tübingen: Niemeyer, 1962).

When psychology demands that projections be taken back into the subject, then this interiorization (into that inner which is a variety of the outer) means in itself, according to the geometric conception, an externalization; the more the projections are taken back, the more depleted of meaning and soul will the world, entire existence, become. Could it perhaps be that precisely by searching *inside* for meaning, precisely by turning *within*, conventional psychology contributes to the total externalization of being and to depriving it of its gods? Are that psychology that strives for an inward life and true humaneness, on the one hand, and that one-sided rationalism which leads to an increasingly inhuman world, on the other, perhaps the same—not despite their opposition, but precisely because psychology sets the inner and the depth of feeling against the outer and the purely rational? Are introspection, inwardness, subject-level interpretations, and analytical self-experience perhaps the most radical ways of increasing externalization, just as is the search for the inner of the piece of chalk if it proceeds "analytically" (by means of division into smaller pieces)?

I mentioned that fairy tales now have their logical place only in the nursery. But is it not precisely psychotherapy that tries to make fairy tales accessible also to adults again? And does Analytical Psychology not overcome the opposition of subject and object through, among other things, the concept of the *collective* unconscious, which surrounds us on all sides? Indeed, does it not teach the alchemical truth of the "above" that is "below" and thus of the true inner? Certainly. But it would be a mistake to think that thereby the split between inner and outer in the sense of geometric thinking had been overcome by it. This overcoming is merely a pious hope. All attempts in that direction, as well-meaning as they may be, have long been *surpassed and sublated by the geometric fantasy*. Thus the fairy tales are being made accessible to adults, but only after they have become children's tales. According to conscious intention they are being fetched out of the nursery into the world at large; but with respect to its true significance the suggestion is conversely that adults occasionally enter the nursery and take an interest in fairy tales *as the children's tales* that they now are, so that the adult world remains protected from the fairytale mentality.

The archetypes of the collective unconscious likewise undoubtedly play a significant role in the practice of psychotherapists. But *are* they what they ostensibly are supposed to be? Do they really surround us on *all* sides? They do this only in theory. In truth, however, they remain reserved, as it were, for the consulting room, just as the cosmic dances of the American Indians, *formally* the same as ever, no longer take place in the cosmos, but only on the reservations, and serve only as entertainment for tourists or as the melancholy remembrance of things irrevocably obsolete. Actual world affairs—the course of the stars, life on earth, political developments, economic growth, technological progress, the recognition of truth, and the determination of the essence of being—have their soul outside of themselves despite archetypes and are in turn excluded from the scope of psychology/psychotherapy. Psychology leaves the actual world to science, technology, politics, and industry, which for their part are left by psychology to their own devices. Psychology contents itself with being a special compartment of knowledge, the theory of a separate (dissociated!) region of being. As long as this is so, the idea of a collective unconscious surrounding us on all sides, not to mention the idea of completeness or wholeness, although they are honestly believed in, have no psychological reality.

*   *   *

When we now look at the second component of projection, the carrier of projection, we are struck, with respect to the ideas of a "distortion of reality" and "correction of one's perception," by the fact that the interest that guides this conception is to enforce the reality principle. Psychology here looks at the phenomenon of projection primarily from the point of view of the correct cognition (almost in the scientific sense). The yardstick and goal is that the inner conceptions of the world do justice to reality, that the inner image matches the physically real. Psychology does not *discover* the reality principle in the individual person as one of its diverse empirical findings; it operates, *prior to* any discovery of individual facts, under its influence. The reality and truth conception of physics is the unquestioned horizon within the boundaries of which the cognitive processes of psychology take place: psychology as the handmaid of "physics."

Now it is a fact that for Jungians the reality principle is not all that important. They stand much more on images from the unconscious, to which an autonomous reality is attributed. But here again it turns out that this autonomous reality is only a partial autonomy within the fundamentally superordinate constitution of "physics": for psychology, individuation, by way of one example, takes place as a developmental process *within* the individual, which is primarily part of the outside world. "The objective psyche" is nothing else but an objectivity which merely is a property of the irrevocably subjective, which in turn is located in the "*really* objective," the physically existent human being. We would be fooling ourselves if we thought that because we *believe* in the "objective psyche," the psyche is indeed objective for us. That which *is* prevails without concern about official dogmas and personal "feelings."

Psychology is an auxiliary science of physics precisely because it is not physics, being occupied with all those phenomena that physics excludes from itself. For in this way it helps to keep reality free from all fantasy images that would be disturbing for physics. Physics, as the secret employer of psychology, gladly grants the latter the right to postulate an inner, psychic reality and even to keep away from it any disdainful "nothing but psychic." For what greater relief could physics wish for *its* reality? The belief in a *special* inner reality besides physical reality is the best guarantee for the inviolability of strictly outer physical reality. The greater the store that is set by self-awareness and introspection, by the development of our emotional and imaginative capacities, the more the soul will be shelved in the private, noncommittal sphere of the consulting room, of the nursery, of "one's own" inner, of subjective believing and feeling, and the more it will be rendered harmless by this very act of internment. At the same time, "real reality" is kept free of it: *Psychology reveals itself to be the mere negative of "physics."* It exists as the one "half" within the neurotic dissociation of the whole into two halves.

* * *

Now we come to the third and fourth components of projection, the content "thrown" and the subject as container. In projection a content moves out from within the subject (this is entailed in the concept of projection). The subject itself thus remains unmoved where it was. At bottom, the subject is in psychology (regardless of whether one accounts to oneself for this or not) conceived as superordinate to the event: as unmoved mover. Inasmuch as the subject is kept out of the projective movement, this movement takes on the character of a mere change of location. The content is displaced from inside out and away, much like in physics mass points are moved on a geometric line. Therefore, the movement of the displaced content is a movement of what in itself is fundamentally *un*moved, just as according to Zeno's proof of the impossibility of movement, a flying arrow is, in keeping with the geometric fantasy, at each instant of its movement at one fixed point on its linear path, and as such unmoved. With respect to the mover as well as to what is moved, movement is a dynamic which takes place within a superordinate fundamental staticness, and thus is not fully real.

All modern science, and along with it psychology, rests upon the Cartesian distinction between *res extensa* and *res cogitans*, between pure extension and consciousness or self-activeness. For obvious reasons, it is psychology's lot to explore the subject, the *res cogitans*. But if this psychology, which investigates the *res cogitans*, construes all qualities as *contents* in the subject, and correspondingly (although tacitly) the subject as the featureless *container* of these contents, as the pure function of holding and containing, and if it conceives of consciousness as a "field," what does this mean if not that the *res cogitans* for its part has turned into pure *extensio*? It is true, psychology is not concerned with outer reality the same way physics is; it is concerned with the inner, with thoughts, feelings, wishes, fantasies. But this inner is already externalized, that is, imagined from the point of view of extension. The psychical contents, complexes, and agencies are inside the psyche or the featureless field of consciousness, just as the mass points are in the empty space and the neutral time of physics.

It appears that the distinction between *cogitatio* and *extensio* cannot simply remain statically what they were in such a way that the *res cogitans* could survive in its originally intended opposition to *extensio*. Rather, this distinction displays an internal movement in the sense that the *res extensa* as the living, seminal germ has an effect upon the *cogitatio* and that the whole distinction is affected and transformed.[3] Thus there still is, to be sure, a *res cogitans* in contradistinction to the *res extensa*, but it has meanwhile settled, along with its difference from its other, within the principal idea of geometric extensionality and

---

[3] Cf. what has been said above and will be said below about "duplication."

obtains its essence and definition from the latter,[4] as we saw above in our discussion of the inner and the outer.

∗   ∗   ∗

The insight to be gained from our examination of the idea of projection is: *we do not have a real psychology as yet.* Our present psychology, although (and because) it is the opposite of physics, has long and fundamentally been in physics' service; indeed, at bottom it is itself a physics of the inner states and ideas, but one not characterized by the precision and certainty prevailing in real physics. And if at those points where psychology and physics have been pushed the farthest ahead, namely in Jung's notion of synchronicity and in nuclear physics, respectively,[5] an approximation of physics and psychology and a mutual mirroring of matter and psyche can be demonstrated,[6] the question can be raised whether this does not merely mean that here a secret identity of psychology with physics is coming to the surface for the first time and is at once cemented; in other words, whether here psychology is being driven into physicality even more decisively than heretofore. The results that physics has come up with are in most cases taken over just like that, *without first having been critically reclaimed for psychology*, and this despite the fact that physics itself comes, after all, from the soul. That approximation seems to amount to an overcoming of the geometric opposition of inner and outer, but it is its codification because the "geometric" inner (psychology) and the corresponding split-off outer ("physics") are the starting-points, because both enter into the approximation *unaltered* and the approximation, as the result of the process, does not retroactively subvert its starting-point.

---

[4] The "from the latter" of course applies just as well if the inner in psychology is meant in a *metaphorical* sense, by way of analogy: after all, it derives its metaphorical meaning from the literal meaning. In the *meta-phora* ("transference") qua analogy the original meaning or faulty meaning is precisely preserved.

[5] Nuclear physics amounts to a supersession of classical physics. However, does this supersession have the character of a real about-turn—or not perhaps that of a deepening and radicalization of the mechanistic approach of classical physics beyond the previous superficially mechanistic thinking?

[6] The concept of synchronicity could lead into a completely different direction, namely to a bursting apart of "physicalized" psychology. I have presented a few suggestions concerning this in my article "Die wissenschaftliche Psychologie als subjektivistische und zudeckende Psychologie. Erwiderung auf einen Artikel über Synchronizität," in *Zeitschrift für analytische Psychologie* 8, 1977, pp. 262–283.

And yet conventional psychology wants to be called psychology and believes itself to be psychology. This general contradiction is the analogue of the specific contradiction in the case of projection. On the one hand, it interprets this phenomenon as pro-jection, which at bottom entails the recognition that the soul, unsatisfied with its internment in the "inner" of humans, pushes its way out into the world. But on the other hand, and simultaneously, it demands that the projection be taken back and in this way cancels the very movement of the soul inherent in the idea of projection. Then it is no longer dealing with a living concept which, comparable to the Kundalini serpent, could revive psychology *from within itself*, get it moving and push it beyond itself. It is dealing only—how comforting!—with a fixed technical term that although it speaks *about* a motion, nevertheless has this motion outside of itself and does not draw psychology out, shaking the certainty of its self-understanding as a "theory about ...." But even this backward movement, this behavior *contra animam*, still contains an indication of the *actual* direction of the movement, and we have to follow this indication.

*   *   *

We take our lead from a scene in the Middle High German *Nibelungenlied* in which Brünhild and Gunther/Siegfried compete in several sport disciplines, a competition which is supposed to bring the decision about whether Gunther's wooing of Brünhild will be successful or not. The one discipline that is of interest to us here consists in throwing a (heavy) stone and then immediately leaping after it. We have, here, not an incidental sequence of two independent sport disciplines as, e.g., in a pentathlon. Rather, it is one complex but homogenous action, a single sport, which, however, combines within itself two acts. We could call this sport the throw-leap. It is as if the momentum of the throw swept the thrower along with the throw and pulled him into itself, so that the thrower does not retain his independence vis-à-vis his act of throwing, but is himself absorbed into the throw and, as it were, becomes the throw. To leap here means to follow the throw in the sense indicated.

Is the demand that the projection be withdrawn inherent in the idea of projection? Is the idea of projection not, much rather, an invitation? Does it not entice us out of our shell? It seems to me to be the point of projection that psychology should leap after it in order to catch up with, and bring in, its final meaning. Such a leaping [*Sprung*] would be the origin [*Ursprung*] of psychology, the primordial leap [*Ur-Sprung*] out of "physics" into the movement of the soul.

What can the idea of projection teach us if we comply with its phenomenology and follow it in the direction of its finality, that is, if we think from within the leap that catches up with the throw? To begin with, the throw is in itself a jump across the borders of the "geometric" inner. The soul reaches out, penetrates forward into the open and conquers a new soul space for itself. What was inside, all of a sudden is outside, and the outer is all of a sudden becoming important for the soul's experience, being adopted as a part of the psychical sphere. Projection brings about a reversal of the relation of subject and content. The content is now precisely no longer something safely contained "in" us, but something that happens to us from outside; and the subject is no longer the containing vessel, but is the person on all sides surrounded by and *exposed to* the psychic reality of this content. The idea of projection "wants" to transport us and psychology into a situation where we do not have the soul in us, but are in it.

Inasmuch as a projection—according to its own idea—is never made, but is suddenly there, and inasmuch as the externality of the so-called contents is also phenomenologically always first and originary, the question arises for an originary [*ursprüngliche*] psychology that complies with this phenomenology whether the withdrawal of the projection indeed amounts to a *return* home of the projected content, and whether, before, this content had ever been in us. Is a projection, as something that befalls us, not in truth an epiphany through which a psychological experience comes to us *for the first time*, not *from* our inner, but *into* our inner experience? And is it not only that active intervention, called withdrawal, that *makes* it a content in the first place? Whereby the concepts "content" and "projection" and the talk of a withdrawing are the first decisive step towards this incorporation? For if an experience can from the outset be conceived as a content coming from within us, then its internment in the ghetto of the inner has in principle been achieved and is psychologically already real.

Jung already had this insight and made it perfectly clear. "The word 'projection' is not really appropriate, for nothing has been cast out of the psyche, rather, the psyche has attained its present complexity by a series of acts of introjection" (*CW* 9i § 54). But a mere insight is not enough. As a mere insight it would be a dead theory, psychologically unreal. It becomes real only if it is "originally" caught up with and brought in, so that it can have, as a living force, a retroacting transforming effect on psychology and fundamentally revises psychology's paradigm, mentality, and language (terminology). This insight should have consequences. If it were heeded, then the soul could not still be localized *in* the human being and it would be impossible, e.g., to keep insisting that the primitive "did not sufficiently distinguish between inner and outer" merely due to a deficient development of consciousness. Like any insight that has been caught up with and come home to consciousness, it would be dynamite: it would burst open from within our *own* present habits of thinking, the "inner" in our context, and force psychology to an about-turn— away from its "enlightenment" (egoic, scientific) fundamental stance and into an (I would almost like to say) "animistic" one (if this word were not hopelessly stuck in a wrong pejorative understanding).

Withdrawal is thought to be necessary because the imagined fear is that the individual loses the content that has been "projected out." But is the "content" that is ascribed to an other really lost for the subject? Is the outer really foreign? And does something become my own only if it has been introjected? Where something is projected, we are already dwelling with this other. No one is closer to an inimical shadow and more personally affected by it than he who experiences it in projection upon somebody and is nagged by it constantly, even deep into his sleepless nights. During the time when the man in the moon was still projected upon the moon, the latter was much closer to us than it is now, when it is possible to travel to it with spaceships and lunar modules. Projection precisely overcomes the split of the inner and the outer and opens up to my soul the whole world as its inner space; it procures for the soul an extendedness over the world so that it begins to carry its title *anima mundi* with full right. The idea of projection entails within it the impulse to bestow again upon psychology a cosmogonic, ontological dimension and upon man an exposed position in the middle of the cosmos (or chaos), to expel him from the safe observer position outside and vis-à-vis ("objectivity," etc.) and to bring the subjective inner into the objective outer. It is not insignificant for psychology that Jung reminds us that the Pueblo

Indians had to help the sun, through their rituals, to rise anew every day and to traverse the sky (*Letters 2,* pp. 596f., to Miguel Serrano, 14 September 1960). This refers to the *real* sun, not merely to the sun "in ourselves"—but also not to the positivistically conceived sun of physics or astronomy. In Jung we read, "The psyche creates *reality* every day" (*CW* 6 § 78, my emphasis).

Already the geometric inner contained within itself a pointer to the fact that it fundamentally cannot be found anywhere, and to its irreality. The true inner is obviously no geometric place, no literally conceived *topos*, but *ou-topos*, "u-topian." That is, as a leap that takes the mind inside it is in truth a mode of *relating* to events. Not *where* we encounter something—whether *in te ipso* or *foris*, out there in the world—is what counts, but whether we view it externally (in terms of a geometrical-physicistic fantasy) or internally, i.e., imaginally (poetically): the true inner is the "poetic" image. However, the image of that sort is the inner not because it could be thought to be an image of something *in* the human person (this would be the unpoetic, external image), but *because it has conversely the world and ourselves within itself—thanks to the leap into it.* It is for this reason that in the cults of the Indians the real sun can be meant, for the image includes the latter, contains it within itself, does not have it outside of itself; it takes us back behind the narrowed-down conception of physics into a more primordial realm.

There can be no doubt that projections distort reality. But is the distortion perhaps something that should *not* be corrected, but rather caught up with and come home to consciousness? When the soul spills over the edge of the "vessel" of the subject and pours into the world, is there not a final meaning inherent in this event, too? Projection reduces the reality principle to absurdity; it takes hold of the world and delivers it over to the weaving, cocooning, poetic nature of the soul. Perhaps projection does not at all want to produce a knowledge about something in external reality, nor to make consciousness aware of a hitherto unconscious part of the personality. Perhaps we have such an expectation only because we presuppose that the scientific view of reality is simply the only one. Perhaps what it brings us is a new *light* by which the whole world can be illumined and perceived differently. To leap after the projection does not merely mean to accept it, but to allow it to have a retroacting effect on our reality conception and to transform it. Each projection, according to the particular light that it emits in each case, designs and wants to initiate into a differently constituted reality within which the same people, things, and conditions can be freshly perceived.

Projection is first of all a shine, a light radiating from the soul, an illumining of the world. Is the world gilded by the evening sun less true than the world as it appears in plain daylight? Is there *the* true light? Does the pale, silvery light of the moon produce a lie, the pallid light before a thunderstorm a distortion of reality? Indeed, do not even the infamous rose-colored glasses provide a true, although rosy, picture of the world? The lesson of projection could be that there are *many* truths, many worlds, i.e., many faces of the one world. What so far was accepted as reality pure and simple is not *the* reality, but in itself only *one* kind of poetry; in this case, however, not poetry in the Romantic, lyrical, visionary style, but in the style of Naturalism or of *Neue Sachlichkeit* (New Objectivity), which, too, are *poetic* styles in their own way! It is the world as it appears in the shine of the ever same neon light of the laboratory.

What the idea of projection can offer to psychology is a new understanding of the nature of truth. The true is not the opposite of shine and appearance, but what shows itself in whatever shine and appearance. And the appearance is likewise not the opposite of truth, although it includes the possibility of mere semblance and although it can, by revealing the particular truth belonging to it, *ipso facto* conceal other truths. Certainly, projections make us biased. But if for that reason they are withdrawn into the subject, the truth and consciousness that they can offer are withdrawn along with them, just as the earth would lie in total darkness, if the sun were to withdraw the light it projects upon it. By making accessible to us the appearance-nature of truth and the insight into the fundamental inseparability of truth and "subjective" bias ("personal equation"), the idea of projection destroys the ego's belief in an abstract absoluteness of truth and reveals this faith as an appearance of its own, an appearance that makes possible the particular truth in the sense of physics. Thus, it brings us closer down to the earth because along with the *notion* of absolute truth in the abstract sense (which is, to be sure, understood to be on principle unreachable, but nevertheless remains in power as an ideal), it divests us a bit of our godlikeness.

*   *   *

The astounding, paradoxical, but for psychology indispensable insight is that *despite the fact that we already dwell with the projected content, we nevertheless have to leap after it in order to get to it.* How is this to be understood?

With the image of the leap after the throw a radicalization of our understanding of the nature of psychology, in the sense of the "psychological difference,"[7] is aimed for. If there is not only one thing, a throw (view, theory), but in addition also a leap, which, however, is in itself precisely nothing but the *explicit* re-enactment and repetition of the throw, then the nature of psychology is not a simple unity, but characterized by an internal difference, a duplication, potentiation, as the word *depth*-psychology may already suggest. If this be so, psychology is not simply psychology; it must on top of that be *psychological* psychology. It is then not sufficient for psychology to have to offer, as physics does, hypotheses and teachings about its objects of study (feelings, ideas, dreams, etc.). This would be only "the throw." For it to become psychological at all, something else beyond is demanded. Psychology *exists* only if and inasmuch as it catches up with its own conception through its leap into it, because it is its nature to always at first be ahead of itself and therefore to be an internal tension and dynamic movement. The throw (theorizing), too, is motion; each new discovery takes us beyond familiar knowledge. But the throw is, in contrast to the leap, a movement in which something retains its static, fixed form: this something is science itself as the theoretical subject. The throw alone, without the leap, still remains in the dimension of "the world of physics."

But the leaping must itself be understood in terms of the leap, or else it would merely be an external addition to the throw or a mere iteration of the throwing movement, only that now the thrower would throw *himself* instead of the stone. Here we run again into the phenomenon of duplication. The pair of concepts of throw and leap can again be conceived in terms of the one term of the pair, the

---

[7] The difference of man (or psychic behavior of the organism) and soul. See Chapter Five below. Or it is the difference between "first" and "second half of life" in that figurative sense in which I treated it elsewhere ("Principium individuationis und Individuationsprozeß," in Ursula Eschenbach (ed.), *Die Behandlung in der Analytischen Psychologie I*, Fellbach-Oeffingen (Bonz) 1979. Or it is the difference between positive fact and image.

throw (i.e., in terms of "physics," literalistically, externally), or in terms of the other term, the leap (i.e., inwardly, dynamically). In the first case our thinking of the leap remains unaffected by what it thinks (the leap itself). The leap is something that has—apart from our thinking about it and independent of the throw—its self-same meaning. To leap could here mean in practice to complement our (theoretical) discoveries by our drawing practical consequences from them, applying them, e.g., on ourselves. In this way we would undergo a change, to be sure, but only a change in our condition, not in our essence, because in the case of a mere application of knowledge, the essence preserves itself as something fixed: theoretical knowledge as well as practical application are states or activities of "the ego," which is the persisting substrate of both.

The second case is different. Here the leap, as leap after the throw, is dynamically and intrinsically connected with the throw. Here psychology as that which thinks the leap and the throw must abandon itself to the inner dynamics of the idea, stirring from within itself, of the throw, so that the throw gradually absorbs psychology into itself (leap). The inner movement of the throw continues in the leap (so to speak as a throw to the power of two) in such a way that its beginning (the idea of the unmoved thrower as the origin of the throw) is exposed to its result and seized and intrinsically transformed by it. With this recoil, the movement returns again to its beginning (origin), thereby completing itself, because everything that "previously" was static goes under in the motion and nothing remains outside of the latter. Psychology is immersed in its own thoughts. The (cognizing or applying) subject goes under and disappears in psychology and psychology as theory disappears in therapy, which in turn is again only "theorizing" (*Theoricieren*) in the sense of Paracelsus, even where it takes practical measures.

Once we follow this dynamic we do not find ourselves in a different location in "geometric" space, but all of a sudden in a totally different space. Through the intrinsic raising of the throw to the second power, through this catching up with the throw and expressly reenacting the throwing movement by leaping into the center established by the throw, the new, exotic space of a "real psychology" and of the true inner has "leapingly" been conquered and opened up, and from within this space throwing and leaping mean something different from changes of location. *Ontic, literalistic* movements in analogy to movements in the sense of "physics" have turned into a *psychological, imaginal*—we could also say: *ontological*—movement. How difficult this origin (*Ursprung*, originary leap) of psychology is shows in everyday life in the fact, e.g., that many young people do not succeed in performing it when they want to gain personal independence from their parents and think that it could be achieved either through mere discord or through moving away. They change something—but on the ontic-literalistic level ("physics"), so that psychologically everything remains as before. A true psychological freeing oneself does not necessarily demand, as we all know, an estrangement or a geographic separation, but the putrefaction of the whole "world" and a new "cosmogony," along with which the *idea* (determination of essence) of the relation to one's parents can be differently defined.

What turns projection into a psychological problem is that the movement stops with the throw. For the throw means that the subject is vis-à-vis the object thrown and becomes its observer (from the outside). Accordingly, projection is seen as perception; one sticks to what is seen, to the "facts," which, however, in the case of projection precisely are not facts, but distortions. So it is easy to see why the demand that projections should be withdrawn suggests itself. By contrast, if the throw is from the outset understood in terms of the leap, then the projection throws out into the world "not what the eyes can see, but what opens the eyes" (*Kena Upanishad*), not something seen, but a light. The confounding of the shining light with what is seen in this light is the essence of psychological literalism, of "geometric-physicistic" thinking in psychology. Psychology begins when it, for its part, steps into this light, starts to see *by means of* it and in this way disappears in it instead of wanting to see it the way one sees a thing. The leap gets theory itself into the act; it makes what is seen retroactively destroy and transform our former view.

Here we have an additional justification for our assertion above that we do not as yet have a real psychology. Conventional psychology is not concerned with its own seeing, but is interested only in what is empirically seen. It only pro-jects, *ent-wirft*, designs (e.g., theories about psychical phenomena), but does not catch up with and expose itself to its own throw or pro-ject. Instead of leaping, e.g., into the theory of the archetypes *so that it would be subordinated and exposed to this its own theory*, that is, instead of taking the archetypes as the light in which and by means of which to see *itself*, it leaves them in their ("pro-jected") initial form where they have been objectified or substantiated into empirical facts to be perceived *in front of* us or even— with an ultimate intensification of the empirical-physical into something quasi-metaphysical—into *trans*empirical "archetypes-in-themselves"; with the result that psychology in the last analysis remains "physics." By believing that it has to prove archetypes and, e.g., when working with dreams, to demonstrate the archetypal images in them, it banishes us to the grandstand and keeps us, as mere observers, out of them. The act of leaping would bestow upon psychology the inness in the images. Psychology would begin to *see* archetypally instead of seeing "the archetypes" or the archetypal images. Psychology would expressly admit *within itself* the play of the archetypes; instead of merely dealing with images, myths, fantasies as its *topics* and practicing active imagination as a method, it would *itself become imaginative ("fantastic") and poetic*. As the theory of the soul, it would go under in the image-producing soul itself and catch up with and integrate the insight that psychology is itself an expression of soul (the soul's life). The psychical would equal the psychological. Psychology would *really* hold the special status ascribed to it by Jung, the status that consists in the fact that its object is the observing subject itself. It would have jumped out of the rank of the sciences back into the freeplay of the imagination itself, from which the sciences, too, have sprung as one particular idea.

Psychology knows, of course, that mere observation is therapeutically unproductive, but for the most part the only recipes that it has to prescribe against it are "to feel" and "to translate into action": the dream images are not only to be viewed, but also "emotionally experienced," and not only to be understood, but also to be "given creative expression to by the ego complex" and "implemented" so as to become real. But both responses are only alibis for the avoided leap. "To feel" is precisely what the spectator on the stand does. The feeling experience is not a sign that the mere observer status has been overcome; it is of a mode, essentially belonging to this detached viewing, of how the ego maintains itself in its egoic stance by emotionally objectifying the world, i.e., by keeping it at a distance vis-à-vis itself and subjecting it to itself. The emotional experience seems to indicate that one is intensively affected by a reality, but it is, this is my interpretation, *as* such stirring of the emotions, the avoidance of a genuine (psychological) being affected. The "practical implication" or "application to reality" of the dream ideas as well as "the ego complex's giving creative expression to the images" are necessary only in those cases where the ego does not give free play to the inner dynamics of the "throw" (production, projection) of the images, but wants to substitute its own activity for it, in other words, where it defends against having to suffer the decomposing recoil upon itself.

The thought of a psychology that is *in itself* poetic or even speculative creates fear. But then we forget that speculation is derived from *speculum*, mirror, and that it is the sole element in which, if at all, consciousness and true critique can happen. For without the mirror of the speculative we see only the visible object, but do not become aware of the light *in* which we see, and thus also lose the chance to discover in what *is seen* our own *seeing* or perspective. Why was the sight of the Gorgon Medusa not fatal for him who saw her in a mirror and for him only? For the mirror image could, after all, not show the Gorgon any more amiable or harmless than she was. But the mirror, by distinguishing the *image* from the positive-factual thing and opening up the in-between space of the psychological difference, could represent the object seen *as* what is seen by us and thus explicitly draw attention to the collaboration of our mode of seeing. The lesson of the myth is that the petrifying effect of the Gorgon does not lie in *her* as empirical object, but in the empirical, unreflected, difference-less mode of viewing. And he who looks in this fashion, sees the Gorgon everywhere, much like conversely that Faust who, permeated by a love potion, had to see a Helen in every woman. He already has the Gorgon within himself and looks with *her* petrifying glance into the world.

The leap after the throw shifts the focus of attention from the objects or contents to the perspective with which we see them. With this realization we catch up with our own initial comments about the spirit of psychology in contradistinction to its contents. The greatness and depth of a psychology does not lie in its answers, but in the spirit of its questions. Not the fact that by way of the *contents* of its teachings it can offer us, e.g., archetypes, individuation, wholeness, the meaning of life, indeed maybe even God, makes it great, but whether it comes to its own psychological ideas with the reason of the heart, the depth and fluidity of the mind, a rootedness in the "cosmogonic" imagination, a fundamental openness for what may show itself and the in-between space of the soul as its advance concession.

What good is it to talk of wholeness if the mental style of talking is not itself characterized by wholeness? Psychology must cease to preach wholeness as part of its ideology and instead begin to view even the singular and one-sided in a holistic way. Wholeness must not be sought as an object before us (mandala symbolism, etc.); it must be the spirit of our psychological viewing. What good is the magnificent conception of the *unus mundus* if it remains only a *theory* about the world, a content of thought that we can marvel at reverently, which, however, is not "caught up with," that is, which does not subversively come home to our thinking and being by removing us from our encasement in the scientific mentality and placing us directly into the open? What good is all talking *about* creativity if this talking merely parrots again and again uncreatively what can be read in Freud, Jung, Neumann, etc.? A shining example to prove the opposite is Freud himself when he addressed himself to the most insignificant phenomenon, the slips of everyday life, in a creative *manner*. This shows there is no need to be connected to a special creative unconscious. The creative depth is everywhere; anything can become the origin of creativity if it is seen in an originary way.

Psychology must itself become creative again; it must not be *about* psychodynamics, but itself *be* psychodynamics, living movement of the soul, as it had originally been with Freud as well as with Jung. The latter wrote in reaction to the attempt by certain Jungians to give precise definitions to some of his concepts, "From such discussions we see what awaits me once I have become posthumous. Then everything that was once fire and wind will be bottled in spirit and reduced to dead nostrums" (*Letters 2*, p. 417, to Baroness Vera von der Heydt, 13 February 1958).

If that which psychology is dealing with is fire, then psychology will be set on fire and consumed by its own contents. The fire is content and container, subject and activity at once. A lion is something that, in addition to its being, also devours; fire, by contrast, *is* in itself the process of consuming, it is nothing else. In this way, the image of fire becomes a bridge for the understanding of psychological being, and at the same time of true psychological movement. In it, as the ontological movement as which we have already characterized it, that which is moved cannot be distinguished from the motion, the subject not from its state. If psychology truly comes about, then the subject is not *in* motion like something that is given (e.g., like the development of an existing human being), but it is *as* movement; and it is not *in* time,[8] but *as* time, namely, as imagination.[9]

This is a movement as we find it in a poetic work or also in a circle. As to poetic works, I am not so much thinking of works whose content is a thrilling, eventful story, but of such quiet works as, e.g., Adalbert Stifter's *Nachsommer* ("Indian Summer," 1857), in which, through 800 or so pages, hardly anything happens, and which nevertheless is in truth one incredible internal movement. As to the circle, I am not thinking of a merry-go-round, for *it* moves *in* a circle, along a pre-existing circular path. Instead of this derived (physical) movement I have in mind the original movement of that circular line that is at rest and is *as such* an internal movement, in other words, a *concept* of movement that has been transmuted by the movement itself. Every lyrical image, every dream image is in motion in this sense, even if it is an image of calm or even rigidity.[10]

It seems to me that the question of whether a true psychology (or, what amounts to the same thing, individuation[11]) is possible or not depends on whether we can give way to this type of movement. And conversely, the coming about of such a movement depends on the condition that it must not be the movement of the person, but is allowed to be the movement of psychology, i.e., imaginal, ontological movement, a movement in which the person is encompassed. Jung said: "There is no linear evolution; there is only a circumambulation of the self. A unidirectional development exists, at most, only at the

---

[8] Of course not either in (whatever kind of) timelessness!

[9] See on this Martin Heidegger, *Sein und Zeit* (Tübingen: Niemeyer, 1977); *idem, Kant und das Problem der Metaphysik* (Frankfurt a.M.: Klostermann,1973); Hermann Mörchen, *Die Einbildungskraft bei Kant* (Tübingen: Niemeyer, 1970); Emil Staiger, *Die Zeit als Einbildungskraft des Dichters* (Zürich: Atlantis, 1953).

[10] An example for the imaginal dynamism of the rigid could be the idea of the dead object, the *res extensa*. Its internal movement is what is behind the historically singular dynamics of our scientific and technological development!

[11] Cf. my paper "Principium individuationis und Individuationsprozeß," in Ursula Eschenbach (ed.), *Die Behandlung in der Analytischen Psychologie I*, Fellbach-Oeffingen (Bonz, 1979), pp. 141–170.

beginning; later everything is a pointer to the center" (*MDR,* pp. 196f., transl. modif.). With this insight Jung has originally caught up with his projected conception of individuation as a self-evolution. It is no longer conceived of as a movement directed towards a goal, but not either as one's resting after one's arrival at the goal. It is the simple "intensional" circumambulation which has its goal not outside and ahead of itself, but already within itself ("true interiority") and is thus open for the most diverse experiences, for the multitude of the gods (see James Hillman's article "Psychology: Monotheistic or Polytheistic?" in *Spring 1971,* pp. 193–208).

But the thinking and practice of conventional psychology does not get beyond that idea of a linear, unidirectional development, i.e., an external and derived movement conceived in analogy to locomotion. When striving for individuation, it thinks in terms of process, goal-directedness, maturation, development of the personality, self-evolution, quest, and it does not think all this imaginally, but literalistically. Here a goal is thus *pre*scribed to us, a goal that we ought to be striving for and that is hoped to become the *content* of our experience. In this way, we remain in the sphere of "should" and "ought"; but a state where that which should be actually is will never be a present reality. "The throw" is all there is. The leap that would catch up with individuation does not take place. Of course, as long as individuation is seen as a task for the person and not for psychology, we will stay with the idea of linear evolution. For such a circumambulation on the part of the ego-personality as suggested here would not only be impossible, it would also be utterly boring. It is precisely for this reason that the leap is needed, the leap that leads out of the personal world into the Inner Space of psychology, of the imaginal.

*   *   *

The overarching goal that modernity is heading for is to eliminate the originary psychological motion and to replace it with the geometric "movement of the *un*moved." With breathtaking speed we are veering towards an ever more radical translation of the essence of man into a physicistic mode: feasting and gorging oneself, but without getting fat; "learning Russian without effort"; receiving news from all over the world, but without having to leave one's television armchair at home;

flying at top speed through the air in airplanes, but calmly sitting there as if in one's living room; being shot to the moon, but, by virtue of a spacesuit, taking terrestrial conditions along and remaining untouched by the reality of the moon. Further examples could be added *ad infinitum*. In all these cases the point is a lack of "psychology," nay, an active elimination of "psychology," that is, the systematic elimination of an originary being-in-motion. The intent is always to achieve change, but to keep the subject as something fixed out of the process and to immunize him. The ultimate goal is to enforce totally, in all areas of reality, a being-human as already *a priori* finished and closed, a being-human that for all physically existing individuals of the species *homo sapiens* is guaranteed, by religion and the Constitution, certain rights as a native inalienable possession and that therefore, in principle, is not in need of still having to *become* human (in the sense of a being-human to the power of two) through an initiation.[12] On the side of the world of objects, the analogues to this *a priori* finished, closed being-human are prefabricated houses, ready-to-serve dishes, "prefabricated parts in the sense of modular systems," etc.

Is it, under these circumstances, astounding that psychology, too, which of course takes place within this development, partakes of this lack of psychology, indeed, that it is put in service of the process of the physicistic conversion of the essence of man? "Physics" is nothing else but the detailed, methodically consistent elaboration of the content of that archetypal fantasy that is called "the ego," nothing else but the world as seen by "the ego." And is conventional psychology in its deepest essence anything else but ego psychology, as the total *establishment of "the ego"* within one's own inner and *as* the "inner"— even in those cases where it talks of the evolution of "the self"? Even where all the ideas discussed by us under the image of the leap (the decomposing recoil, the psychological movement, the "poetic" image, the true inner, the psychological difference and the duplication) are accepted and striven for by psychology (including the ego's going under in the self of the individuation process), it nevertheless shrinks, almost everywhere, back from the ultimate and decisive step, from that leap

---

[12] This explains the popularity today of the idea of the development of the personality. It permits us to continue to be content with a merely empirical humanness (for "development" is a process that the *a priori* "finished" human being undergoes); at the same time it is supposed to serve the purpose of a vicarious satisfaction of the desire for a true deepening of human existence.

which does not merely make the ego *of the individual* enter the unconscious and experience it, but would retroactively decompose even the fixed theoretical *concept* of the ego, would putrefy "the ego" as psychology's paradigmatic conception (along with ego development, ego strength, ego-self axis, ego-consciousness, emotional experience of the archetypal images through the ego complex, etc.). Modifying a dictum by Nietzsche for our present context, I would like to say: *I believe we cannot get rid of the rationalistic egoic attitude* (despite "self-development") *as long as we still believe (in our psychological theory) in "the ego."* If the individual is not really changed, nothing is changed," Jung said (*Letters 2*, p. 462, to James Gibb, 1 October 1958). But the converse must likewise be asserted: if psychological theory is not really changed, if the (egoically) fixed thoughts of psychology have not come in motion because psychology has not leaped into them and instead shied away from getting affected by them, then nothing is changed, despite the most beautiful personal individuation processes and the greatest openness to myths and images.

And yet—in the midst of this overwhelmingly powerful development, the idea of projection, of a throw out into the open, still continues in psychology. The soul is still waiting for the time when the impulse that the soul gave with this idea will be kept faith with, so that it might itself be allowed to transport us: into the leap after the throw, the originary leap or *Ur-sprung* (origin) of pschology.

CHAPTER FOUR

No Alibi!
Comments on "The Autonomous Psyche. A Communication to Goodheart from the Bi-Personal Field of Paul Kugler and James Hillman"

You have shown that Goodheart's stance is enraging, because it violates a basic psychological *credo*; untenable, because its ontology leads to an infinite regress; uncritical, because it exempts itself from being seen through as a text; therapeutically problematic, because it implies a psychology of blame; atavistic, because it revives an outdated view that has long been overcome in philosophical, psychological, and scientific theorizing. I would like to raise a further question: "Is psychology, as a field of study, really free to adopt *or* to reject the idea of an autonomous psyche, or is this idea not an indispensable prerequisite for doing psychology at all?"

Editor's Note: In an 1984 article published in the *Journal of Analytical Psychology*, entitled " 'C. G. Jung's First 'Patient': On the Seminal Emergence of Jung's Thought" (vol. 29, no. 1), the Jungian analyst William Goodheart developed the thesis that Jung's notion of the autonomous psyche was a derivative of transference interactions which Goodheart, drawing upon the work of the psychoanalyst Robert Langs, attributed to "the bi-personal field." A year later, in an article published in *Spring 1985* entitled "The Autonomous Psyche: A Communication to Goodheart from the Bi-Personal Field of Paul Kugler and James Hillman," a spirited critique of Goodheart's thesis was presented that employed the conceit of a therapy-like consultation between an enraged James Hillman and his interlocutor, Paul Kugler. This exchange was then followed by responses from Goodheart as well as from ten other prominent analysts. The present article is Giegerich's response to Kugler and Hillman on the autonomous psyche versus the bi-personal field question.

The classical example for the origin of a science is mathematical physics. What made physics an "exact" science and the model for all other sciences was neither the empirical method nor the application of mathematics to nature, but something more fundamental, which alone made the empirical-mathematical method possible in the first place: physics' unconditional surrender to its underlying pre-conception of the world, its own *a priori*: "nature." With an absolute commitment, physics followed the principle that "nature" has to be explained exclusively from "natural" causes. At no point during the investigation was science allowed to take recourse to any factor outside of its own vision. It had to fall back on its own resources. For this reason, physics had to ruthlessly rid itself, one by one, of such ideas extraneous to its fantasy as fate, Spirit, God, ether—not because these are 'theological' or 'mythical' ideas whereas physics' "nature" is not, but simply to be true to its own myth ("nature" as pre-conceived by modern science). It is as if physics had, with respect to *its* root fantasy, strictly obeyed Jung's advice concerning fantasy images in general: "Above all, don't let anything from outside, that does not belong, get into it, for the fantasy-image has 'everything it needs' within itself" (*CW* 14 § 749, transl. modif.).

If nothing from outside that does not belong is allowed to enter physics' nature, this means that nature is here conceived as self-contained, its own origin, a spontaneous and autonomous reality. Never must it be thought of as the result, e.g., of the workings of an outside God; it carries its ultimate cause, its "God," within. Physics thus acts out as its unconscious underlying axiom the idea "deus *sive* natura" clearly articulated by Spinoza.

By uncompromisingly refusing to take refuge in an "alibi" (an explanatory factor "elsewhere": outside of itself), physics was constantly thrown back on itself (on its fantasy). This had two consequences.

First, this guaranteed that "nature" was *a priori* "opened up" as something fundamentally unknown, an endless labyrinth to be entered, and that this basic vision would be perpetually enforced. Both mythical Mother Earth and theological "God's creation" had been ontologically present and complete because their ultimate (divine) essence was given, in the one manifestly as an epiphany, in the other only to faith as God's revelation about the world. Thus, the only meaningful mode of relating to them, as already given, was reverence, not science. Physics' nature by contrast is ontologically absent and incomplete: its ultimate essence has to be sought, the *"deus sive natura"* being an irrevocably absent God, so much so that science has even been thought to be atheism. This is the *a priori* condition that made science, scientific *investigation* possible and absolutely necessary. The fantasy of "nature" drove man into an inescapable search, a real *petitio principii*: the systematic uncovering and unfolding of its fantasy of the world in search of its unknown first principle at ever new levels of sophistication. If, as Jung said, the anima is the mediatrix to the unknown, physics is a single gigantic anima adventure and highly psychological.

Second, by being entirely thrown back on itself, physics had no escape. It was cornered, given over to Necessity, forced onto an inevitable course, the course of an analytical insearch for ever deeper, more hidden causes contained in "nature," i.e., in physics' fundamental vision of the world. The strict obedience to its own myth is what provided the ontological basis for the application of the scientific, mathematical method and thus for physics as a truly exact and "certain" science. Physics did not, as Goodheart wants for psychology, *avoid* tautology; it *settled* in a tautology (to explain nature from nature), allowing itself to be irrevocably enclosed by it and making the unknown of its root fantasy its very fundament.

If anything can be learned from physics for other fields of study, then this is not the mathematical *method* which is the exclusive property of physics' myth. Rather, it is the total dedication with which each field must bind itself religiously to *its* respective fantasy as its exclusive *prima materia*, i.e. as that which has "'everything it needs' within itself" and which therefore has to be kept free from any extraneous idea; it is the faith in its own tautology, its own *petitio principii*; and the courage to let itself fall into the unknown of its root fantasy without reserve. The imitation of physics' scientific method would do the very opposite of what physics itself does and teaches us: that the style of a field must be exclusively derived from its own *a priori* vision.

Returning from here to psychology, the concept of an autonomous psyche seems to me not only a question of personal preference, of one's ontology, of epistemological logic, theoretical and therapeutic valuableness, or empirical evidence. It, above all, seems to me a simple necessity. In order for psychology to be, it *must* posit an autonomous psyche, because only then is psychological inquiry possible in the first place. For only if the psyche is granted autonomy and spontaneity does psychology relentlessly bind itself to the unknownness of its own root fantasy, having to explain everything psychic "tautologically" from the psyche herself, and only if psychology strictly refuses to base itself on anything outside the idea of "psyche" (*whatever* "psyche" may be) will it be inescapably forced into the depth of its subject matter and be able to establish its own (psychological) version of exactitude and certainty. Denying the autonomous reality of the psyche would be abortive. It would mean to saw off the branch one is sitting on. It would mean a psychology divided against itself; a study of the soul deprived of its unknown and cut off from the anima; a broken commitment, since the name of our field, "psychology", *has* already *committed* us to the psyche as our unknown *a priori* and our self-contained *prima materia*, whether we admit it or not.

Any psychology taking for its fundament anything "known" ("ontologically present and complete" in the sense of having to be taken for granted and not itself subject to psychological questioning, i.e., reflection), be it Freud's bedrock of the biological or Goodheart's bi-personal field or whatever, will be fundamentalist and have unwittingly fallen into a "medieval" state of science (nature to be explained in terms of a factor, e.g., God, that by definition lies without the responsibility of the science in question). In this way, the door is *systematically* opened for uncontrolled projections. The repressed faith in the autonomous psyche is not simply gone; it is now experienced outside, in the power of conviction with which the bi-personal field, e.g., demands belief in itself as the actual cause of everything psychological. Precisely because psychology based itself on something "concrete," it has become arbitrary and dogmatic in Kant's sense: you now have your pick from so many primary causes: brain, birth trauma, reincarnation, the mother's breast, the bi-personal field, etc. If the *petitio principii* or tautology as the bedrock *on* which any field of study must base itself is denied and avoided, it seems to return *in* this field of study as a logical fallacy and as the unrecognized problem of the infinite regress.

In this sense, psychology has no choice as to acknowledging or denying the autonomous psyche. A psychology that would deny it is "impossible." And yet, such a psychology *is* possible inasmuch as it does exist. In physics, any attempt to establish a science of nature denying the autonomy of nature would simply be laughed off. But in psychology it is possible to propose in all earnestness a study of psyche declaring the idea of the autonomous psyche as a reaction formation derived from the bi-personal field, and there will be many psychologists who will take such an attempt seriously. I think this fact cannot simply be dismissed, but must be understood. It seems to indicate a fundamental difference between physics and psychology, "nature" and "psyche." It cannot have been an *intellectual* need that gave rise to the psychology of the bi-personal field, since intellectually it is untenable and obsolete, as you have most convincingly shown. So it must stem from a *psychological* need, the autonomy of the psyche not being allowed to appear *before* the theoretical vision now exerting itself from behind *in* or *as* this act of psychological theorizing instead. This, however, suggests that it must be inherent in the nature of psyche that it can or even wants to turn against itself and produce neuroses not only in people, but also in psychology, theories about itself that deny its own autonomous reality. It must be compatible with the psyche to produce the incompatible, an insight which could give rise to further reflection.

CHAPTER FIVE

The Present as Dimension of the Soul
'Actual Conflict' and Archetypal Psychology

When the whites came to Melanesia in the course of colonialism and later again during World War II, and with their ships or airplanes brought in the whole abundance of their material goods—food, appliances, cars, weapons, prefabricated houses—"cargo cults" sprang up among the natives: people believed in an immediately imminent millennium that miraculously would bring an unlimited wealth of "cargo" (pidgin English for Western consumer goods). Because of this religious expectation, traditional means of livelihood were often destroyed and storerooms for the expected riches built. What had happened here? The sight of the Western abundance of consumer goods had overwhelmed the natives, and their consciousness, used to a Stone Age life as it had been, was not capable of comprehending the goods as what they were, namely the results of ordinary human production rather than goods of supernatural, celestial origin.

This example drastically demonstrates an important fact to us. The character that an object has for us is not simply dependent on its real nature, but even more on the consciousness that views it. One swallow doesn't make a summer, but even one thousand swallows do not make one either. Applied to psychology this means: not everything that is about the mother-child relationship, complexes, the anima, and individuation is *ipso facto* already psychology. The concepts and contents of psychology do not constitute *per se* the essential character of psychology. What is decisive is much rather that the orientation of consciousness within which these contents are perceived is already a psychological one.

I object here to empiricism in psychology, to that stance that believes that psychological problems can be solved scientifically and directly, within the framework and on the basis of empirical-practical experience, without one's *simultaneously* having engaged in reflections about foundational questions of a philosophical-archetypal nature. But the subject matter of one's presuppositions must not thereby be ignored, because it is precisely an integral part of the constitution of psychology: the psychological objects *and* the archetypal structure of the consciousness viewing them are the two moments that only together make up psychological *phenomenology*. Without being able to enter into this topic more closely, I would like to state that in this spirit and along with Hillman[1] I stand up for an archetypal psychology that reflects its presuppositions, in contrast to an analytical psychology operating with an empiricist fantasy. The latter believes itself able to see in what is "objectively given" the whole of the psychological phenomenon, whereas it is, after all, only a partial aspect, and an abstraction on top of it. My concern is about the particular direction in which a psychological investigation would have to move in order to become psychological in the first place. I am searching for the dimension of the soul and of psychology; I want to find, and consolidate, the particular space that alone makes a psychology as psychology possible and allows it to thrive.

With the notion of the "actual conflict" Jung seems to have provided one cue for a truly psychological way of viewing. I consider the "actual conflict" theorem not only as a theory *about* the psychological topic "neurosis," but at the same time also as an *expression of a particular intellectual orientation* that produced this theory in the first place.[2] This second aspect is what we will be concerned with here. Our attention is thus not aimed directly at the empirical object

---

[1] James Hillman, "Why 'archetypal' psychology?' in *Spring 1970*, pp. 212–217.

[2] The "actual conflict" (*Aktualkonflikt*) theory of neurosis proceeds from the assumption that neurosis is not rooted in a trauma from the past, but in a person's unresolved pathogenic conflict, which, because it is unresolved, is a pressing (but repressed) *current, present-day* problem for him or her. The literal meaning of *Aktualkonflikt* is a conflict that is effective at present, currently, acutely.

"neurosis," but, bent back, at the very perspective that sees in neurosis an *actual* (current) conflict. Since our task is to work out an entire mentality (which is only intimated by the notion of the actual conflict), our investigation must not confine itself to studying what Jung himself in fact stated and explicitly intended, but must attempt, as it were, to amplify, unfold and, as far as possible, to think through to the end what in his texts is only hinted at.

Thus, I profess my commitment to an "overinterpretation" of Jung's thoughts (if one wants to call it that). My overinterpretation is in principle something similar to that of Jung's archetypal dream interpretation. Jung shows how collectively significant archetypes and gods loom up behind inconspicuous dream images with an example by Dr. Buder: the seed grain that a woman in her dream finds in the pocket of her modern leather coat points *pars pro toto* to the whole mythic world of Demeter, although such mythological ideas are completely alien to this dreamer. Just as amplification must make conscious the larger background of the (often quite meager) hints contained in a dream, so we also have to amplify the often inconspicuous concepts of our psychological theories in order for that which is represented in them merely by "a subsidiary attribute" (*CW* 9ii § 55) to become visible in its entire extent, its full "collective" significance, and its larger context.

Jung, with his concept of the actual conflict, speaks out against the tendency to "trace" the fantasies of the neurotic "back to the cradle" (*CW* 10 § 345). "The true cause for a neurosis lies in the Now [the today], for the neurosis exists in the present. It is by no means a hangover from the past, a *caput mortuum*, but it is daily maintained [or fed], indeed even generated anew, as it were. And it is only in the today, not in our yesterdays, that a neurosis can be 'cured.' Because the neurotic conflict faces us today, any historical deviation is a detour, if not actually a wrong turning." (*CW* 10 § 363, transl. modif.). Jung thus remits psychology to the present. In what follows I want to try to delineate the meaning of "present," that is, the meaning that "present," *within* the framework and at once *as* the framework of archetypal psychology, must have. However, here I can discuss only a small part of this whole theme, so that the meaning of "present" can accordingly also only become visible in a fragmentary way. I confine myself to the one single aspect of *present and phenomenon*.

Jung's notion of the actual conflict first of all sets the present against the "historical deviation" emphasized in Freud, which we also know under the name of the causal-reductive mode of interpretation. The latter looks backwards and is aetiological. Jung introduced beside it and in place of it the final point of view, which is usually conceived as looking forward into the future. However, if Jung stresses the present, then *this* kind of finality is excluded. It is in fact the mere converse and at the same time continuation of the causal point of view, and not something fundamentally different. In the genetic model, both perspectives are indeed united, in the psychoanalytical as well as in the Neumann version. We can imagine this model as a straight line which leads from the past (childhood) to the present, possibly neurotic, condition and which thereafter, so one hopes, will in the future bring a belated maturation. In the background of this view there is always an ideal picture of normal development, which leads, via certain fixed phases, to a goal which is called, as the case may be, genitality, solar rationality, completeness of the four functions, or whatever. Wherever this model is operative in the background of one's thinking, a fixed specific goal has been set for psychotherapy. This goal is at the same time the standard by which the patient is measured. The question then is: where does he or she stand—maybe still stuck in the oral phase, in matriarchy? And one will be able to more or less accurately determine the point on the developmental scale at which the patient got stuck as well as where he or she should actually be. This means that there is unwittingly a moral value judgment inherent in the genetic model, a "should" and "ought," and so this model inevitably exerts a moral pressure and produces corresponding guilt feelings in those cases where this pressure is unconsciously sensed by the patient. For he "ought to," but is not, which is why he must at once make up for his missed maturation and development. This model at bottom turns the analyst into the long arm of society, inasmuch as his goal, however it may be spelled out specifically in each given case, is in the last analysis normalization.

The corresponding view of man does not comprehend man from the idea of the *imago dei*, but conceives of him as created in the image of the plant, for development and ripening are concepts taken from the vegetable kingdom. Despite this, the moral spirit inherent in this thinking suffices to make apparent how much secularized Christianity, how much theology it contains. This whole model represents a way to salvation translated into this-world terms, an eschatology, which comes best to the fore when at the end of the strenuous path of hard analytical work the sublime goal of individuation is expected to be fulfilled. This model promises salvation through development. It exclaims, as it were: come unto me, all ye that are stuck in an early phase of your development; your "lacunae" (Schultz-Hencke) shall be worked through, your "inhibitions" removed and what is "undeveloped" in you shall be differentiated, so that you shall at long last enter the state of freedom from disorder, of accomplished maturity and completeness.

All these concepts: inhibition, lacuna, disorder, incomplete development show how psychic phenomena are being judged on the basis of a norm that is taken for granted and how they are disparaged when they do not fulfill it. The meaning of phenomena lies in the final goal of one's development; only as a *"partial* drive" or as a *"preliminary* phase" that already points to the final state, only as a not-yet does something that is below the norm have meaning here, but not in itself. Masturbation is "wrong" or only in place during a certain phase; sexual intercourse is "correct." Therapy here means correction, leading the patient up to the pre-set goal; for example: Where there was masturbation, there sexual intercourse shall be. The mentality that shows itself here is the same as in colonialism and Christian missionizing, for which everything that does not correspond to the norms of the Western world is "*under*developed" and which wants, e.g., to free the primitive head hunters of their fear of demons, prohibit the Indians from ritually burning their widows and, as a first and foremost measure, to introduce monogamy everywhere. Just as the genetic approach measures one phenomenon by another one that has been set up as the norm, so the corresponding form of therapy is supposed to replace one ("wrong") behavior by another, "mature" one. In quite the same way, psychological theory explains one phenomenon by another one, e.g., the mystic love of God by sexuality. The substitution of the one for the other is the principle of the developmental approach.

The norm originates here from isolating one single phenomenon from within the range of phenomena (behaviors) and placing it above the others, much as the intolerant religions (e.g., Islam, Christianity) in each case single out one religion (namely themselves) among all the many factual religions as the exclusive one and proclaim it as *the* true, the absolute one. What serves as legitimization for this setting up of one religion (which to begin with is just as "finite"!) as the absolute one? Nothing else but the doctrine of this religion itself! In the same way, the developmental fantasy can distinguish what is "fully developed" from what is "undeveloped" only on the basis of that genetic prejudice that it has itself set up and that constitutes its theory. The belief in development posits and "verifies" itself.

Of course the developmental conception is not *intended* as a moral one. But I am not talking about how we therapists understand our concepts and with which intentions we apply them in therapeutic practice, because the subjective self-interpretation appears to me to have a low reality value. Rather, I am interested in what a given perspective objectively entails and what it in fact states. My standpoint is thus not that of the people who may develop certain conceptions, but that of those conceptions themselves which may be operative in a person.

If Jung emphasizes the present, then this means in our context that the psychic phenomena must be removed from our explanatory systems. No phenomenon is supposed to be understood in terms of another one or replaced by another one. "Present" means: to stay with the phenomenon itself, to understand it by itself and in its own terms. A symptom or condition must not be clamped onto the Procrustean bed of a whole development scheme, so that we always know from the outset what was "before" and what in principle would have to follow it, which means that it would be *a priori* pinned down to a fixed meaning. *The present returns the innocence of the phenomena to psychology and frees them of the curse of the "not yet."* Then there will be no longer a "wrong" and a "correct," but whatever is *is* what it is. It carries its meaning within itself and does not need to obtain it from something that it is not. The zoologist does not view animals from the point of view of their evolutionary past or their future, i.e., not as what they are not yet, but apperceives and appreciates them as a present, as what and how they are, each "after his kind," as the creation story in the Bible so aptly puts it. He studies them in their own habitat and views each as the center of its own environment. In the same way psychology, too, has to appreciate the individual phenomena, each after its kind.

Jung always fought against that interpretation of anxiety that explains it as a result of repression and thereby dismisses it as inauthentic. He insisted that anxiety is in itself legitimate and an authentic psychological way that one may have to follow. "To be freed of anxiety" therefore cannot be a truly psychological goal. To stick to the phenomenon, in the sense of the present, thus also means to give up the goal of being free of symptoms, of a *salvation* from complexes and symptoms. For the symptoms precisely contain, as Jung puts it, "a precious piece of soul." Jung even went so far as to declare that "[t]o lose a neurosis means as much as to become redundant; life loses its point and hence its meaning" (*CW* 10 § 355, transl. modif.). For the pathological phenomena are not foreign bodies, as the medical fantasy must think, but originate in the soul. The soul sometimes even *hungers* for anxiety and produces it from within itself where there is nothing real to be feared. Where the soul is left to its own devices, there it produces rumors, belief in witches, stories of dismemberment and other grotesque ideas. It is fascinated by horrible and perverse things and drives people to places of accidents, into horror movies and to pornography. Where this happens, there soul is at work. To affirm soul thus also always means to affirm psychopathology. This is probably one of the main reasons why, as Jung states, we have a downright panic fear of the soul and seek to protect ourselves in psychology from it, e.g., by taking a medical or scientific stance.

We approach symptoms from the outset with the idea that they are disorders and should disappear. The patient is supposed to lose, e.g., his or her fear of the other sex. We prioritize the "normal" or "healthy" state striven for and view the symptom as something that actually should not be, at least "not any more." What is needed here is a shift of emphasis. It is, on closer look, a scandal if an analyst refers to himself as an advocate of "reality." This would be as if a biologist were to comprehend himself as an advocate of industry. The biologist must obviously be an advocate of the animal and plant kingdoms and seek a place where animals can *be* when modern civilization tends to displace them. In the same way, the psychotherapist must side with the soul's impulses, *even if* they are "archaic" and pathological. Just as it is not a question of domesticating all wild animals, so it cannot be the prime concern of a therapist to transform the soul's pathological and archaic impulses through development into so-called healthy and human ones. No doubt, psychotherapy does have the task of changing something. But in the spirit of the necessary shift of emphasis it must not ask how, e.g., the fear of the other sex could be removed, but where it belongs. It must take care of this fear, attend to it and find a place for it where it is allowed to be. For this fear is perfectly right, inasmuch as sexuality *is* a mystery and mysteries can legitimately be accompanied by fear. The evil is not the fear itself, but rather that, we, in our psychological ignorance, do not know of a place where this fear can be authentically experienced. Let us keep in mind that in the rituals of primitives fear and horror were often especially induced. But of course, primitives have knowledge of where the fear in each case belongs, in the domain of which god or demon, and this is why they do not need, as we do, to neurotically locate that which is feared in harmless human beings and place the burden of archetypal demands and mightiness that only gods can carry upon one's mother, e.g., or on women in general.

But, if we are supposed to stick to the phenomenon in the sense of the present, how can the perspective of finality, which Jung insists on just as much, still be possible? It is possible only if it is understood as the finality of the *symptom* or, more generally, of the psychic phenomenon and not of the analysand. The question is not how the *person* in each case would have to develop in the sense of finality, but how the psychic impulse can unfold and "complete" itself. What is the final aim and end (*telos*) of the symptom? Where does it find its "divine equivalents" (*Letters 2*, p. 545, to Victor White, 25 March 1960)? Which structure of consciousness is necessary for it to receive a home in us? Psychology, thus, will not aim for a redemption and liberation *from*, but for the *deepening* and *strengthening* ("amplification"!) *of* the symptom. The final point of view understood in this way does no longer look to the future end at the right-hand side of the horizontal developmental scale, but dwells at the present spot, the phenomenon, and with an inevitable turn directs its attention into the vertical dimension of depth. The alteration that psychotherapy wants to bring about is thus not a modification of behavior through *our* development, but the *fulfillment* of the phenomenon that at first appeared only in distorted and stunted form.

The coexistence of "present" and "finality" in Jung's psychology implies that "present" is not the flat, one-dimensional here and now, but means the intrusion of a new dimension.

By distinguishing the finality of the symptom from that of the analysand we have come across an important fact. Generalizing and modeling my formulation on a (only formally) similar one of Heidegger's, I would like to refer to it as the "psychological difference," i.e., the difference between soul and human being. Soul and man must be distinguished. Man *is* not the soul, and does not own it as his property or quality either. He can have soul, and yet also easily lose it too, a fact that primitives referred to as loss of soul. Obviously, the soul is something that the human being himself *is* not, but something which can have a relation to him and, if it is working in him, can give his life depth, meaning, interiority. With this distinction, the soul is, however, not supposed to be split off from the human being and, with a hypostasis, be construed as an entity among other entities, as an invisible second human being, as it were, besides the visible first one. It is, rather, possible to conceive of the soul as a quality or modality that is more a task than a given. It is nothing but a *"wesenloser Schatten"* (an insubstantial shadow), one possible perspective from which man can view his life. ...

It is my thesis that conventional psychology wants to eliminate the psychological difference and do without it. It acts as if the demonstrable human being were identical with the soul, containing it within himself as a part of himself, or as if the demonstrable human being *per se* implied the soul. It is for this reason that it likes to call itself humanistic psychology. The full independence and autonomy of the soul, the fact that it, as mythology teaches us, does not have its true home in the human being and upon the horizontal earth, but that it is native to the underworld (in the vertical), is not heeded. Psychology has *a priori* committed itself to the standpoint of the human being.

When, in the spirit of humanistic psychology, one says "human being," then what is intended with this phrase is in truth nothing else but what Jung often terms the ego-personality,[3] for with "human being" we mean *ourselves*. This same psychology also likes to call itself

---

[3] Cf. "... the ego—that is, the empirical man—..." *Memories, Dreams, Reflections*, p. 346.

ego-psychology. Since it abolishes the difference, it must translate everything that was intended in terms of the vertical dimension into the horizontal dimension. In this way finality, which is actually a property of the impulses of the soul (in other words, of that which the human being as ego-personality is *not*), is ascribed to this very ego-personality. This has the result that now *I* have to develop and mature; it is the well-known unfolding of the personality, which is identical with ego development, just as Analytical Psychology sets for itself the goal of the complete differentiation of the "*ego* functions." It does not matter if in one psychology the human being is seen as "*Dasein*," in another as organism, in a third as a social being, in a further one as person—these are all aspects of ourselves, i.e., of the ego-personality. The fact that in our psychology the collective unconscious and the non-ego play a great role does not change this. These concepts remain mere lip service (despite the fact that subjectively they are honest), *as long as* the perspective is that of the human being and the ego. For then what actually is supposed to be non-ego comes under the spell of the ego; it is interpreted in terms of it and thus subsumed under it. Even the non-ego can in this sense be annexed by the ego. The anima is then *my* feeling side, *my* relationship function (it therefore in truth belongs to the *personal* unconscious!), and individuation turns, with a fundamental misunderstanding of Jung's conception, into a process in which I realize myself (horizontally). *Selbsterfahrung* (self experience), even if one writes this word, as Barz did, with a hyphen (*Selbst-Erfahrung*, which implies experience of the self) is nevertheless not the experience of the self in the Jungian sense, but only another word for *Icherfahrung* (ego-experience) which can just as easily be hyphenated. The experience may be as intensely emotional as possible and for the ego as alien as possible (as alien, e.g., as it is reported to be in primal scream therapy), yet it always is and remains the ego that experiences itself and its own private unconscious.

Jung's concepts of individuation and of the self, as well as his work as a whole in general, can be understood in this way or that way, either personalistically or in terms of the psychological difference and of the vertical dimension. I believe that only an interpretation in the spirit of the difference can do justice to Jung's overall intention. For this reason I professed at the beginning my commitment to what then I still had to call an "overinterpretation." Instead of reducing the topics Jung speaks about to factual realities, it seems more appropriate to comprehend them as a statements about something ultimately unknown and unknowable, something *imaginal*, and to take this into account by following an "anagogical" hermeneutic. We should not think that psychological phenomena are, as a matter of course, about the empirical person: what else could be the meaning of a "transpersonal psychology"? Thus, we must get accustomed to the idea that individuation in a certain sense has nothing to do with us. It does not mean *our* wholeness; *we* do not have to become models of completeness. The *coniunctio* is, as Jung says, a hierosgamos of the gods rather than a love-affair between mortals (*CW* 16 § 500). Likewise, "becoming self" in Jung's sense means an "*Entselbstung*" (a being de-selfed), and integration into consciousness means the exact opposite of that subsuming of a content under the ego that it is frequently thought to mean, namely, that consciousness abandons itself to the alien content and allows the *latter's* consciousness structure to become real. One could almost say: Where there was Ego, there Id shall be. Jung himself expressed it in the following way: "I have to be everywhere *beneath* and not *above*" (*Letters 2*, p. 35, to Erich Neumann, 5 January 1952).

"To be *beneath*" does not apply to therapy only, but also to our *theoria*, our psychological perspective. This means that psychology has to view things from the standpoint of the psychological phenomena, thus also of the symptoms. Instead of being the advocate of reality, of the human being, and of life, it will then comprehend itself as the advocate of the symptom and attempt to see *with its eyes*. Only when psychology ceases to defend the interests of the human person, and therefore of the ego, can it begin to become *objective* psychology, because then it is no longer speaking on its own (or the human ego is no longer speaking through it), but rather allows the psychological phenomena to have their say. "To be *beneath*" therefore implies that psychology adopts a passive, receptive, listening attitude. "To hell with the Ego-world! Listen to the voices of your *daimonion*. It has a say now, not you," Jung once wrote (*Letters 2*, p. 532, to Charteris, 9 January 1960). It is from here that we can understand Jung's tendency to personify psychic phenomena: the anima, the old wise man, the gods, spirits, goblins, partial souls. For only thereby is the phenomenon granted *the full reality of a subject*, the irreducible autonomy of a person with respect to which we are objects. This highly "unscientific" personification underlines once more the radical difference of Jung's psychological stance over against the empirical (personalistic) psychology that wants to do without the psychological difference. For the latter type of psychology, there must exist an *empirical*, factual object *whose* states or properties are to be investigated. It must therefore, even when it speaks of "anima," comprehend it as a state or "property" of the human organism, because this is the only empirically demonstrable object that is relevant here. The human being functions here as *hypokeimenon*, *subjectum*, as the foundation on which all of psychological phenomenology rests (which in turn is reduced to a mere appendage).

With that, psychology ceases to be real psychology. It betrays the present by not staying with itself, but falling back on something else, something external to psychology: on the existential-philosophical concept of *Dasein*, the biological concept of the organism, the sociological concept of group dynamics, etc. This is pure reductionism, analogous to the materialistic attempts to explain the living organism exclusively with the basic concepts of chemistry or physics. Psychological statements are then in the last analysis not statements about the soul as a reality *sui generis*, but about the human being (conceived as a fact), or about a partial aspect of it. Psychology all of sudden turns into a form of anthropology, and psychotherapy becomes either a medical method for curing people or a humanistic-educational development of the personality. But, to overstate it a bit: what is *ultimately* the object of psychology, the patient or the soul, the dreamer or the dream? (Which of the two is the foundational conception? Is the soul to be comprehended in terms of the *idea*, taken factually, of the human being—or the human being in terms of the *idea* of soul?) This is, it seems to me, psychology's crucial question. Is, e.g., the dream to be absorbed into the "reality" of the dreamer, or not perhaps conversely the dreamer and his "reality" into the imaginal world of the dream? Is the symptom supposed to adapt to normal thinking, or not perhaps one's normal thinking to the symptom?

By anchoring the soul, with a dogmatic prejudgment, on the human being, personalistic psychology succeeds in avoiding the tension given with the psychological difference and the odium that lies in the fundamental undemonstrability of the soul, and in holding on to the conventional, so reassuring one-dimensional world view—despite the fact that psychology was actually supposed to provide the second dimension of vertical depth (*depth*-psychology!). In personalistic psychology one thus behaves toward the soul pretty much like a mother who conceives of her child, even if it is at times headstrong, maybe even naughty, as her own personal property, as a part of herself, and who evades the disconcerting insight that her child is in reality a second being in his own right. Do we not, e.g., look upon anxiety as something that *we* "have," much as we have lungs and kidneys, that we, to be sure, do not have under our control, either, but which nevertheless are doubtlessly *our* organs? And do we not view the soul as if it belonged, just as our life indeed does, to the individual organism? Is it not our secret view that the anima exists for the purpose of making it possible for *us* to have intensive relationships with other people, and the great mother so that *we* might have a sense of basic trust and embeddedness—just like certain Christians see in God a means for their personal well-being?

For a true psychology, only the soul, which is certainly undemonstrable, merely "metaphorical" and for this reason a seeming nothing, can be the "substrate" and subject of the phenomena. The human being is then their object; he or she is nothing but the place where soul shows itself, just like the world is the place where man shows himself and becomes active. We therefore must shift our standpoint away from "the human person" to the "soul." (*N.B.*: I am talking of a shift of *our standpoint, perspective, or of the idea in terms of which* we study, just as before, the concrete experience of individuals or peoples.) Anxiety is then not any more a part of me than is a lion who attacks me. It is this way of thinking that is meant when Jung calls his psychology a natural science. And to acknowledge the reality of the soul implies to view it as an "environment" just as autonomous and filled with all sorts of animals, plants, persons, and things as nature is, a "microcosm," *in* which we live and whose part *we* are, not the other way around. This microcosm is the imaginal, the world of the images. This view finds its clearest expression in personifications. Without the spirit of personification, this clear manifestation of the acknowledgment of the psychological difference, the psychic (*Seelische*) as psychic cannot be sighted at all.

At least in one point, Freud perceived with the eyes of the pathological phenomenon and not from the standpoint of reality, namely when he remembered where incest belongs: in the myth of Oedipus. Freud's perspective was here neither that of medicine, nor of law, nor of morality, but it was psychological. He recognized the psychological legitimacy, indeed necessity, of incest, by understanding it in terms of a myth. It will be the task of the future to elaborate in this sense the psychology of each psychic phenomenon, each of the archetypal worlds into which our symptoms want to initiate us. To elaborate the psychology of a symptom means to amplify it—not in the miserable sense of a mechanical listing of mythological parallels, but in such a way that a given miserable symptom, this tiny peephole into another world, turns into a whole mode of living, a perspective, or a kind of living philosophy, i.e., as I already indicated, into a complete psychology (just as psychoanalysis as well as Jungian psychology are elaborations of mainly *one* particular form of pathology). For what is Freud's psychoanalysis, seen as a whole, if not the comprehensive elaboration of his own Oedipal actual conflict into one grandiose theory and view of life? And does Jung's work not boil down to a grandiose amplification and deepening of his personal psychopathology, those experiences which have by some psychoanalysts been referred to as "prepsychotic states"? The pathology that each of them had taught Freud as well as Jung to see. It is the inner substance that they circumambulated, that they lived on a whole life long, and that they sought to creatively exhaust. In both cases they did not fight their actual conflict, but devoted their life, in the sense of the present, to it. From out of their pathology they formed their life's work, which thus became a vessel for the pathology and preserved and transmitted its substance for us. Since we do not each of us possess the psychology of Freud or of Jung, we are called upon to stay with our own pathology and to develop, through its deepening and expansion or "amplification," our own psychology—each after his or her kind or, as Jung calls it, after his personal equation.

In closing, I want to summarize what I presented. By committing us, through the concept of actual conflict, to the present and blocking our glance from straying off to the left or to the right on the developmental scale, Jung forces us to dwell at the one point "between" the causal past and the final future, i.e., dwell on the phenomenon at hand, but thereby discover the vertical dimension of depth and the autonomy of the soul's life in the sense of the psychological difference.

These were my reflections about the subtopic "Present and Phenomenon." In order to complete the picture of "the present," additional topics would need to be contemplated: "Present and Time," "Present and Interiority," "*Aktualität*" (topicality), and "Presence" would be the headings of further chapters.

CHAPTER SIX

The Provenance of C. G. Jung's Psychological Findings

How did Jung arrive at his psychological insights? What is their ground of knowledge, his means of gaining knowledge? From what do they derive their "claim to truth"? For these questions there is a clear answer. And because it comes from C. G. Jung himself, we may take it as authoritative. The answer is: from empirical experience. The sentences from a leading English article—"Facts first and theories later is the key-note of Jung's work. He is an empiricist first and last"—meet with Jung's full approval (*CW* 18 § 1502), because indeed, they convey the quintessence of Jung's scientific self-image. Jung always conceived of his psychology as empirical psychology and as a natural science.

However, in conflict with this view there is the strange fact that the general scientific community in no way agrees with this assessment by Jung concerning the character of his psychology. To be sure, Jungians in San Francisco as well as in Zurich, in London as well as in Stuttgart advocate the conception of Jungian psychology as an empirical science, but these researchers themselves come from the Jungian school. If, however, we look around among those scientists who do not feel under any obligation to the Jungian approach, be it psychologists from other schools or scientists from totally different fields, we find with very few exceptions only two reactions: either Jung is attacked as predominantly unscientific, as a mystic, a "prophet of the unconscious" or the like and dismissed, or he is simply ignored, as if he had not existed.

This is a strange, remarkable situation. For if we do not try to get by with the excuse that all these scientists are either too stupid to understand the empirical character of Jungian psychology or that they maliciously do not *want* to see it, then the question arises how it is possible that serious scientists who probably for the most part are willing to provide an impartial assessment do not acknowledge Jungian psychology as a full-fledged empirical science, if this psychology in fact is such, as Jung and some of his disciples claim.

It seems to me that we must not refute and combat this disregard for Jung, but understand it and learn something from it. It is a fact and as such a sign of something real. In it, something of the nature of C. G. Jung's analytical psychology manifests itself. The way in which something is received always reflects to some extent something of the peculiar character of what is being received.

The mere possibility of having doubts concerning the scientific character of Jungian psychology, as well as the need that Jung felt to again and again protest its empirical character, or the necessity that some of his followers felt to *prove* its scientificity apologetically, with the help of the whole apparatus of the modern theory of science, put a big question mark behind the conception of Jungian psychology as an empirical natural science. For where could such an odd thing as that be encountered in, e.g., physics? Would it be at all imaginable that doubts about its scientificity might emerge and protestations and apologetics be necessary? The scientificity of physics, just as of any genuine natural science, is simply not in question, but a self-evident vested certainty; and it would not be a genuine science if doubts and different opinions about its status were possible in the first place.

All true science has the acquisition of its scientific nature, i.e., its *identity* as science and thus the acquisition of it *truth*, fundamentally *behind itself*, which is why it needs only, imperturbably, to provide evidence for the correctness of its individual statements about the facts and the big picture of its respective field, but not the proof of its scientificity *per se*. However, where one still needs to struggle to provide this proof, it becomes clear that the particular discipline has not yet attained the steady gait of a science, to use Kant's phrase, and that the question about its identity and truth is still a fundamentally open one.

THE UNKNOWN NATURE OF PSYCHOLOGY

So there are with respect to Jungian psychology at least two conflicting views: the view of Jung and some of his disciples, that it is an empirical science; and that of public opinion, that it is not. Given this state of affairs, we can fall back on an important psychological insight from Jung himself. "Now when opinions about the same subject differ so widely, there is in my view ground for the suspicion that none of them is correct, and that there has been a misunderstanding" (CW 18 § 1500). Maybe neither the opinion that C. G. Jung's psychology is a natural science, nor the one that Jung is a theologist, Gnostic, mystic, guru, or a prophet of the unconscious, but that in any case his teachings are unscientific, is appropriate.

Maybe both the pro and the contra miss the point and rest on the same misunderstanding and merely give opposite answers to an absolutely unsuitable question, one and the same question. Both are maybe only opinions about this psychology, but not this psychology's apparent truth that speaks for itself. The coexistence of such divergent opinions seems to imply that psychology is still in the state of "ought" and not "is."

Maybe Jung's psychology is, therefore, neither the one nor the other, but a third thing, something unknown and new, which requires us simply to forget the customary patterns of thought and categories, in order to approach Jung with completely fresh, different categories and expectations, categories yet to be derived immanently from Jungian psychology itself. Just as abstract painting is not degenerate representational art, so, too, Jungian psychology does not have to be poor science, but could have a different *Stilwillen*, i.e., immanently aim for another "style."

At the same time, this would indicate that "psychology," properly understood, would possibly neither have to be put into the old familiar pigeonhole (that of religion, philosophical speculation, spiritual disciplines), nor classified among the likewise familiar sciences as an additional one. Rather, it would still be a task of the future for us to *learn* what Jungian psychology in truth is. We do not know it yet, and psychology itself has obviously not yet found its own identity, an identity that would allow it to be fully at one with itself. The individuation process, its self-actualization, that process through which it would enter the state of its simple truth, is still in store for it.

If we want to catch a glimpse of the as yet unkown nature of psychology, we must not develop theories on our own, but must direct our attention to where psychology in fact is already in action. Where it takes place, where it happens, there we must observe it and what it does. For only psychology itself can inform us about what and how it is and what its source and origin is. It is in this sense that I want, by way of example, to take one single instance in order to try to see how Jung approached psychic phenomena and where he derived his insights from, in our case particularly the idea of archetypes, which is so central for him. Therefore, rather than presenting my own conception of psychology in a dogmatic way, I will try to derive and develop (one aspect of) the nature of psychology exegetically, as it were, from one existing example of psychology.

THE NON-EMPIRICAL NATURE OF THE ARCHETYPE

When Jung wanted to demonstrate the genesis of his concept of archetypes and, at the same time, give reasons for its legitimacy, he liked to fall back on the case of that schizophrenic who had the vision of the solar phallus. For our purposes it is not important if this case was in fact *the* origin of the later doctrine of the archetypes or if Jung merely adduced it as a particularly striking example. (It is also not important for us if the facts of the case were exactly as reported by Jung. We know now that there has been quite some controversy surrounding Jung's description and the discrepancies between his various reports of the same case. The point is that we are not concerned here with the factual, historical origin of the theory of archetypes, but with how Jung's psychological mind worked. And this comes to the fore for us best in a report that shows how Jung himself *imagined* the origin of and proof for his theory, regardless of what the exact historical facts were.[1]) Be that as it may, what Jung describes is that this schizophrenic saw a tube descending from the sun and swaying back and forth when the patient moved his head

---

[1] The text in brackets is an insertion dated 2005.

to and fro, and from it a wind was blowing. A few years later Jung discovered, in an only just then published Gnostic text, a parallel to this strange delusional idea that corresponded to it down to many details. Individual features of it also recur elsewhere, e.g., in medieval paintings. It can with certainty be excluded that the patient could have had knowledge of those earlier occurrences of this idea (be it only subliminally), and these earlier examples must in turn be viewed as having come about independently of each other. With this, Jung has at bottom furnished proof that this idea has "a collective existence" (*GW* 9/I § 108, my transl., omitted in *CW*) and is not a personal acquisition (through education, tradition) nor a new creation. As a potentially *semper et ubique* (always and everywhere) occurring idea— this is at bottom Jung's argument—it is demonstrated to be an archetypal idea or, phrased differently, it has at least in this one case been proven that there are ideas of archetypal origin. Jung was able to convince himself by means of many further examples of the correctness of this theoretical assumption, especially when he found in the dreams of American Blacks who had been untouched by Greek mythology striking parallels to motifs from Greek mythology.

This, and all other perhaps more extensive empirical proofs for the concept of archetypes, were, however, not able to convince the general scientific community of the archetypes. From this fact I would conclude that the empirical proof is flawed, and furthermore, that if the empirical proof is not valid, then even Jung himself did not arrive at his theory of archetypes or at his sticking to it through empirical demonstration. Its source and origin, as well as its ground of knowledge must lie elsewhere. The empirical support does not only come after the birth of the concept of archetype—just as in science the first thing is usually to establish a hypothesis and validate it empirically afterwards, but it is also external to it and more or less irrelevant for it. For the empirical proof misses, I think, the decisive substance of the notion of archetype.

Or is it really so that the mere evidence for the independent occurrence of mythological motifs during different ages and at different locations is enough to capture the central meaning of the notion of archetype? Do the determinations "parallels," "independence," "mythological character"—in other words, purely formal aspects—exhaust the idea of archetype? All these features can probably indeed be "empirically" demonstrated, but this would in all likelihood even be admitted by most adversaries of the archetype concept, without their feeling thereby forced to acknowledge the concept of archetype. For the empirical proof, this is how we could express it, leads at most up to the demonstration of the *-typos*, but not to the demonstration of what is suggested by the much more significant first part of the word, *arche-*. We do not even have to refer to the classical prehistory of the archetype concept (it was used in the Platonic school in the sense of the Platonic Idea or Form) or to the deeper philosophical as well as emotional overtones of the Greek *arché* concept (or the corresponding word element *Ur-* in *Urbild*), although the Jungian concept of archetype resounds with both, at least as connotations. It suffices to observe how the archetype concept is in fact used in Jungian psychology and what is indispensably included in its meaning beyond the aspects already described: namely (a) a meaningful structure, indeed one that establishes or endows with meaning, and (b) numinosity.

NUMINOSITY

Now it is a fact that, to begin with the last-mentioned feature, a heightened emotional state that occurs together with a so-called archetypal idea can at times be empirically demonstrated, but, first, this does not by itself amount to an empirical proof of "numinosity." For this notion does not simply ascribe to the idea a causal efficacy, but beyond that also a worth or dignity, which of course is not an empirical concept. As Jung himself stated, "the numinous quality, so indispensable to the recognition of an archetype, is an indefinable imponderable like the expression of the human eye, which is indubitable yet indescribable" (*Letters 2*, p. 490, to Abrams, 5 March 1959).

Secondly, it is not a proof of the numinosity *of the archetypal idea*. For even if one is willing to concede that such a worth and dignity are at times ascribed to an archetypal idea by those who have this idea, or that this idea *de facto* has for them an emotional value, it is by no means determined whether this numinosity indeed derives from the archetypal image (or an archetype in itself that might be expected behind it) and is intrinsic to it. It could also have been subjectively conferred upon the image by the persons concerned due to whatever kind of affective disorder (in which case the image might possibly have to be viewed as a mere epiphenomenon), especially if one takes into account that the regularity that exists in the biological sphere between key stimulus and pattern of behavior (innate release mechanism) is lacking in the psychological sphere as far as archetypes are concerned, where one and the same archetypal motif (trinity, solar phallus, mandala, etc.) without apparent reason is accompanied by deep emotion in one person, but is only an empty word or an intellectual game for another.

Only *ex post facto* statements can be made about the archetypes and the effects that they produce. If one confines oneself to the empirical, then one's argumentation necessarily amounts to circular reasoning: solely from the deep emotional state and effect can one conclude that an archetype must have been constellated, which on its part, however, is precisely supposed to provide the explanation for the emotional effect. "But is this—an answer?," so one might wish to ask with Nietzsche (*Beyond Good and Evil*, Aph. 11), "An Explanation? Or not much rather merely a repetition of the question?"

How far the concept of archetypes is at bottom removed from truly empirical thinking is shown when one contrasts "archetypal effect" with "nexus of empirical conditions." The natural sciences under certain conditions postulate an (inferred) causal connection between two empirical events. But what does the archetype concept, if it is conceived as empirical, produce? It asserts an effective relationship between one single empirical event (namely the occurrence of an emotional state and/or of a mythological motif), on the one hand, and a merely hypothetical, intangible archetype on the other. Thus, here it is not only the nexus that is hypothetical, but also that to which the event is supposed to be causally connected. This means that there is not, in the last analysis, a connection at all. The concept of archetypes stands, as it were, only with one leg on the "empirical" ground. The other leg, if we see it from the empirical point of view, projects up into the air, the sky—into nothingness.

The archetype, therefore, does not explain at all. It is only hypostatized causal inexplainability, or, better, an objectifying name for Jung's vertical orientation and his renunciation of the will for horizontal-causal explanation and his turning instead to the question of significance and meaningful substance. In other words, instead of establishing an explanatory relationship between two separate events, the theory of archetypes makes only one single event *transparent* by holding it in front of the 'illuminating' archetypal background. In this way, the concept of archetypes arrests at bottom that causalistic movement of thought that resorts to ever other things in order to explain through them the event at hand, and instead detains the movement of thought at the one and only phenomenon itself, thereby forcing our glance into the phenomenon's depth.

This lets us understand why we have to confine ourselves to *ex post facto* statements when applying the theory of archetypes. If Jung attributes the psychosis of a young catatonic patient, who, as she later told him, had lived on the moon under the spell of a winged demon (*MDR,* pp. 128 ff.), to incest with her brother, then this sounds of course like a causal explanation. However, this statement is only possible in retrospect. The prediction "if incest, then psychosis" is not feasible, because experience shows that not every incest that has occurred has led to a psychosis, and that even if we introduced additional conditions, we would never arrive at a lawlike explanation. However, what we have to realize, and this is the crucial point, is that Jung here does not refer to incest as an empirical event ("in the eyes of the world," p. 130), but from the outset as a *mythological event "in the realm of fantasy" (ibid.).* This means that the "explanation" does not at all break out of this one *fantasy* that the patient had and does not proceed to an empirical occurrence preceding the fantasy, an occurrence that could serve as a cause (*Ursache*) of the delusional fantasy, but it dwells with this fantasy itself, enclosed within its circle, so that the experienced incest is only the meaningful immanent prime matter (*Ur-Sache*) of the fantasized drama: a purposive *petitio principii.* Jung does not explain the delusion by the empirical incest, but views conversely the empirical incest in the light of the delusion and as an integral part of it.

Jung himself was clearly aware of this state of affairs and repeatedly expressed himself accordingly. He said, for example, "... [I]ts [the archetype's] activity cannot as a rule be predicted; one never knows when an archetype will react, and which archetype it will be. But once it is constellated, it produces 'numinous' effects of a determining character" (*CW* 18 § 1492). Or: "But the supremely important motive power which is needed for this, and which sets the archetypal possibilities in motion at a given historical moment, cannot be explained in terms of the archetype itself. Only experience can establish which archetype has become operative, but one can never predict that it *must* enter into manifestation" (*CW* 14 § 488).

MEANING

We arrive at a similar result as in the case of the discussion of numinosity when we turn to the archetype concept from the point of view of the meaning aspect. As far as the amassing of parallel examples is concerned, we can say that a hundred times the same delusional idea, a hundred times the same nonsense, does not yield one single archetype. In order for us to be able to talk legitimately of archetypes, one indispensable condition must be fulfilled: it must be possible to consider the motif in question as in itself meaningful; it must deserve the predicates objectivity and truth. The view that the vision of the solar phallus is meaningful and that it is a truth is tacitly presupposed, but it is on principle not to be determined by means of empirical methods, because substantial meanings do not happen to be anything empirical. They belong to another (vertical, depth) dimension. What might possibly be determined with empirical methods is at best that certain people *experience* an event as meaningful. But in our context, what we are interested in is not how archetypal motifs are experienced, but whether they *are* meaningful: the fact that they have "a collective existence" (*GW* 9/I § 108) and "a human meaning" (*MDR*, p. 110)—contracted: that they have a universal human and objective meaning.

For this reason, generations of psychiatrists could heedlessly bypass the archetypal-psychologically most fascinating delusional ideas, and still bypass them today, even if one shows them the mythological parallels, because such a thing as a solar phallus is for them a delusional idea and thus nonsense, and not the greatest accumulation of independent examples can demonstrate its archetypal meaning to them. *Quod erat demonstrandum*, namely that it is an *archetypal* idea, an idea of numinous meaning and depth, cannot be made evident, even through the most numerous amassing of independent references. It has its origin in a different source of knowledge than natural-scientific empiricism and requires other eyes than those that are adjusted to establishing the positive-factual.

(Jung tried to bypass the problem given with this situation by taking recourse to an equivocation: "collective unconscious." The word collective indeed points to the empirically demonstrable frequent occurrence, but has in Jung simultaneously and tacitly the unempirical connotation of general human truth and objectively meaningful. For this, "collective" is of course the most inappropriate term, inasmuch as the literal meaning of "the collective" is actually the accumulation of the merely individual or subjective, that is, the crowd or mass, something that Jung precisely does not have in mind. The actually intended meaning finds an expression in the words "*Ur*bild" [primordial image] and *arche*type: that which is irreducible, which is only to be comprehended in its own terms, which leads into the depth.)

PROVENANCE FROM PSYCHOLOGICAL FAITH

In fact a totally different picture of the provenance of the idea of archetypes emerges if one analyzes the process of how this insight came into being on the basis of how Jung himself describes the case of the solar phallus. In the *Tavistock Lectures* we read: "One day, when I was still at the clinic, I saw a patient with schizophrenia who had a peculiar vision, and he told me about it. He wanted me to see it and, being very dull, I could not see it. I thought, 'This man is crazy and I am normal and his vision should not bother me.' But it did. I asked myself: What does it mean? I was not satisfied that it was just crazy ..." (*CW* 18 § 85).

The first thing to learn from this passage is that Jung took the delusional idea seriously. He was, as he himself states, "the only person with any sympathy for his abstruse ideas" (*CW* 9i § 107). But Jung did not take this delusional idea seriously merely out of respect for the human person who had them, and for his sake. Rather, we see in the quoted passage that he took it seriously for its own sake and substantially! This is what is special, indeed unheard-of. Obviously, he felt himself that it was important through what its message was. The delusional idea was at this time, to be sure, like a sealed book; however, like a book whose message he absolutely wanted to get to know. Jung reacted to the demonstration of the insane person in the same way as he would have if an important scientist had wanted to present to him his newest experiment or inform him of revolutionary insights. For this reason, Jung was honestly trying—and one has to consider what this means!—to *see* the solar phallus. We for our part see here that with Jung's behavior we are already dealing with a totally different temperament from an empirical-scientific one.

The basic attitude of the scientist is that of distrust vis-à-vis nature. He approaches reality with the fundamental (not personal, but methodological) doubt and demands that the phenomena first of all prove their identity and legitimize themselves, if he is supposed to acknowledge them as existent, true and as facts, not altogether unlike many a bureaucrat for whom we also only begin to exist after having shown our birth certificate or passport. Science insists on verification and validation. Confronted with a primary experience, it wants, in addition to and beyond its having been experienced, an official certification, as it were, of its status as empirical-factual experience. If at all, an empirical scientist therefore would have reacted to the vision of the solar phallus with an attempt at verification; he would have sought confirmation that the solar phallus factually exists. And because this confirmation cannot be furnished, he could at best have empirically established that patient X *claimed* to have seen a solar penis, that is, he could have provided proof for the existence of the subjective idea of it.

The approach that Jung takes is fundamentally different. He meets the phenomenon with a basic trust. Long before he has himself seen the solar penis, indeed, even after having found out (as he of course new from the outset) that (with one's ordinary eyes) there is nothing there that could be seen, he gives credit to the vision, or rather, to be more exact, not "credit" at all (which is something that would still have to be redeemed sooner or later), but relentless faith. It is a faith vis-à-vis the immediate psychic phenomenon: it is sufficient for Jung that, at least by the insane person, something has in fact been *seen* and that *something* has been seen. This he takes seriously; he allows himself to be affected, indeed disconcerted by it and he does not try to reassure himself after the fact by devaluing the original phenomenon through rationalistic critique as a nonentity, or as merely a subjective delusional idea, a personal experience, a private feeling of the patient.

What Jung takes seriously is precisely not the subjective idea of the patient and that it means something to him, but *the solar penis*

itself seen by him in his delusion. What he took seriously was that this
idea had a real meaning (just as the insane person, too, implied): "I
was not satisfied that it was just crazy." In more general terms, it is
the psychic image (the objective content of the image as such) in which
Jung shows faith. Doubt about the solar penis cannot arise from the
outset when this attitude is present, because then nothing is believed
in or asserted, or, if doubt should enter from outside (namely from
out of the scientific stance), it could not hold its place: "His vision
should not bother me. *But it did.*" A search for proofs or explanations
is therefore completely alien to this way of thinking. The desire to
obtain a validation of the sun penis would, given this type of bond of
trust as it exists between Jung and the phenomenon, be just as
inconsistent, tactless, indeed deadly, as if one would suddenly demand
of a friend to prove his identity through official documents.

The fact that Jung took the content of the vision (the solar penis
itself in its truth) seriously and not only the vision as a subjective
idea of the schizophrenic *in nuce* already contains within itself the
whole archetypal concept. Jung was only able to wish to see the solar
phallus because he instinctively—without calling it so and without
explicitly knowing about it—started from the assumption that this
was an archetypal idea, i.e., an idea backed up by a psychic *reality*
(namely the solar phallus). In his stance, the archetypal concept had
been real and at work from the beginning, and only through and
by virtue of this stance, only for this stance—this is my thesis—can
there be archetypal ideas. The archetype concept has its provenance
in the faith that Jung brings to the phenomenon as such, and not
in empirical research.

The concept of archetypes is also not a scientific hypothesis, not
a "working hypothesis," but the hypostatizing name *for this stance*! It
is the name of an ethos, in Aristotelian terminology the name of a *hexis*
that through such a naming *awards* to the image unfathomable depth
and numinous reality. The word archetype is not simply a designation
for an objective factor of the life of the soul, a factor that Jung could
be said to have discovered. Rather, it is equally also an *act* of
acknowledgment on the part of the psychologist himself, an outlook
or perspective. That this is so is the sole feature that establishes the
term archetype as a truly psychological concept in the first place. For
the peculiar characteristic of a psychological notion lies in the fact that

it says just as much about the subject as about the object; that the subjective attitude of the speaker expresses itself (and is supposed to express itself) in it *to the same degree that* it also reflects the aspect of reality that it is about. By contrast, scientific concepts—although these also of course betray the perspective of the subject (scientist), even if involuntarily—are supposed purely to represent the objectively real and eliminate the subject. Truly psychological concepts, as concepts that intrinsically implicate the subject, have inevitably the nature-of-being of a *hexis*. They are never only theoretical, but also "ethical."[2]

For this reason, the concept of archetypes is not in need of being proven at the outset, and any attempted proof after the fact, by means of an accumulation of independent parallels, does not add anything essential to the (initially still implicit) concept, and as a theoretical proof it will also never be able to transport a person into that stance. Above all, such a proof cannot demonstrate the "correctness" of the idea of archetypes, as I have shown, inasmuch as it is an attitude that can never be correct or false, but is in any case merely something that one can adopt or not.

The conclusiveness that the Gnostic parallel to the solar penis vision had for Jung does of course not lie in the demonstrable parallelism and independence, but in the fact that Jung had been deeply affected and moved by this vision already, when first confronted with it, and that he again took it seriously in its substantial content when he came across it the second time. It is a comparison of two examples *that have already been apperceived in their archetypal depth* and that, for this reason, only "verify" what has *a priori* been conferred upon them through the attitude of trust and faith. In reality, the parallel examples do not in any way provide a validation. What they provide is merely an "amplification" in the sense of electrophysics: a reinforcement and underlining of what had been there from the beginning. The second appearance of the solar penis vision gives a greater weight to it, intensifies the impression that it makes on Jung and nourishes the trust that he brought to it—just as a new friendly act of a friend only strengthens the bond of trust, but neither creates nor verifies it. And in addition, it allows

---

[2] As a matter of course, "ethical" must here not be confused with "moral" (in the sense of being in accordance with a specific moral code), as if implicit in psychological concepts were ethical norms (imperatives and prohibitions) for human behavior.

the otherwise isolated, erratic idea to be placed in a context, thus providing a clearer idea of the richness of its meaning.

It is about time to accept, and to allow oneself to be taught by, the critique of the opponents of the archetype theory. This theory *is* not an empirical-scientific theory, and it is misleading to call it that, or to try to turn it into one. With empirical arguments one can at best verify what is not essential and superficial about Jung's insights (the positively tangible and obvious); however, that which is Jung's deepest concern (the archetypal depth and truth of, e.g., the idea of the solar penis itself) can at most be foisted on the empirical proof.

By encouraging the empirical approach, one successfully ensures that nobody except insane people will see the solar phallus and we all will remain "too dull." It is wrong to view the theory of archetypes in terms of the correct-false or truth-error opposition. The opposition that is appropriate to it is that of being able to see vs. being blind, or truth (in the sense of *Offenbarkeit*, disclosedness) vs. occludedness, concealment. Thus, Jung himself states about religion that it "consists of psychic realities which one cannot say are right or wrong. Are lice or elephants right or wrong?" (*Letters 1*, p. 327, to Anonymous, 6 January 1943).

Does one really understand the sentence "the solar phallus is an archetypal idea" if one has not, like Jung, attempted to see the solar penis and if one does not take it relentlessly seriously as having a legitimate content? He who wants to open people's eyes to psychic reality—regardless of whether it is the reality of the solar phallus or of other archetypes—must precisely get them off the empirical approach and direct them to that which alone is the source of all truly psychological insight: to the attitude of trust, which as faithfulness toward the immediate psychic phenomenon deserves the name "psychological faith," a name first used by Grinnell.[3]

What is psychological faith? It here reveals itself in the fact that Jung places more trust in the vision of the madman, who has been

---

[3] Robert Grinnell, "Reflections on the Archetype of Consciousness: Personality and Psychological Faith," in *Spring 1970*, pp. 15–39. In this important paper Grinnell derives the concept of psychological faith directly from Jung's dove dream of the year 1912 (*MDR,* pp. 171 f.) and shows that the gift of the dove to Jung was this very faith in psychological reality, which from then on supported Jung's life and thought and made his psychology possible.

displaced ("*verrückt*") from the normal world by the soul, than in his own eyes' empirical sight. This is the beginning of psychology.

When I give so much emphasis to psychological faith, one might get the idea that Jung was after all a preacher of a belief. But this would be a misunderstanding. Psychological faith is not a creed. Within the limits set by this paper, I discuss the Jungian attitude only in the direction of its one aspect of trust, and with respect to its equally important other side must confine myself to the following brief remark. Jung's attitude is *also* and at the same time characterized by great soberness and down-to-earth-ness. He does not only abhor all rapturous enthusiasm, but, so I think, founded also the most *critical* of all psychologies known to me. Psychological faith does not mean that Jung would have *believed* in the solar phallus or the archetypes. He did not presuppose the archetypes as something positively subsisting; on the contrary, he emphasized that psychology is dealing only with images, fantasies. However, and here psychological faith comes in, he also believed that the images, *as* mere images, *as* fictions are not null and void, but an essential reality, and he called this reality "psychic reality, which has at least the same dignity as the physical one" (*CW* 15 § 148, transl. modif.). That is to say, Jung believed in the gravity, dignity, and independent reality of that which, like the solar penis, has no physically real basis at all. Jung's attitude is thus close to that of a poet, who, like Homer, describes and sings the praise of the gods and in this way takes them utterly seriously, without, however, believing in their existence or wanting to make the audience believe. "It goes without saying," we hear from a scholar of Homer, "that the only truth that myth still had even for the original audience of the *Iliad* was poetic truth" (W. Bröcker).[4] In much the same way, myth and archetypes have for Jung only a poetic, or as he would say, *psychological* truth, but thus, to be sure, also a psychological *truth*.

PROVENANCE FROM BEING TOUCHED AND AFFECTED:
"PSYCHOPATHOLOGY"

All sciences approach their object by means of a method, which is applied systematically and is at one's free disposal. But is it

---

[4] Walter Bröcker, *Theologie der Ilias*, Frankfurt/Main (Klostermann) 1975, p. 23.

possible for us to believe that there could be a method by which the soul can be captured? Would "psychological method" not be an absurd notion, because if there were one, it would either have annihilated itself as a method the moment it truly exposed itself to the "object" soul, or because if it maintained itself as a method, it would have to bypass the actual nature of the soul? For the second possibility there is of course enough illustrative material in scientific psychology. Be that as it may, it seems to me at any rate that Jung's behavior vis-à-vis the solar penis vision suggests a totally different conception: psychological research, seen from the standpoint of Jung, is not the application of a method to an object by a scholar who remains more or less untouched, but is only possible as an attitude, indeed as a mode of *being*, of the scholar himself.

This comes out in our example in the fact that Jung was affected and disconcerted by the idea of the solar penis, and to such a degree that his being affected is not just an unessential side effect not pertinent to the matter at hand or which even interferes with the scientific process—which would be the case with an empirical scientist, but is an essential and integral element of that reality that is here to be experienced. Precisely through it Jung becomes a psychologist, somebody who is open for the soul-content, somebody who is touched and moved by psychic reality and for this reason beholds something there where empirical eyes cannot see anything. In the "But it did (bother me)" *psychology unexpectedly happens*, it originally (out of its own origin) gives itself to Jung, as the soul's speaking to the soul about the soul, a speaking for which the people concerned are merely the place and vessel.

What I want to drive at here is the following: psychology, as we find it in Jung, is not a methodically applicable science, but event, happening! And it is not theory or doctrine (textbook knowledge) that would have to be secondarily applied in a separate practice, but as a *theoria* that is rooted in a *hexis*, it belongs *a priori* to "ethics." Therefore, it also cannot be taught and learned, but requires an authentic initiation, one's being moved and touched by psychic reality. For this reason, I could speak elsewhere of psychology as the "third autonomous person" of psychotherapy.[5]

---

[5] Wolfgang Giegerich, "On the Neurosis of Psychology or The Third of the Two," see above Chapter Two.

This being affected means that Jung is addressed in his soul by this vision, as by a reality. He senses that it has a message even for him himself, and he acknowledges this being called by this idea and he places himself under this call. He accepts that he is, as it were, "meant" by this idea. He does not maintain the posture of the scientist who diagnoses from a distance what odd fantasies "this patient over there," vis-à-vis himself, produces. He is also not the personalistically thinking psychotherapist who tries to have empathy with the patient, but in the last analysis does nothing other than analyze what kind of unconscious problem has now been constellated in the patient and on which stage of ego or libidinal development the patient is at present. Rather, Jung becomes himself the addressee of the message contained in the vision. What the insane person saw has some kind of meaning for him himself. It bothers him. The content of the fantasy is in some way binding for him. What we see here comes close to what in Gadamer's hermeneutic is called "*applicatio*," the speaking of a historical text into the personal situation of the interpreter.

The being affected or the "*applicatio*" cannot be excluded from the concept of archetype, if not no more than a meager, merely formal skeleton of it is supposed to remain. The actual concept of archetype originates in a *relation* (and essentially implies this relation) into which the psychologist is immersed, involved. It is not a relation that he establishes through a method, but rather, one that happens to him. Whereas science interrogates nature and, taking it to task, sits in judgment, as it were, on it, demanding from it answers to science's questions according to its aiming for correctness,[6] Jung conversely allows himself to be addressed by nature and get drawn into a conversation. All activity is on the side of the psychic phenomenon, not on the side of the scholar and his methodological procedure. Jung is and conceives himself first of all as one who listens, hears, and if he does at first not succeed in perceiving the message that wants to impart itself to him, as in the case cited, then he does not blame the delusional character of the idea (here of the solar penis), but rather considers himself "dull." This word "dull" can be spoken only by someone who has already conceived of himself as one who has to listen and learn. At a later date Jung wrote in this spirit: "We have simply got to listen to

---

[6] Heidegger discussed this aspect of science at length.

what the psyche spontaneously says to us. What the dream, which is
not manufactured by us, says is *just so*. Say it again as well as you can.
Quod Natura relinquit imperfectum, Ars perficit" (*Letters 2*, p. 591, to
Read, 2 September 1960).

That *ars* is the soul-work, soul-making, which does not interpret,
not explain, but "says again." The relation of the psychologist to the
phenomenon is that of receptivity, or even, if we think of the "being
touched and affected," one of suffering the infliction that the experience
of the phenomenon entails. For this reason, I called the attitude out
of which psychology becomes possible a *"psychopathological attitude,"*[7]
a phrase that first of all falls back on the literal meaning of the word
(*pathos, passio*, passion, being seized by a deep emotion), not on
psychopathology in the narrower sense, which, however, is supposed
to include the psychologist's closeness, indispensable for psychology,
to pathology (as an intensification of one's being seized by a deep
emotion). Psychology is possible only out of *Ergriffenheit*, one's being
deeply affected and moved by the soul, just as Jung, too, stated about
himself in a certain context ("I myself am haunted [*ergriffen*] by the
same dream ..."—*MDR*, p. 206). In the phrase "psychopathological
attitude" the word attitude can consequently not mean, in an active
sense, our gearing ourselves up for ..., but rather passively being put
into the appropriate frame of mind as one's suffering to be affected
and touched by psychological reality: passion in its twofold sense.

Natural science *subjects* nature to all sorts of experimental
conditions and forces it to answer scientific questions. It is not only
essentially contraception, but also on top of it in a certain sense use
of violence, which begins in a still external sense with the dissecting
of corpses and the pinning of butterflies, and goes, via physics'
experiments with inclined planes and the experiments of people like
Skinner with rats, to sublimated forms of violence such as locking
realities in definitions and terminology. As Gadamer aptly stated:
"... [T]he terminological use of a word is an act of violence
committed upon language." Science is "'*Herrschaftswissen*'
[domination knowledge], i.e., appropriation as seizure."[8] Psychology

---

[7] Wolfgang Giegerich, "Über den Gegensatz von Psychopathologie und Neurose.
Oder: Von der Analytischen zur Archetypischen Psychologie," unpublished manuscript
1976, especially p. 80.

[8] Hans-Georg Gadamer, *Wahrheit und Methode*, Tübingen (J. C. B. Mohr [Paul
Siebeck]) 1974, p. 392, 295.

as we primordially find it in Jung, by contrast, submits to, and tries to serve, the demand or call that comes to us from the phenomenon, where the word "serve" can remind us of the literal Greek meaning of the word therapy (*therapeia*), so that it becomes clear that here psychology as theory is in itself already therapeutic.

Although Jung had initially still conceived of his own confrontation with the unconscious as a scientific experiment, he realized later that it had been an experiment that had, conversely, been conducted on him (*MDR,* p. 178). In the same vein, he says with respect to psychotherapy: "Nature experiments with the doctor in expecting an answer from him" (*CW* 10 § 532). In exactly this sense the question came, in our example of the solar penis, from the phenomenon, and Jung had to meet the challenge. It was not that *he* approached psychological reality with hypotheses and theoretical models. It was the other way around. He allowed himself to be addressed by it and listened to what it had to tell him. "It has a say now, not you" (*Letters 2*, p. 532, to Charteris, 9 January 1960): this is what one could put as a motto over Jung's entire attitude as a researcher and therapist.

PERSONALISTIC VERSUS OBJECTIVE PSYCHOLOGY

The attitude of the psychologist is receptivity; the relation into which he is placed is the conversation through which he is addressed and experiences a challenge. That is, the phenomenon does the talking: the phenomenon and not, as one might think at first, the patient. I have already said that Jung's interest and sympathy was for the delusional idea (the solar phallus itself) and not in the first place for the person who had this idea. What touched Jung to such a degree was the content, the matter, that expressed itself and demanded his (as well as the patient's) attention. And we can probably say that Jung was in general of the opinion that a patient is then, and only then, taken seriously if the *message* that is contained in what he says and the *message* that comes to him through a dream, for example, is taken seriously in *what* it says, in its content and substance. "Of course, it is most unorthodox from the psychiatric point of view to take psychotic things seriously. But for the patient it is much better to be unorthodox ...." (*Letters 1*, p. 252, to Bertine, 9 January 1939). About the solar phallus patient Jung says: "He was kindly disposed towards me; he liked me as the sole person who showed any sympathy for his abstruse ideas" (*CW* 9i § 107, transl. modif.).

For us it sounds offensive when I state that Jung's interest and sympathy was in the first place for the delusional idea itself and not for the person who had it. Does this not mean that the real human being is overlooked? Is it in this way at all possible to have a therapeutic relationship, or does such a stance not amount to an exploitation of the person for the scientific interests of the researcher? It may, perhaps, seem so. But the opposite is the case. Jung's patient liked Jung precisely because Jung showed genuine interest in the content of his delusional ideas. The psychotic does not want to be understood and accepted in his subjectivity; he wants to be taken seriously in what his contents are. The contents of the soul want to be heard and received. Thinking about this a little longer, we will soon realize that this is at bottom true all the time. To take the stories, memories, dream images, and other psychic productions seriously only for the patient's sake, that is, only because one wants to understand and help *him*, but not because one wants to understand *them* in their substance and in their truth, is at bottom the most hurtful betrayal, the greatest disparagement.

Of course, many patients want to be accepted only in their subjectivity and as ego personalities, and they would feel themselves hard done by if a difference between the ego-personality and the soul should be made. And, of course, this need for acknowledgment of the person that identifies himself as ego must in some way or other be taken into account, too. But a therapy that would simply gratify this patient need would not do the patient a favor. It would, in a deeper, therapeutic sense, precisely betray him. He would not have been understood at all, inasmuch as to understand a person means to understand him in his deepest essence, which is not what he, from his subjective, egoic, personal point of view, considers his own truth. And just like Jung's solar phallus patient, there are in today's therapies, too, off and on people who almost refuse to accept personal (person-centered) understanding and compassion, because they are driven to insist on the substantial right of their depression or whatever their symptoms may be and to fight for a state where the therapist understands and takes seriously the content of their pathology. Here,

---

[9] Wolfgang Giegerich, "On the Neurosis of Psychology or The Third of the Two," see Chapter Two above.

apparently, the Third Person of psychotherapy (as I called it once[9]) comes to the fore.

The fact that a real communication and understanding between people is in general to be differentiated from an orientation upon the ego-personality as such of whoever one's vis-à-vis happens to be was pointed out by Gadamer. "Thus it is inherent in an authentic conversation that ... one wants to understand him (the other person), to be sure not him as the individuality that he is, but as that which he says. What is to be comprehended is the material right of his opinion. ... Where, however, we truly focus on the other person as individuality, e.g., in a therapeutic dialogue [here we must be more specific than Gadamer: in a therapeutic dialogue *of the personalistic variety*] ..., there this is not truly a situation of communication."[10] But this comment does not apply to therapy in Jung's sense. For it is precisely an *authentic* communication: a dialogue or dialectical relationship in which two persons try together to come to a real understanding about what the psychic phenomena say to them. The point of this communication is thus not the individualities as such, but a third thing, a matter, the contents of the objective soul, such truths as, e.g., that of the solar penis. Nevertheless, the therapeutic situation is different from ordinary communication in Gadamer's sense. In ordinary communication it is, according to Gadamer, a question of understanding the other person as what he says, of the substantial right of his opinion. In psychotherapy, by contrast, we have to view what the patient says not as *his* speaking, *his* opinion, but as something that is itself spoken to him by the soul.

To what extent Jung did not focus on the individuality of the patient, but on the content, and to what extent he felt less affected and touched by the former than by the latter—and so even in his therapeutic endeavors—comes out beautifully in his description of how he demonstrated to Freud the case of Babette (*MDR*, p. 128).

Freud visited Jung in Zurich, and Jung demonstrated his more interesting cases to him, among them the old, completely crazy

---

[10] Hans-Georg Gadamer, *Wahrheit und Methode. Grundzüge einer philosophischen Hermeneutik* (Tübingen: J. C. B. Mohr [Paul Siebeck], 1975), p. 363 (my translation). In a footnote to this passage Gadamer adds, "This putting oneself into the position [of the other person], which means the other person and not his substantial right [the legitimacy of the content of what he says] is matched by the inauthenticity of the questions asked in such conversations."

Babette. When Freud asked Jung, "how in the world were you able to bear spending hours and hours with this phenomenally ugly female," Jung, so he relates, "must have given him a rather flabbergasted look, for this idea had never occurred to me" (transl. modif.). This was so because Jung did not first of all look at the human being as a person, but at "the interesting things" that she said and at her "such lovely delusions" behind which the ugly outer appearance of the patient totally paled, indeed, which even threw a transfiguring light upon her so that she could appear to Jung as "a pleasant old creature." This interest in psychic reality for its own sake made it possible for the person herself to receive her due too.

Even quite generally Jung emphasizes the priority of the substantial matter (the objective psychic reality) in therapy (and thus the authentic communication). "As a doctor I constantly have to ask myself what kind of message the patient is bringing me. ... The doctor is effective only when he himself is affected" (*MDR*, p. 134). So the patient brings a message to the therapist; there must be something in what the patient tells him that moves the therapist even for his own sake—another example pointing to "applicatio" in the sense of hermeneutics. Because it is the material message that is at stake, and because Jung wants to hear it for its own sake and does not use it merely for the purpose of interpreting the individuality of the patient (where *he* psychologically stands—i.e., diagnosis—and what he should do— i.e., the therapeutic step to be taken), he has every right to call his psychology objective psychology. In the same spirit, his written works deal with the objective contents and not, as in case reports and personalistic studies, with people who experienced such contents: e.g., with symbols of transformation (not with the transformation of the particular patient), with the divine child (not with childhood development), with mandala symbolism (not with the self-actualization of a patient), with the philosophical tree, with the spirit Mercurius, with the *mysterium coniunctionis*, etc. Even his typology, where it would be most likely to assume that it focused on personality and personal differences, deals in nine chapters with notional contents and not with personal matters, with the Holy Communion controversy, Schiller's aesthetic ideas, the Dionysian and the Apollinian, etc., and in only one chapter (which was expressly designated as not central) with personal things.

For us, who are ourselves deeply rooted in personalistic thinking, it is difficult to really understand and heed this. Time and again we lose objective psychology and slip back into a subjectivist, personalistic mode, by automatically using the symptoms, dream images, and memories of the patient as means to understand him as person, in his present developmental stage or psychic state. Even when we work with mythology and archetypes, the vortex of the Ego is so strong that we again and again feel tempted to view the dream and the other psychic material as an expression of the personality of the patient instead of him as an expression of those psychic images. This amounts to a slipping away from objective psychology and into ego-psychology—despite "archetypes" and the "collective unconscious." This way of thinking, into which we so easily lapse, lies on this side of the psychological difference (the difference between human being or ego and soul) and has not yet acknowledged the true autonomy and objectivity of the reality of the soul, but takes it continuously prisoner for subjectivity by chaining the material to the empirical person (ego).

If psychotherapy is not personalistically focusing on the person, but if, as psycho-therapy, as *therapeia* of the phenomenon, of the persons in the soul, it feels first of all an obligation towards the contents of the objective psyche, to the units of meaning and truths that they represent, then it is clear that practical therapy and theoretical psychology are one and the same. For both are a ministrant ("therapeutic") listening to psychic reality, an attempt to communicate with it, and both move within the same affection and *passio*. As belonging to "ethics," psychological "theory" is in itself therapeutic-practical.

I have already pointed out that with this objectively psychological orientation the patient, too, receives his due in the deepest sense of the word. For what is it that therapy should bring him? He, too, is supposed to learn to listen and hear and gain the insight through experience that his ideas and feelings are precisely not personally his own, but are addressed to him, pretty much in the sense in which Jung states: "Consequently, man derives his human personality only secondarily, as myth states, from his descent from the heroes and gods, that is in psychological terms: his consciousness of himself as a personality derives from the influence of quasi-personal archetypes" (*CW* 5 § 388, transl. modif.).

THE SHINE OF THE BEAUTIFUL, THE APPEARANCE OF
THE GUEST

We heard that Babette had such "lovely" [lit. *schöne*, beautiful] delusions. The little word "schön" is in truth a very significant attribute because in it the relation in which Jung stands toward psychic reality reveals itself. The delusional ideas, the dream images, the images in general in which the soul speaks to the soul about the soul are "beautiful" for him; they belong to the realm of the beautiful. What is called beautiful here is of course not the literally beautiful, the ideal, the aesthetically transfigured. It is the imposing, that which radiates, shines, gleams. It is that which, coming forward, makes itself manifest, shows and presents itself—*phainomenon* in the original sense. It is the "coming to light," which allows forms, contours, images to become visible. The archetypes are for Jung that which shines into our life, or they are the shine, the light itself, that possibly shines into us. Above all, the beautiful is something that attracts of its own accord and invites us to devote our attention to it. This "loving" relation to the images must not be omitted from our understanding of Jung's theory of archetypes.

We may remember here Jung's words quoted in the following, although they are specifically dedicated to the situation of artists: "It is the great dream which has always spoken through the artist as a mouthpiece. All his love and passion ... flow towards the coming guest to proclaim his arrival" (*Letters 2*, p. 591, to Read, 2 September 1960). Notwithstanding all the differences between the artist who proclaims the great dream and the psychologist who particularly attends also to the small dreams and who does not proclaim them, but merely "says them again," these words throw a light upon the style of thought and the basic orientation adopted by Jung. Jung met the delusional idea of the solar phallus as a coming guest whom one had to receive hospitably.

Seen from here, Jung's comparison of the archetypes with the pattern of behavior is a very remote analogy indeed. This comparison would be terribly reductive if this distance were not taken into account as, however, in Jung it is. (Even where he presents the archetype as biological fact, he nevertheless immediately spells out the difference: the biological pattern, he says, describes above all external phenomena;

the archetype, by contrast, the mental image, for which reason a concept of its own is needed for the "psychological pattern"—*Letters 2*, p. 152f., to van den Berg von Eysinga, 13 February 1954.)

As we all know, Jung introduced the distinction between the archetypes in themselves and the archetypal image. Although this distinction is questionable inasmuch as it raises difficult, maybe even hopeless, problems of a metaphysical nature and rather obscures the central issue, underlying this distinction there is, nevertheless, a legitimate objective concern, namely that the beautiful within itself posits the opposition of *Urbild* (prototype, model) and *Abbild* (copy, reproduction), of Idea (constant and superior to flux) and appearance (subject to change). However, it also cancels this opposition within itself! This latter aspect does not get, in Jung's distinction, the attention it deserves. It is essential to the beautiful that it manifests and represents itself. "From this it follows that as regards its beauty [*Schönsein*], the beautiful must always be ontologically comprehended as 'image.' It does not make any difference whether 'it itself' appears or its copy," states Gadamer, on whom I rely here in my discussion of the beautiful.[11] The beautiful precisely *closes* the hiatus between Idea and appearance, and where the psychologist is reached by the beauty of the psychic images he does not have to insist on the opposition of archetype in itself and archetypal idea: the image is itself the appearance of the primordial image; it all by itself has the archetypal depth and primordiality within itself (and not in an "archetype in itself" behind itself).

Here it becomes very clear once more that Jungian psychology, where it is at work spontaneously and in an originary spirit and has not yet been secondarily deformed by external influences, has its provenance in a mental world that is totally different from that of scientific empiricism. The real home of the theory of archetypes is the world of the beautiful that shines from within itself and speaks to the soul; that is lovable and is not in need of any proof, because as the *Wahr-Scheinliche* (the shining truth, the *verisimile*, not to be confused with the *Wahrscheinlichkeit* in the sense of probability!) it "illuminates" and convinces *per se*. Jung's thinking has its home in the powerful, but usually subterranean tradition of the Platonic, neo-Platonic

---

[11] Gadamer, *op. cit.*, p. 462.

metaphysic of the beautiful (which is also corroborated by his closeness to alchemy and to the Romantic thinking of Schelling, Creuzer, Carus), in contradistinction to the official Western tradition from which the natural sciences sprang. The latter's main concern in its struggle for "correctness" and "certainty" (predictability) is, as is well-known, to avoid all appearance, therefore even the beautiful appearance (i.e., the beautiful shine). Where the theory of archetypes is supposed to be construed as a scientific theory in accordance with the theory of science and with epistemology, there it will be expelled from its home and sent into exile, removed from that intellectual tradition that naturally gave rise to it, and it will be implanted into a completely different tradition, in which it will not be at home. Certainly, this can be done; but the consequence would be that the theory of archetypes then loses its immediately convincing, illuminating character while not gaining the intended empirical persuasiveness, as can be seen from the fact that its non-acceptance is widespread.

The fact that Jungian psychology stands in the neo-Platonic tradition means nothing less than that is has a different ground, that is, that it is based on a different *ontology*. This is the imposition of Jungian psychology. For this reason, many of the concepts taken over from Jung, mostly without explicit acknowledgment, into other psychologies (e.g., the self, the soul's religious need, mid-life crisis, life-after-death theme, etc.) are something totally different even if their immediate definition might be almost identical.

Scientific thought, which insinuates and sub-poses human opinions to reality ("hypo-thesis") and thereafter has to "*make* them true" ("veri-fication"), obviously is diametrically opposed to Jungian thought, for which the psychological truth *appears and shines per se*, so that, although as unproven appearance, it *a priori* comes with its own unquestionable evident nature (its *Augenschein*, i.e., as what it seems to be). Jung time and again emphasized that he did not want to establish a scientific doctrine, a theory, but that he only wanted to describe and name phenomena. This needs to be understood in terms of the shining-and-seeming of the phenomena. His concepts are designations, "mere names" (*Letters 2*, p. 293, to Jacobi, 13 March 1956), not constructs or hypotheses. He says, for example, "If I speak of the collective unconscious I don't assume it as a principle, I only give a name to the totality of observable facts, i.e., archetypes. I derive nothing from it as it is merely a *nomen*" (*Letters 2*, p. 567, to Bennet, 23 June 1960). By merely naming the phenomena—the same way we give names to each other—he does not substitute his own models or conceptions for them, he does not cover them up, but he precisely allows them to speak for themselves. He releases them into their own shining/seeming.

A corresponding view is Jung's concept of truth, which is so alien to empiricistic thought—just think of the lack of understanding with which, e.g., Erich Fromm[12] viewed Jung's idea of "psychological truth" because he was impervious to an objective psychology. Jung says, e.g., "An idea is psychologically true inasmuch as it exists"; "An elephant is true because it exists" (*CW* 11 § 4 f., modif.)—we could also say: because he appears, i.e., presents himself of his own accord. This is the self-sufficient truth, the same truth that poetry, myth, the phenomenon possess; it is not the truth of a judgment (*adaequatio rei et intellectus*) and not the correctness of propositions. The image, it is once explicitly stated, "has 'everything it needs' within itself"; therefore "one should above all take care not to let anything from outside, that does not belong, get into it" (as, e.g., our associations!) (*CW* 14 § 749, modif.).

To what extent Jungian psychology has its native home in the world of shine/appearance of the beautiful also shows in many of its specific concepts, which obviously name the figures, archetypal persons, *daimonia* and *animalia* of the soul that appear of their own accord: shadow, anima, great mother, divine child, *puer aeternus*, old wise man, etc. For the beautiful appears as visible figure, in other words, personified, not as an abstract concept. Only the person-like figure speaks, confronts us with a question, a demand, and only to it can we enter into a loving relation. According to Plato it is the fate of beauty that it is what shines forth the most and must be loved the most (*Phaidros* 250 d f.). When Jung once raises the question whether later generations might suspect that he, Jung, had been a great lover, then we do not have to take it only in terms of love between persons, but can recognize it particularly in his psychological conception, which throughout bears witness to a love for psychic reality, a love for the phenomenon and for the figures in the soul, in clear contrast to many

---

[12] See Erich Fromm, *Psychoanalysis and Religion* (New York: Bantam Books, 1967), pp. 14–20.

other psychologies, which, where they comprehend themselves as "emancipatory," seem to be born out of (logical) resentment and hatred.

Once it has been understood that for Jung in theory as well as in practice this kind of relation is at issue, then it should be clear that not only an empiricist theory of science, but theory of science as such is out of place in such a thinking. It would want to answer questions that for a psychology oriented by the shining/appearance of images simply do not arise. However, it is true, Jung himself emphatically insisted that his psychology was an empirical natural science. But after all the evidence to the contrary that we demonstrated so far, the question comes up why Jung could nevertheless insist on the empiricist-scientific character and status of his psychology. His statements concerning this are, after all, not occasional and casual ones. Rather, they express a firm standpoint held consistently and with full awareness till the end of Jung's days. In a second part of the original manuscript from which this paper is taken I tried to examine this question in different directions and to bring out the (limited) factual right of Jung's position, without, however, in the least moving away from the views presented here. The question in which sense Jung's psychology is an empirical science after all, *that is, how "empirical," "nature," and "science" must here be understood* and how they were understood by Jung so that these attributes indeed apply to his psychology, must here be excluded for reasons of limited space. The one hint may suffice for the time being that on the main it is, as indicated, a matter of how terms are basically defined and a matter of the necessity of avoiding equivocal use of words.

If, however, we retain the concept of empirical natural science as we find it today in the general scientific community—and at bottom only this concept is relevant for us, because it is the psychologically real (the ruling) one[13]—then we can say that this predicate is only afterwards stuck or imposed upon Jungian psychology, without,

---

[13] The reproach that Jungian psychology is unscientific is generally not expressed on a high theoretical level, but rather, has its ground in unreflected but emotionally quite powerful collective ideas. I purposely do not here start out from logically highly differentiated definitions of "empirical natural science," as they have been presented by diverse theories of science, nor from Jung's own concept of science either (which still has to be worked out), because these definitions, as concepts acquired through intellectual effort would simply pass over the understanding of "science" that today in fact is the ubiquitous, tacitly accepted, emotionally decisive one.

however, its being able to hide fully, under this covering, its true phenomenal, hermeneutic character (shine/appearance, being approached with a demand, receptivity, attending to, being affected). What is taking place here could be compared with what Niklas von Flüe did when he tried to adapt his original vision of an archaic god to the conventional Christian God image—it could be compared if Jung had indeed transformed the original phenomenal character of his psychology into a genuinely empiricist form, which, however, is not the case. Even at those few places where Jung comes close to the empiricist-scientific manner of speaking and thinking, the empirical science character always remains foreign and external to the substance and spirit of his psychology. And Jung himself was well aware that the belief that he came to his insights on the basis of empirical findings is a fiction, because in reality they come from an inner source (cf. *CW* 4 § 778), and he also knew that the inner experiences "cannot be dealt with by rational argument, scientific evidence, and depreciative diagnosis" (*Letters 2*, p. 602, to Lasky, 19 October 1960).

The Opposition of Empirical Natural Science and Jungian Psychology

So it is and remains established that Jungian psychology and natural sciences belong to two totally different worlds, temperaments, mentalities. In order to characterize once more the perhaps most essential difference: The empirical sciences begin in the human being, who on his own responsibility puts forward his propositions and op-poses or (as the word hypo-thesis indicates) sub-poses them to the phenomena. Jungian psychology, by contrast, according to its own self-understanding has its provenance in a real "pro-*venance*." When the science fantasy calls its concepts constructs, it makes it clear that scientific research is comprehended as the establishment of an essentially "fabricated," artificial world, the establishment of a second world that both as theory and as its application (technology) stands vis-à-vis reality itself, which is the reason why science is necessarily burdened with the task and the problem of validation.

The fantasy within which Jungian psychology sees the relation of the psychologist to the reality explored by him is completely different. According to it, it is not at all our task to establish, and prove as correct, a system of propositions. It has a different concern. Inherent in the mere word arche-type is the acknowledgment that psychological insight does not begin with us and our talking, but always *has* already begun. Psychology's essential propositions are not pronounced by us, but by the soul itself, in dreams, in our pathology, imagination, emotions, etc. Thus, the fantasy underlying Jungian psychology conceives of psychological research from the outset in a manner that can be expressed by means of, e.g., the metaphor of the arrival of a guest (cf., of the idea of the solar penis), who asks to be received in our consciousness; or by means of the metaphor of our being approached and addressed by psychological reality, a being addressed that calls for our answering and responding to it in our attitude of consciousness. Jung tries to adopt an attitude such that the phenomena themselves can have a say: the soul's soliloquy, the *diálogos* (or *lógos*) *psychês pròs hautén*, as Plato words it, so that here there is no fundamental vis-à-vis of theory (subject) and reality (object) and thus not either a necessity of validation. "Correctness" here simply does not exist as a category. The point is "to say again," an appropriate echo, a friendly reception. That is all. Jung's diction and concepts are so pictorial and exotic (anima, shadow, putrefaction, raven's head, etc.) for the sole reason that they are not supposed to be scientific constructs, but rather vessels and home for that which comes to us of its own accord, and, to be sure, a home in which the arriving guest, as I want to put it metaphorically, can feel to be under good care. This is, as will be noticed, the very converse of the basic scientific stance.

However, it is not only the directions that differ, but above all also the intangible element, the atmosphere, the shading. If such concepts and metaphors as faith, happening, arrival, and reception are needed to describe the Jungian attitude, then the fundamentally different sphere in which Jung's thinking moves is evident. Jung does not only talk *about* the anima, the very *style of his psychological thinking and speaking is characterized by it.* It is indispensable to mention the anima when it is a question of the provenance of the insights of C. G. Jung, for it is the anima's presence that makes psychological faith possible in the first place. *She* is the founder of psychology, by bringing it about that the researcher does not only turn to the psyche as his object, but that even he himself as subject has become psychological in his perspective, indeed in his whole mode of being.

A number of additional aspects of the provenance of Jungian psychology need be discussed, important and instructive ones. But I have to confine myself here to mentioning them only briefly. From our assertion that psychology has its provenance in the anima, it is not very far to its provenance from 'history.' Jung's psychology is distinguished from (I dare say) all other psychologies, especially from those natural-scientific ones that aim for timeless truths, in that it is consciously aware of standing in a historical tradition, derives inspiration from it, and reflects itself, as well as today's psychological reality as such, through its constant retrospect to history. "... [W]ithout history there can be no psychology ..." (*MDR*, p. 205).

This in turn leads us to the biographical provenance from the problematic of his immediate ancestors, especially his fantasy, taken over by Jung as his heritage. Only one quotation on this topic: "I feel very strongly that I am under the influence of things or questions which were left incomplete and unanswered by my parents and grandparents and more distant ancestors" (*MDR*, p. 237). And it is quite obvious that the fundamental concern that motivates his whole psychology is most closely connected with his father's religious predicament (at least the way Jung himself saw this predicament).

In the context of the provenance from 'history' the question of the provenance of Jungian psychology with respect to its source of knowledge becomes easily accessible. In the case of Jung, psychology's individual insights are rooted in the *consensus omnium*, in the *sensus communis*, in *memoria*. Jung does not want to construct concepts by himself ("constructs"), but derives them from the Western or universally human "common sense": a concept, such as 'psychic energy' or 'archetype,' does not simply become legitimate on the basis of our empirical observation of present-day case material, but is legitimate only if the concept (or an idea corresponding to it) is backed up by collective ideas existing from time immemorial. So it is in the case of 'archetype,' which can be traced as far back as St. Augustine, Cicero, and the Middle Academy, and in the case of 'psychic energy,' which has its equivalents in the *mana* idea, etc.

As far as the psychology of his personality is concerned, Jung's psychology has it provenance from what he termed his "personality No. 2."And with respect to its material substance it is derived from the magma of his own experience. "But then I hit upon this stream of lava, and the passion that was contained in the heat of its fire, reshaped my life and gave it its pattern. That was the prime matter and as such the compelling force of my life. ... My whole later activity consisted in elaborating what had in those years burst forth from the unconscious ... It was the prime matter for a lifetime's work" (*MDR*, p. 199, transl. modif.). Jung's work is the vision that he had been caught up in (*MDR*, p. 356). Thus, his procedure as a researcher did not, according to the methodology of science, consist in the propounding and validation of hypotheses and in step by step adding one insight to, and basing it upon, another ("progress"). No, his life's work had, in its basic substance, all been set for him from the beginning. The stone that had crystallized from out of the fiery-liquid basalt of his imagination and dreams was only worked, elaborated, circumambulated. There is no progress here, but only a deepening and differentiation of one and the same. In this sense, Jung's work is closer to that of a poet than to that of a scientist proceeding according to the methods of empiricism.

ONE EXAMPLE

I want to once more contrast the two fundamentally different temperaments and mentalities with the help of a concrete example: the different reactions that Freud and Jung had to the so-called *Klopfgeisterspuk* (poltergeist) experience during Jung's visit to Vienna in 1909 (*MDR*, p. 155 f.). The course of events was, briefly put, as follows. While Freud during a discussion about parapsychology in general propounded arguments against parapsychological phenomena, Jung all of a sudden felt a glowing heat in his diaphragm, and there was, simultaneously, such a loud banging noise in the bookcase that both of them feared that it might topple over onto them. When Freud denied the parapsychological nature of this event, Jung, out of a felt inner certainty inexplicable to himself, predicted a repetition of the loud bang, which then, in fact, immediately occurred.

This event made a powerful impression upon Freud, as he himself confessed in his letter to Jung (16 April 1909, printed in *MDR*, p. 361 f.). Jung, too, reports that Freud "only stared aghast at me" (*MDR*, p. 156). This means that a "being touched and affected" (*applicatio*) had happened and Freud had been reached by the phenomenon. But Freud does not continue to think along this line. He does not dwell with the immediate phenomenon, namely, that something had happened and appeared to him (as his terror showed), whereby it is totally irrelevant whether this was an "illusion" or a "fact." He does not investigate the question *what* it was that had appeared to him (cf. *MDR*, p. 156). Rather, he veered back into the rationalistic mode of thinking of the scientist and argued that that kind of banging noise also happened occasionally without there being any connection to Jung. With this thought he tries to reassure himself; with it he tries to put his terror to rest.

To be sure, Freud's objection might be completely correct. Anyway, empirically speaking one single event or experiment is never decisive. Reproducibility and intersubjectivity are normally indispensable prerequisites for an acknowledgment by science of an experimental finding. Only, for the psychologist Jung it is here not at all a question of what is correct and valid. Rather, the issue is that a "terrifying" experience of the soul occurred and waits to be acknowledged, even if it was an illusion. Jung therefore remained faithful to the immediate, singular phenomenon that is tied to an irretrievable situation, and allowed himself to be moved by this event, an event that *comprises* the subjective reaction as part of itself and for this reason can never be verified. "The experience has to be taken for what it is or *what it seems to be*" (*MDR*, p. 191, modif., my italics), he says in another context, but this statement may be viewed as his general formula for that attitude that is supposed to make it possible for the phenomenon to emerge as a psychological experience and to be preserved as such. Any verification, control, or explanation would destroy it as a *psychic* phenomenon and treat it like something physical. Just as Jung took the solar phallus seriously as a true phenomenon, notwithstanding the fact that it was, for him, too, a delusion, so he also respected the parapsychological event as a phenomenon and the way it *appeared* to be. For even if nothing of it can be validated, the singular event nevertheless *speaks* to the soul. It touches us, it evokes an image, and only as such is it psychologically relevant. It has then of course no need for proof, ascertainment or repetition—just as the friendly greeting that I receive from someone does not need a proof, a repetition, or a causal explanation.

JUNGIAN PSYCHOLOGY AS CATASTROPHE

With the word *Schein* (shine/seeming appearance) we have named the threshold that one must transgress if one wants to enter the realm of psychology the way Jung conceived it. Jung's basic premise is that to the largest and most significant extent the psyche is not a depiction or reflection of reality or a reaction to it or sedimented earlier experiences of and within it, but that it is originary appearance (*arche*type, *primordial* image); however, a *seeming* or *appearance* that possesses its own dignity and truth. It is not a mere semblance, but that appearance from which—even if it is a delusion—something shines forth that gives a radiance to things and a meaning to life—in short, something that brings *soul* to the world. Here, in the realm of appearance Jungian psychology has its home, on the other side of the concern for correctness and certainty that haunts the natural sciences since the days of one of their most important philosophical ancestors, Descartes. For Descartes, as well as for the natural sciences, the main concern is the elimination of error and appearance (*Schein*).

Now the depreciation of Jungian psychology by the scientific community, which was our starting point, can be understood better. Somehow, it is quite in order, because this psychology in fact represents an imposition, indeed a catastrophe, to the metaphysical fundamental stance of natural-scientific thinking. However, catastrophe, *kata-strophé*, originally means 'going under,' a 'turning downwards' into the underworld, the realm of the souls, the shades, and images. The fact that Jungian psychology is a catastrophe is, seen in this light, not a mistake, but precisely its task as *depth*-psychology, a task set for it ever since Freud placed above the first great book of depth-psychology (and thus above depth-psychology in general) that verse from Virgil as a motto which has no other content than the *kata-strophé* (even if unfortunately with a pose of rebelliousness sometimes characteristic of Freud):

> *Flectere si nequeo superos, Acheronta movebo.*
> (If I cannot influence the upper gods, I will move the underworld.

CHAPTER SEVEN

Jungian Psychology: A Baseless Enterprise
Reflections on our Identity as Jungians

1. The Identity Question as the Distinction of Psychology

The question of one's identity is not only a practical and theoretical concern of psychotherapy in that we have to deal with the identity crises of our patients. There is also an identity problem of psychology itself. Each psychologist has to account to himself for his identity, and that not only in a personal sense, not only in that sense in which he too will always be a patient, but also as regards his professional quality and as a theoretician. He has to account for his identity *as* a Jungian, Freudian, or whatever he may be. This need for an identity (as whatever) is what distinguishes psychology from the sciences. In physics, such an identity problem does not exist. There are no Newtonians, Helmholtzians, Einsteinians, and if a physicist considered himself as such, he would cease to be a serious scientist.

Why does physics exclude and psychology entail a personal profession to the founder of a school? In order to do proper scientific research, the physicist must restrict himself, at least for the duration of his research, only to that abstract and minimal aspect of the total personality that Kant termed "consciousness at large," whereas psychology obviously draws the psychologist into, and involves him in, itself on a personal, indeed existential, level. Each psychological interpretation or theoretical statement is at once also a self-representation of the psychologist. In what I say about my patients, I inevitably betray who I am. The more psychology points forward to its subject matter, the more it refers, in one and the same act, back to the person speaking. Psychology is unavoidably confessional. Jung discussed this fact under the name of the "psychological equation."

2. THE HOPELESSNESS OF THE IDENTITY QUESTION

The embarrassing thing about psychology is that in it one's professional identity is inevitably contaminated with one's personality. Psychology is nothing pure. My professional work, which I of course claim has a certain objective validity, is not only *de facto*, as all human endeavors, but also systematically infused with my personal equation inasmuch as I profess myself to be a Jungian or whatever. And my professed identity as a Jungian entails another contamination, since with a Jungian identity I claim to have an identity with some other, namely with the teachings of C. G. Jung. In other words, my personal equation contains what I am not and is thus turned into a personal *un*equation: I am supposed to be identical with something or someone else. This shows the difficulty of the question of our identity as Jungians, a difficulty that Jung had already fully understood when he said that only he could be a Jungian. How, when, and with what justification can we claim to be Jungians? Which criteria must be satisfied? This is the question we will have to concern ourselves with.

At first glance, there seems to be an easy answer. We are Jungians if the psychological convictions corresponding to our personal equation coincide with Jung's ideas. But rather than being an answer, this statement opens up new questions. For how can I decide whether what I believe coincides with Jung's concepts? For sure, we have Jung's written work. But what Jung actually meant in his written work by concepts such as individuation, self, archetype is and will remain a matter for debate. Different Jungians have given and will give different interpretations of them, so that we see that the personal equation makes itself felt again.

In order for us to account to ourselves for our identity as Jungians, we have to have an answer to the question of what is truly Jungian, but in order to answer this question correctly we would have to be true Jungians to begin with. We are necessarily begging the question.

The identity question throws us into a hopeless circular situation. We cannot reject the question of what truly constitutes Jungian psychology unless we are willing to embrace an unbearable indifferentism, but we cannot give a satisfactory answer either because any answer would amount to giving absolute validity to a Jung interpretation relative to our personal equation.

So we are stuck. We can move neither forward nor back. But if we do not try to steal away from this hopeless situation by means of some defense mechanisms, if instead we honestly endure our being stuck, paradoxically something will start to move. A reversal takes place. At first, *we* had tried to be the ones giving the answer to the identity problem. Now we are immobilized, and what is left to us is to listen to what the hopeless situation may tell us. Through this shift, the hopeless situation ceases to be the problem to be solved and turns into the message to be heard. We begin to understand that the aporetic situation obviously and essentially "belongs" to the question of identity and is very much in place. As long as we try to get out of the aporia, it blocks our way, and rightly so, I would think. But once we allow it to *be*, it itself becomes the way out. It frees us to the insight that there cannot be a positive answer to the question of what is truly Jungian. There cannot be a checklist of essentials, a secure yardstick. Our identity as Jungians, and likewise "the true Jung," are something *fundamentally* debatable. They are not anything empirical or factual, but merely an idea in the soul, a blank space, as it were, that can be filled with all kinds of different contents.

The criterion of our identity as Jungians, namely, "the true Jung," proves to be an absolute *x*. It cannot be defined, and this not despite Jung's written work, but precisely *as* something existing in writing. For the written text requires again an interpretation. What constitutes the true Jung is unknown, and fundamentally unknown, and this is why our attempt to answer the question of our Jungian identity must take the form of the alchemical *"ignotum per ignotius,"* the form of an elucidation of the unknown by what is even more unknown. We must not be seduced by our longings for positive truths to make up some spelled-out formula by way of a reliable yardstick; to this we have no right. Even while still asking the identity question *of* psychology we are already fully *in* the psychology of the unconscious, in the middle of the imaginal, hopelessly, if you wish to call it such, surrounded on all sides by images, fantasies, not facts. Just as Jung made it clear that the unconscious is truly unknown, i.e., an absolute x that cannot be reduced to anything positive such as sexuality or early childhood experiences or social conditions, we must now realize that "the true Jung" is also an image for or personification of the unconscious, a kind of Rorschach blot providing every Jungian with a definite-indefinite outline into which to project his personal equation.

If it thus turns out that we can never arrive at the true Jung interpretation, but will forever have to live with so many different "true Jungs," the idea of the "true Jung" might appear to be reduced to absurdity, and we might succumb to a relativism in which everyone may fashion his own Jung understanding as he pleases. Anything goes. But paradoxically, this would mean we have to keep clinging to positivity. One would stubbornly insist on one's demand for a positive yardstick even after having seen that this demand ends in failure and would merely react to this failure with resignation, content oneself with sort of "zero fulfillment" of the same old wish, instead of allowing this wish itself, and along with it our entire positivistic consciousness, to be changed by the experience of its impossibility. It is not the idea of the "true Jung" that has been reduced to absurdity; rather, it is our literal understanding of this idea as though it refered to something tangible. Where this idea is accepted as an at first empty fantasy in the soul, it can become a catalyst, making a real and responsible understanding of Jungian psychology possible. That it is empty and not known does not disqualify it as a criterion. Rather, the evasive quality of the "true Jung" is precisely what empowers this idea to generate all the differing interpretations.

With this insight, our question has changed. We cannot any longer seriously try to find *the* true Jung interpretation in order to measure our Jungian identity by it. Now we can only ask how each Jungian relates to his own Jung interpretation, to his own "true Jung," independently of whether it be "correct" or not. Our question has shifted from one asking for the true *Jung* to one asking for the true form or *style of identity*. It has itself become psychological. We must now be concerned with internal relations, one variety of the relations between the ego and the unconscious, of which the idea of the true Jung has proven to be one manifestation or personification.

3. Phenomenology of Possible Identity Styles

The phenomenology of possible styles of identity that I will give now has to do with ideal types, not with a portrayal of actual people.

The form of a Jungian identity that comes to mind first is probably that in which the Jungian looks up to his Jung as the unsurpassable master. What Jung taught is considered the highest possible wisdom, so that one has to strive to adopt and to transmit as faithfully as possible what he has said. Here we seem to be in the world of the Pythagorean "*autòs épha*" (he himself, the master, said so). The Jungian here feels himself to be more or less the mouthpiece of the master, the beloved son, in whom the spiritual father would be well pleased. Even if such a Jungian did new research, he would do so only as executor, not on his own initiative and responsibility. We can call this relation to one's own Jung *orthodoxy*. Just as in Christian orthodoxy the printed copy of the Bible is the place of truth, so here Jung's opus is considered the place of truth and Jung the carrier of the philosopher's stone, so that he who follows him closely will indirectly partake in truth too.

We see immediately that this style of identity is not the best. Without having to consider any contents, we can say simply with respect to the formal relation between the Jungian and his Jung that there is an imbalance. All authority rests with "Jung," the philosopher's stone is projected onto him, and the Jungian has lost his own identity. As disciple, mouthpiece, executor he subordinates his personal creativity to the true doctrine, and the amount of this self-sacrifice is equal to the amount to which Jung is raised to heaven. We might say, the Jungian is here fully Jungian, but the one who is here fully Jungian is no longer himself.

So this is no way to gain a satisfactory identity. The Jungian with his personal equation must not go under. If he therefore maintains himself and retains his integrity, we come to the second style of identity. Here Jung's teachings are not adopted without question. The Jungian has critical reservations with respect to his own Jung, be it that he, e.g., finds fault with Jung's lack of interest in clinical questions, or with respect to the topic of counter-transference, or that he thinks Jung's concept of the objective psyche originated from a defense on the part of Jung against binding personal interactions, or that his "self" and "God" concepts remained too deeply rooted in the patriarchal tradition, or that the individuation process does not in the first place, as Jung thought, belong only to the second half of life, but just as much to the first. This form of identity I would like to call *heresy*—not because I, on my part, would wish to condemn such thoughts as heretical, but because the immanent relation of the Jungian to his own Jung is such that he himself sets up an orthodox Jungian doctrine which he then attacks.

Since this relation is the reverse of orthodoxy, it is not any more satisfactory as identity relation. The Jungian, to be sure, has retained his personal equation, but he has paid for this by curtailing his Jungianism. The same imbalance that we found in the first style prevails here too, only in reverse.

The two identity structures discussed so far are dyadic. As long as identity is conceived as a dyadic relationship, an imbalance is inescapable. Once this has come home to us, our need for an identity will be driven beyond itself to the attempt to arrive at a Jungian identity via some third. One could, for example, concencentrate one's efforts mainly on spreading Jungian psychology and gaining new followers, on training as many people in Jungian psychology, or making it possible for them to experience a Jungian analysis, in order to get one's own identity as a Jungian confirmed through this continuously growing circle of initiates. These kindred spirits would be, as it were, the living embodiment, the carriers as well as guarantors, of one's own identity as a Jungian. Here we could speak of the *missionary* identity type.

Obviously, this form of identity is highly questionable, too. One's identity is here delegated to others, and the Jungian himself can keep himself out, especially also out of secret doubts that may plague him deep down in his relation to Jung. On the one hand, the embeddedness in a circle of new followers is reassuring and covers over one's own uncertainty. On the other hand, by *passing* Jung on, one can also *free* oneself of one's own identity as a Jungian, i.e., one can escape the necessity of clarifying one's own position by wrestling with Jung, and then stand up for one's conviction on one's own responsibility.

Another way of obtaining an identity via some third would be to make one's being a Jungian dependent on the assent of other groups. One might then seek recognition from others, e.g., from other schools of analysis that seem to have a higher scientific respectability, from the academic and scientific community, or from society at large. One may feel the need to prove that Jung was "by no means" an obscure mystic or Gnostic, that he, instead, worked as an empirical scientist, or at least that his findings can be corroborated by empirical observation and be expressed in a strictly formalized scientific language. Or one may wish to set up high national and international standards for training in order to prove that the analyst has equal rank with the medical professional. Or one may establish ethics committees to prove, before society, the highest moral respectability of the Jungian school. We could speak here of an *apologetic* identity relation. The Jungian here feels that he has to present an apology, as it were, for being a Jungian. He feels the need to show that as a Jungian he is no backwoodsman.

It goes without saying that this stance does not fulfill the criteria of a true identity either. In the last analysis, the Jungian is, in this case, ashamed of being a Jungian and a psychologist. He looks at his own Jung with an inferiority feeling and feels he must compensate for it. Truth for him does not rest with his own school of thought, but with others. *They* possess the yardstick by which he thinks he has to be measured. So this is really a split identity: he adopts the contents of Jungian psychology, but all worth and authority rest for him with those whose theoretical views he does not share.

There is a further possibility of a need for others, which, however, is not about calming inner doubts, as in the missionary situation, or overcoming inferiority feelings, as in the apologetic situation. The Jungian is here deeply convinced of his understanding of Jung, but he is impressed by the fact that there are so many other views in the total spectrum of Jungian psychology or psychoanalysis at large that he cannot accept. He feels stifled by these other interpretations and feels he must fight against them in order to create free space for his own Jung to live and breathe. It is not merely that he has factual objections to other opinions; rather, he *needs* those other opinions, for by fighting against them, pushing himself off from them, he can find his own. I call this the *polemical* identity form.

On first sight, a real identity seems here to have been successfully realized. For here the Jungian's "own Jung" has full authority without reservation and the Jungian himself finds his very own in his Jung interpretation. Nevertheless, here too, the identity is disturbed. The fact that in the case of the polemical attitude others are needed as opponents, as a springboard to push off from, so that the Jungian may reach his own through his pushing off from them, shows that he has not really come to his own yet and will never arrive at it as long as remains in the polemical attitude. Jungian psychology is, to be sure, his very own; his personal equation may in fact be at one with "his Jung" and find its fulfillment in the latter. But he himself is not where his own, where his personal equation is. Something reserves itself. He has not dropped into his personal equation without reserve, allowing it to become truly his own, and he does not simply enjoy the possession of his own. He constantly puts between himself and his personal equation the fight against other opinions and for the first acquisition of his own.

In view of so many aberrations on the way to a Jungian identity, there may arise the wish to obtain at last something secure on which to rely with a good conscience. It is the wish for a psychology that is an empirical science. As a great ideal for the future, the vision of a general consensus among analysts of different leanings may arise, the wish for a kind of standard psychology based on ideas and findings that may stem from such diverse sources as Freud, Jung, Adler, Winicott, Kohut, Bettelheim, etc. This synoptic, syncretistic, or eclectic direction I would like to term the *indifferent* identity structure.

Here there is no longer an internal imbalance in the identity relation as with the previous modes; rather, the entire identity question has been thrown overboard. Neither my personal equation nor the founder of a school have a home here. They have both been vaporized in the striven-for general validity of abstract scientific findings. Jung is reduced to a precursor of only historical interest. The confessional aspect of psychology has been eliminated. One might want to celebrate this as a great success, as the discovery at long last of a firm ground for psychology. But if one considers *what it is* that has been lost along with the confessional aspect, one will understand that psychology may, to be sure, have acquired the respectable character of an objective science, but only at the price of having ceased to be psychology.

For now it has been cut off from the individual psyche. It is no longer rooted in real concrete persons as its carriers, not in that historical individual C. G. Jung, nor in me as a Jungian with a particular personality. Because, along with the confession, both the feeling-toned bond to the founder or, as we might call it, the loyalty relationship, *and* the connection to myself (*my* subjectivity, *my* needs and my being personally committed) have been lost, it has become abstract. Even if psychology may still talk about feelings, it itself is devoid of all feeling the way it is now constituted. This means it has forfeited its body, its connection to the earth, and now is suspended in the air of abstract intellect. As objective science, it now belongs to everybody, and nobody. Intersubjectivity is the official name for this state.

Without a personal confession and a personal bond to some founder of a school as the beginner of a tradition of thought, the psychologist is reduced to a croupier, setting off the chips of others against one another without staking, in his theoretical work, his own self and fate along with his chip.

Loss of soul is, of course, too high a price, especially for psychology, the "study of soul," even if the gain may be most enticing. How can a psychology turned into a science perform its task of soul-making if it has excluded from its own self-definition the bond to the individual psyche? As embarrassing as it may be, the confessional element is indispensable in psychology, because only through it the connection to the concreteness of the individual psyche is made an integral element of the very *definition* of psychology.

The confessional bond amounts to a contamination of the scientific character of psychology. In the psychologist's having to be some kind of -ian (Jungian, Freudian, etc.) psychology has its Achilles' heel. It is the weak spot in its intellectuality. But this weakness is the opening through which alone psychology's very own, namely, the real, living soul, can enter, the soul which, even though it is transpersonal, is nevertheless always tied to particular individuals and enmeshed with feelings. *The elimination of the confessional element from psychology would be the same as the exclusion of transference from therapy.* For the identity structures are nothing else but the styles of transference on the theoretical level of psychology. That we have to ask about "our identity as ..." shows that transference is not only a content of psychology and an object of its practical observations and efforts. Transference also permeates psychology itself, psychology as a noetic body of theory. Psychology is not, like a science, a theoretical superstructure above therapeutic practice. Theory and therapy do not have the relation of pure idea and application. They are intertwined. In psychology, we are in an upside-down world in which both theory and practice are the generic term of each other, because both are *part of* and contained in the very psychic process that is the *object* of their efforts of study and treatment. And there is no way out. Transference, with all its intellectual uncleanness, is the landmark of psychology. It embroils patient and therapist, theory and practice, psychology and soul-process, general validity of the intellectual doctrine and personal confession in one another.

Once the personal element has been excluded from the definition of psychology, it cannot be recovered through any activity based on this definition. If in quarters where a scientific standard psychology seems to be the ideal, work with the personalistic transference and counter-transference reactions is considered the Alpha and Omega of therapy, this fixation may also be due to the fact that the personal loyalty repressed from the theoretical foundation of psychology returns as a personalistic concern *in* psychology. What is not *erinnert,* is acted out.

4. TRUE IDENTITY

None of the six identity styles presented is convincing. Nevertheless, each one represents one ingredient of a true identity relation. Thus, we could say that each of these styles absolutized a single moment of true identity: in orthodoxy the loyalty to the person and the authoritativeness of his or her texts; in heresy the independence of the Jungian; in the missionary attitude the concern and insight that the identification must not, as with orthodoxy, be the ego's total identification; in the apologetic stance the clear sense for the embarrassing nature of an attachment to a founder figure, which, being something very personal, protects itself behind a sense of shame; in the polemical variety it is the sense for the dangerous, fiery quality that inheres in one's relentless dropping into true identity, into one's own; and in the position of indifference it is the knowledge that "psychology" cannot be merely the utterly subjective reality of a personal creed.

In the beginning we found that the identity question is inescapable. The discussion of the last identity style has shown that it is also indispensable. But so far we have not found a satisfactory form of identity. True identity obviously is no easy matter. Indeed, it is a kind of *adýnaton*, something "impossible," inasmuch is it has to be a reconciliation of opposites. Here I come back to my idea of the unequation that must be contained in the personal equation if there is to be such a thing as our identity as Jungians. "*Our* identity" as Jungians requires that *as* Jungians we maintain our own and do not castrate ourselves by subordinating ourselves to the authority of our master; "our identity *as Jungians*" on the other hand requires that Jungian thought come into its own in our thought and is not arbitrarily selected and fashioned after our personal tastes. And the masterpiece will be to find an identity style that brings both opposites into agreement, an identity that is the oneness of identity and non-identity. I must remain myself and yet at the same time be not myself.

All the identity forms discussed or referred to so far did not endure this contradiction. They either joined one side through subordination or self-assertion, or they interposed some third and thus evaded the pungency of the contradiction. Thus they were able to hold fast to the identity of formal logic, A = A, and rescue this idea even in or for psychology. The world remained intact, safe, logical. The moment, however, that I endure the contradiction and get into the "craziness" of transference, the very idea or definition of identity breaks apart. I intellectually lose the ground under my feet and fall into the depths. The reliability of the world, which rests on the logical exclusion principle, is destroyed. Much the same shaking event as the one that happened to Nietzsche on the level of personal experience now happens to me on the intellectual level of my thought about myself and the world, on the level of my ontological premises:

> Da, plötzlich, Freundin! wurde eins zu zwei —
> Und Zarathustra ging an mir vorbei ....
> (from "Sils-Maria," in: Lieder des Prinzen Vogelfrei).
> (Then, suddenly, friend! One was changed to Two —
> And Zarathustra passed me by ....)

Only if I *plunge into non-identity with myself,* only if and inasmuch as I also am not myself, but encounter my own inner "Zarathustra," as it were, can I find my identity as, e.g., Jungian. As long as I am totally identical with myself in accordance with the formula A = A, I take myself as a positive fact and am essentially closed, irreversibly locked into myself. Only when the solid ground opens under me and

I fall into my own unknownness, into the inner infinity of *my* "Zarathustra," am I at that point at which I can truly be at one with Jung, just as in general an identity between two different ones is only possible in infinity, such as in the love between two people. The example of love, which after all is a possible empirically real experience, shows that I am not speaking of an *otherworldly* infinity, but of that infinity that can be known and experienced on this earth. This is an infinity that belongs to me as finite man and that can be encountered in concrete shapes, such as Zarathustra, Philemon, *lapis*, totem animal or however, if one plunges from his self-identity into his own unknownness. I am speaking of that unknownness that is usually referred to by the term 'unconscious,' especially 'collective unconscious,' a name that, however, has long become dull. The fact that love is the preeminent mode of the identity of different ones, makes it likely that our identity as Jungians, too, is, just as any transference relationship, not possible without the element of love.

Why is it that infinity can grant an identity of the different? My infinity is not mine, Jung's is not his, but we are both its own. As different as the concrete figures and symbols in which one's own unknownness or infinity may show itself may be, the realm of that infinity, however, is one and the same and thus common to all, if only they have been assigned to it as its own. Our Jungian identity is not based on some contents of doctrine, not on anything positive, but rather on a crack, a plunge, a hole, on that infinitely unknown which is a complete X, even when it has been experienced and has taken on a concrete shape.

The breaking apart of our self-identity and the plunge into the bottomless is, in an abstract and general sense, the condition of a possible identity with just any different one. But beyond this, it also quite concretely joins us with Jung in particular. This becomes clear if we remember that what the name Jung means to us is, above all, just that breaking apart in the sense of the "Then One changed to Two." I mention only three well-known facts to support this claim. First, Jung experienced in his personal life the plunge from the One to the Two. On December 12, 1913, he gave up all resistence and let himself fall. Then it was, he reports in *Memories*, as if the ground had literally given in under him and as if he had dropped into dark depths. Thus began his *descensus ad inferos* and the breaking apart in him of the formal-logical identity. Secondly, from early on he distinguished, in his self-conception, personalities No. 1 and No. 2. Thirdly, his entire psychology, with its distinctions between personal and archetypal-collective unconscious, between ego and self, between first and second half of life, is at bottom nothing else but one great formulation and containment, within the vessel of a *theoria*, for this breaking apart.

Now we perhaps understand that our very personal way into the underworld does not isolate us, but grants community, identity, and that conversely our identity as Jungians does not estrange us from ourselves or rob us of our independence. The more I lose myself to Jungian Psychology, the more I gain myself, because my loss of self is here my very own way into the unknown. If that is the case, to be a Jungian no longer means to cling slavishly, in the sense of a personality cult, to the person of Jung or to the letter of his work, because my loyalty does not pertain to what is positively tangible about Jung, but to that inner infinity to which he directs us. To understand Jung means to encounter the objective psyche on one's own responsibility. Just as my self-identity must break apart if my identity as a Jungian is to be possible, so Jung, too, as person and as an opus must change from a self-identical One to Two for me.

5. THE TRIANGLE OF THE IDENTITY RELATION

At the end of his paper in *Harvest 1985*, David Black said with respect to Jung: "Our loyalty cannot be to some precursor, however admirable; it must be to our patients ...."[1] Even if it is true that our loyalty must be to our patients, we must, nevertheless, not go along with the absolute disjunction into which Jung and our patients are brought here. When does one have to think in this way? When is it a question of loyalty *either* to some precursor *or* to our patients? Only when one remains in the realm of positive identity, of A = A. Of course there must be a loyalty conflict if Jung is exclusively identical with himself and my patient is just as exclusively identical with himself. Then I can always be loyal only to the one or the other. But must we not see that precisely if I decide for loyalty to my patient and not to Jung, I have betrayed my patient in a deeper sense, not despite but

---

[1] David Black, "Some Thoughts on the Future of Analytical Psychology or The Exclamtion-Mark of Dr. Schwartz-Salant," *Harvest* 1985, p. 31.

through this kind of (disjunctive) loyalty? For the way I conceive him now, I have identified him with himself, have nailed him down to his positivity, and thus deprived him, from the outset, of his inner infinity. The greatest therapeutic effort cannot compensate for this fundamental castration. The therapeutic process will be limited to what the boundaries of positivity, carefully marked out by this theoretical stance, allow for. If I truly want to do justice to my patient, I must not confuse him with his positive, empirical personality. He, too, is fundamentally more and someone different from himself; he, too, is his own inner "Zarathustra," with whom, however, he is not identical in the sense of formal logic. It is not without purpose that Jung repeatedly quoted the saying, "Ye are Gods" (John 10:34).

How is there to be a *coniunctio oppositorum* in therapy if therapy is placed within a disjunctive frame of mind? Our frame of mind then does not offer a vessel into which the conjunctive process could flow. If there is an alternative between loyalty either to Jung or to the patient and if under these circumstances one necessarily decides for the patient, then one will have created a puritanically clear situation, but one has also, by conceiving the therapeutic relationship as a dyadic one, defined oneself and the patient as unambiguously self-identical, as identical with my or his positivity, respectively. A real psychology of the unconscious, a psychology that takes cognizance of the unfathomableness, unknownness, and infinity of myself as well as of my patient, is altogether impossible on that basis. Only if my loyalty is not clear and unambiguous, but broken, divided, only if I am not dyadically alone with my patient, but if in the sense of a triangular relationship an invisible third person who is not physically and literally present participates, only then will there be, in the brokenness of my loyalty, an opening in the therapeutic relationship through which the infinite nature of the non-ego, the divine in man can enter. Let me refer in this connection to the important book by David Miller about Trinity, *Three Faces of God*. Because there is no single-thread relation to the other here, but a third comes into play, neither one of the two literal participants can fuse with himself or with the other. The third will draw each of them out of a total identity with himself as well as out of an identification with the other. Thus, in the center of this triangle, the triangle "I—patient—Jung" or "I—phenomenology of the soul—Jungian theory," there can now arise something new, a point that exists only by virtue of both the committed bond and the differentiating tension between the three. In this point, which is, as it were, the Fourth of the Three, the *quart*essence, if you wish, all three may find their personal precise shape as well as their *common* identity. This point is nothing positive, it does not exist literally. It is an un- or in-: unknown, unconscious, obscure, infinite, bottomless, and, if the expression were not so burdened with negative connotations, also occult. It is the point sought for by the alchemists under the name of the *lapis*, to mention only one example.

Where this triangle prevails, I do not need to project the philosopher's stone onto Jung, nor do I have to claim it for myself, nor do I have to delegate the task of acquiring it to my patients in the sense of the missionary identity structure. The *lapis*, to use only this one image, does not belong to anyone. But we are its own. It is what gives to each of the three dignity, firm grounding, and uniqueness and what nevertheless unites them too. It is the oneness of identity and non-identity, of independence and loyalty, of freedom and bondage.

For Jung, who could not avail himself of a Jungian psychology existing outside of and prior to himself, there nevertheless was a third to which his loyalty went, in addition to his patients. It was, besides mythology, most of all alchemy, that Jung, as we know, saw as a kind of implicit psychology. Today there is a growing tendency among Jungians to base Jungian psychology, too, on the solid grounding of the scientific observation of early childhood. And thus Jung's grounding his psychology on such traditions as alchemy can be viewed as a crucial weakness. For—and here I am indebted to David Black's paper referred to earlier, which I find very much to the point and excellent in its succinctness, even if I cannot agree with the conclusions he draws—alchemy and similar traditions are in no way stable themselves; they are vague and obscure, nothing on which a science could be based. "We think [says Black] we are looking into the world of Platonic Forms; and actually we are looking at a Rorschach blot." If we try to reflect our psychological convictions by means of alchemy, mythology or the like, "we stand in a wilderness of mirrors" "instead of standing in a landscape." And therefore, Black suggests, we "have to find the thing, other than psychology, with which psychology can be compared," and "the securest 'thing, other than psychology, with which psychology can be compared'" is for him the infant, who, because of his inability to speak, has to be and can be observed scientifically from the outside.[2]

6. BOTTOMLESSNESS

No doubt, one will have to think along these lines if psychology is to be given a solid scientific standing. He who thinks this way is to be likened to a wise man who builds the house of psychology upon a rock, on a positive base. But it is one and the same act that turns psychology into a secure science by means of the thing, other than psychology, with which psychology can be compared, which also excludes from psychology the very thing that psychology is actually about. I would like to show this by means of the metaphor of the Rorschach blot.

In the Rorschach test, we are not interested in the positive, empirical blot whose size we could measure and whose shape we could determine exactly by means of a system of coordinates. What interests us are the statements about what is seen in the blot by each person. And for our evaluation of the test we do not compare the statement with the blot, but we compare the different statements with each other. The blot is only the concretely given, otherwise indefinite prompt that allows the unknown psyche, as our actual object of interest, to show itself. The blot is like a bridge that one burns once he has gone over it. If we long for an Archimedean point outside of psychology; if we do not compare psychology with psychology, verbal statement with verbal statement, but the psychological statement with the so-called 'real' landscape outside, i.e., with the pre-verbal behavior of the infant, then this is not psychology at all. It is at best a physics of behavior and feeling. It would mean to study empirically the literal Rorschach blot that in itself is of no psychological interest whatsoever. It would further mean to tie the soul back to the very thing from which it was just about to push off, indeed, to bury the soul again in the physical factualness of the blot. And at the same time one would fall prey to the very danger that this entire move was suppose to avoid. For the child who does not speak is of course just another kind of Rorschach blot to project our fantasies onto, and a most obscure one at that, and the scientific observation of this blot therefore amounts to nothing

---

[2] *Ibid.*, p. 29.

more than a huge, even though methodologically guided, performance of one extended Rorschach test. We now even begin to see through physics and to understand that physics has nothing to do with knowledge (in the narrower sense) and truth.

Psychology, instead of placing us before landscapes, has the opposite task, the task of transforming everything positively given into a mirror or Rorschach blot and of teaching us to see it as such, so that by virtue of our interpretative (and that always means projective) viewing, the unconscious objective psyche can come to the fore. Without our subjective involvement, without our risking ourselves in interpretations and theorizings, there *is* no psyche at all. Psyche, and I have in mind here especially the objective psyche, does not exist, like a thing, out there, independent of our subjectivity, since the objectivity in question here is the objectivity of psyche, not physics.

Psychology must build its house on sand, and only then can it hope to produce the incorruptible in the sense of alchemy. Such are the 'perverse' ways of psychology. It must reflect itself in a wilderness of mirrors, because in the upside-down world of the psyche, it is the mirrors that *produce* for the first time the object to be mirrored between them. It must compare obscure psychological statements with obscure psychological statements, because only as the result of such *comparing* can the objective psyche as an intangible third become visible. In physics we talk about what exists positively in front and outside of us, and what physics talks about is also its ultimate object of interest. The object of psychology, however, is not what our statements are about. Rather, the object is what through such statements or images of ours is only pointed to or hinted at from behind, as it were, as something irreversibly unknown. The actual object of psychology is always the inner non-identity of what our psychological statements and images say.

The moment we choose some objective, positive thing outside of the psychological as a fixed point of comparison, we have broken out of our entanglement in the therapeutic triangle with its inner infinity, or unknownness, or non-identity. A true psychology finds its identity only in its non-identity. This is why Jung can say quite impertinently: psychology "must sublate itself as a science, and precisely by doing so it achieves its scientific goal" (*CW* 10 § 429, transl. modif.). This statement is said from within the insight into the identity of identity and non-identity. It is the unfathomable impertinence of psychology to expect the natural mind to swallow this insight, and to demand this not only once and for all in a moment of theoretical reflection, such as here, but at every step. We have our identity as Jungians (or should I say: as psychologists, which would be the same thing) if in everything we experience One changes to Two for us; if we experience not only ourselves, our patients, and Jungian psychology, but also every particular phenomenon and each individual statement as double-bottomed, bottomless.

But then the reverse applies too: each person, no matter of what psychological school, for whom One has changed to Two in the way he sees the world, each person who on his own theoretical base penetrates so consistently into the depths that he plunges into the bottomlessness of his own ground, is *ipso facto* a 'Jungian' even if he has never heard of Jung. This also implies that a Jungian does not need to shut himself off from other psychologies. It is his task to take them in too, not syncretistically of course, not in just that positivity in which they may present themselves, but in such a way that they are dissolved or broken down into true psychology, that is to say, in such a way that they stop being descriptions of a 'landscape' seen from outside and enter into the primal wilderness of mirrors and the play of their reflections.

CHAPTER EIGHT

Jung's *Thought* of the Self in the Light of Its Underlying Experience

In this lecture I do not want to talk about what Jung's ideas about the Self were. I want to go behind his teachings about the Self to their background in the underlying experience, in order to attempt to *reconstruct* some aspects of his teachings about the Self. The word "underlying" here has two different meanings. First, it refers to the *experience* of the idea of the Self in contradistinction to the worked out *theory* of the Self. There is, I submit, an experience underlying the explicit theoretical statements Jung made about the Self. Secondly, this experience of the Self has again a background in another experience, and the experience of the Self has to be seen against this background experience, because in a way the experience of the thought of the Self is a reaction or response to this earlier experience. Accordingly, my talk today will have two parts. First I will discuss the earlier background experience, then I will come to the actual experience of the thought of the Self.

PART I: THE EXPERIENCE OF JUNG'S THAT PRECEDES HIS
EXPERIENCE OF THE SELF

Jung relates the fundamental experience decisive for all of his subsequent work in his *MDR*. In the time after his separating from Freud and after extensive studies in comparative mythology, in 1913, the question forced itself upon him:

"But in what myth does man live nowadays?"—"In the Christian myth," the answer might be.—"Do you live in it?" something in me asked.—"To be honest, the answer is no! It is not the myth I live in."—"Then do we no longer have any myth?"—"No, evidently we no longer have any myth."—"But then what is your myth? The myth in which you do live?" At this point the dialogue with myself became uncomfortable, and I stopped thinking. I had reached a dead end.[1]

This is one half, the negative half, of the experience preceding and underlying Jung's experience of the Self. Its message is: we have fallen out of myth. Myth is once and for all a thing of the past for us. We do not even live in the Christian myth any more, which strictly speaking is in itself already no myth any more to begin with, but *sublated* myth. I should briefly explain what "sublated" means, since I will use this word several times. Sublated (in German: *aufgehoben*) is a Hegelian term. A reality is sublated when it is negated or canceled as the reality that it was, but when *as* this negated reality it is also preserved and transformed into a logically higher reality, in which the negated original reality is now only a subordinate moment or ingredient. We live, as Jung never tires to stress, *extra ecclesiam*, outside the containment in the Church, where there is *nulla salus*, no salvation. This is the starting point of all of Jung's later work in psychology and *the* problem that he struggled with. It is all over, all lost.

The other positive half of his experience is expressed in another report in *MDR*. On his East-Africa expedition more than a decade later he was confronted with a fantastic view in an animal reservation.

> To the very brink of the horizon we saw gigantic herds of animals: gazelle, antelope, gnu, zebra, warthog, and so on. Slowly moving, grazing, heads nodding, the herds proceeded in an incessant stream. There was scarcely any sound save the melancholy cry of a bird of prey. This was the stillness of the eternal beginning, the world as it had always been, in the state of non-being; for until then no one had been present to know that it was "this world". I walked away from my companions until I had put them out of sight, and savored the feeling of being entirely alone. In this moment I was the first man [*Mensch*]

---

[1] From *MDR,* close to the beginning of Ch. VI, p. 171(transl. slightly altered according to the German original).

who recognized that this was the world and who had created it in this moment through his knowing.

There the cosmic meaning of consciousness became overwhelmingly clear to me. ... It was only man, I, who in an invisible act of creation gave to the world what made it complete, objective existence [*das objektive Sein*]. ... My old Pueblo friend came to my mind. He thought that the *raison d'être* of his pueblo had been to help their father, the sun, to cross the sky each day. I had envied him for the fullness of meaning that his existence had and had been looking without hope for our own myth. **Now I knew it**, and knew even more: man is indispensable for the completion of creation; in fact, he himself is the second creator of the world, who alone gives to the world its objective existence, without which it would, unheard, unseen, silently eating, giving birth, dying, heads nodding, have gone on through hundreds of millions of years in the profoundest night of non-being to its unknown end.[2]

Here, in Africa in 1925, Jung finally received the answer to the earlier question that had tormented him: "But what is your myth? The myth in which you live?" Now Jung *knew* his, our own myth. It is, to say it with the title of a book by Aniela Jaffé, "The Myth of Meaning," where "meaning" is in itself to be translated (according to a chapter heading in this book) as, "Meaning as the Myth of Consciousness."

The two experiences, "no, we do not have a myth any more" and "now I knew our own myth," are the two extremes or poles between which Jung's entire psychology project as the therapy of neurosis has its place.

One might think that with Jung's African experience, our loss of myth ended and that we returned to the ranks of all those cultures that live from within myth. But this is by no means the case. For the "myth of consciousness" is not really a myth in the same sense. Genuine myth moves within natural imagery. Consciousness could never be a content of mythology. Consciousness is already an abstract *concept*, it presupposes reflection. As a concept, it belongs in the sphere of *logos*, in philosophy, psychology, anthropology. It does not have its place in the imaginal. We may *interpret* certain imaginal, mythological images

---

[2] From *MDR*, Ch. IX p. 255f (transl. altered according to the German original. Bold print not in the original)

as being about consciousness. But that is our modern psychological interpretation. Myth itself speaks, e.g., about the sun or sun god, about the separation of the world parents, etc., but it does not speak or know about such an abstract concept as consciousness.

Similarly, the counterpart to consciousness in Jung's report, "objective existence or Being," is just as much a *concept* (not an image) that could never occur in the sphere of myth. Both, "objective" and "Being" belong to the sphere of *logos*, thought, reflection.

Not only the content of his so-called myth, but also the moves Jung makes when confronted with the animal herd are anti-mythological. The mythological experience would have been to see *in* the visible *phenomenon* (here in the herd of animals) the epiphany of a god or archetypal truth, here, in all likelihood, the Great Mother as the Mistress of Animals. But what does Jung do? He *pushes off* from the phenomenon. In his thoughts he thrusts the animal herd into "the profoundest night of non-being." Incredible. He throws the whole natural course of life, giving birth, dying, eating, in other words, that world that was the basis and locus of mythological experience, he throws all this into nothingness and condemns it to pointlessness. The whole sphere of the phenomenal and imaginal is negated, *sublated*. And instead, in his thoughts Jung turned literally around to *himself*, i.e., he *reflected* upon himself, as *subject* in the modern sense. The phenomenon, the sight of the animals, is reduced to a mere occasion making it possible for him to become aware of himself as consciousness and of consciousness as a second creator of the world. In other words, the epiphany was for Jung no longer in the phenomenon, but in what the sublated phenomenon gave occasion to *reflect* about, in the human subject as observer.

We can still speak of an epiphany in Jung's experience, because *as* the second creator, human consciousness is given the status of a kind of divinity. The modern subject is of course not an imaginal phenomenon (one cannot see the subject with one's eyes or with sensory intuition), it is a conceptual thought. And so we have to realize that *thought* (the idea of human subjectivity) has here for Jung become the place of epiphany, where before, for myth, either sensory intuition (phenomenal reality) or imagination had been that place. Jung always insisted that he was an empiricist and that only *facts* count for him. But here he shows himself to be not an empiricist but a thinker, inasmuch as the idea of consciousness as the second creator of the world is not a fact, neither a fact established by perception or the sensation function nor a fact of the imagination. It cannot be seen or demonstrated. It is also not a vision. It is a thought, and as such, we can *think* it, and *only* think it.

So Jung's African experience did not undo his earlier experience of the loss of myth at all. On the contrary, it is firmly based on it and confirms it, but also proceeds far beyond it to entirely *new* territory. The fact that he still uses the term "myth" even for his fundamentally different experience is greatly misleading. Myth, on the one hand, and meaning in Jung's sense, on the other, are mutually exclusive. The experience within the sphere of myth is determined by the fact that all phenomena have their meaning in themselves. They are self-sufficient and in this sense perfect, even if they are phenomena of death or illness. And because they are *in themselves* perfect, the world of myth is the world of eternal repetition or recurrence, that goes on "through hundreds of millions of years" "to its unknown end." Jung's idea of meaning by contrast is the narrative of an overall movement towards a known end. Only to the extent that the individual phenomena are within the larger narrative of this goal-oriented movement do they now, too, partake of meaning.

Jung's African experience was possible through two acts of abstraction. The first abstraction is literal, external: he isolated himself from his companions. This can be interpreted as his separating himself from the ordinary and familiar consciousness or familiar mode of being-in-the-world. He needed to cut himself off from what was (also in himself) the ordinary or *natural* consciousness, in order to become able, in the resulting absolute loneliness, to say: "In this moment I was the first man who recognized that this was the world and who had created it in this moment through his knowing." The fact that it needed this separation shows that the consciousness of which it can be said that it is the second creator of the world is not our habitual consciousness. Rather, it is a radically new and higher consciousness, one that results from the explicit negation of the habitual natural consciousness.

What Jung here performs is a *revolution* of consciousness. Natural consciousness, that in this story is for Jung represented by his companions, is still on the same level as mythic experience and thus also with the world of the animal herds, which Jung pushes down in order to rise above it. It is on the same natural level, even though as modern consciousness it is no longer able to positively experience the world mythically. As such it is only the simple negation of mythic consciousness. It cannot perceive the divine image in natural *phenomena* any more, but it still stays on the same natural *level* of phenomena, which, however, now that they cannot be experienced as mythic any longer have become reduced to empirical facts. Jung, with his severing act, by contrast, now negated this simple negation, too, and thereby also the whole level of natural consciousness. This amounts to a revolution of consciousness.

Because of this revolution Jung is "the first man", i.e., *Adam*, again. He experiences the first day, indeed, first "moment", of a newly created world. This is his experience of a cosmogony. But what a difference to cosmogonic myths! Here, for Jung, the cosmogony does not, as in mythology, happen out there in the cosmos itself and as *its* emergence. It happens "invisibly" in here in consciousness, in the human mind, in subjectivity, namely in and as the *recognition* "that this was the world" and in and as his *knowing* "that it was 'this world'." Here we come to the second abstraction on which Jung's African experience was based. Jung pulls himself out of the presence of *this* moment in which he actually is while seeing the animal herds and rises above it, indeed above the whole *infinite* manifold of the world at large in both its temporal and spatial extension, and thus above the corresponding whole level of consciousness. And he contracts or condenses, indeed collapses, this manifold, this infinity of moments and of phenomena, into *one* single abstract thought: "that it was 'this world'." The whole phenomenal richness of the world is compressed into his *knowledge*, on the one hand, and into the demonstrative pronoun "this," on the other.

I said above that Jung's experience was not a vision but a thought. Here this becomes obvious. There is no apparition happening to him, but he performs the logical act of sublation. He sort of kicks the herd of animals (and along with it the whole manifold of the phenomenal world) into meaninglessness and through the same act rises to a new level of consciousness and a new sense of meaning. His new insight is thus the *result* of the logical act of sublation that he performed and not the irrational intrusion of a vision or image. The whole natural experience of the world, and this means the *basis of all mythology*, is sublated into this *knowing about* the whole natural experience of the world, and this knowledge is nothing else but the logical *abbreviation* of the former world, the world of myth and meaning. We could also say what once was the manifold of a whole world is now reduced to a moment of, a content in, the new consciousness that has become knowing (knowing consciousness) in this sense. This consciousness is, *ipso facto, extra naturam* and *extra ecclesiam*, where nature, in our psychological context, means as much as "imaginal or mythic world." For this consciousness, the imaginally experienced world, the world filled with divine meaning is irretrievably lost and no more than a sublated moment or content of its knowing, not a real presence. The level of "where psychologically the action is" has been relocated from the imagination of the natural world to consciousness itself.

By the same token, Jung did not "stick to the image" of the phenomenon that he saw before himself, the grazing and slowly moving herd of innumerable animals. This slowly moving, grazing, head-nodding herd was reduced by him to no more than a visual aid that, much like the fingers used by children when adding or subtracting, *facilitated* the thought process for him, but also obscured for him the fact that it was a thought.

For this stance, nature as such and myth have become psychologically an obsolete past. But almost as if as a consolation or compensation for this loss, this stance opened up for the first time a sense of "future," future in the sense of having a completely new, hitherto unheard-of task ahead of us and thus having to live forward towards its fulfillment in the future. This task, as we will see, is the realization of the Self. The age of myth and ritual did, of course, not have a real sense of future. Man during that age had a task too, but it was not future-oriented, not the task of bringing a new reality into existence for the first time. The task was, on the contrary, to *accompany* the natural course of events with ritual, as the Pueblo Indians, e.g., helped their Father, the sun, to move across the sky, and the task was to repeat, to re-enact, the rituals that had been instituted by mythical ancestors at the beginning of time. So the mythological and ritualistic world is determined by an orientation "backwards" to "eternal" or at least "timeless" models, paradigms, archetypes. The Self, as the task that Jung sees and that is in his eyes the task of the future, is very different. It is, as he makes clear, the movement forward to an as-yet-unknown continent.

Jung's East-African experience is the ground on which his later psychology of the Self rests. It is not yet the experience of the Self-concept itself. However, it contains one feature, which we have not yet mentioned, that traces out lines on which the thought of the Self will later on proceed. This has to do with a reversal or dialectic.

"In this moment [that is to say, in the moment when I had removed myself from the others and when my whole previous mode of existence came to me as *condensed* or *contracted* into my knowing, into one single thought of my consciousness], in this moment I was the first man ...." We already know that as such he was a second Adam, the first man created by God. But now comes the amazing reversal: as first man, as Adam created by God, he is himself at the same time "the second creator of the world," in other words, a creator god. The abstract opposition of creator god, on the one hand, and created creature, on the other, has been sublated. In religious as well as in everyday thinking, God and creature are unambiguously separated and stand vis-à-vis each other on different sides. This absolute separation is now over. Jung is talking about an event of becoming conscious in a very special sense in which man gives to the world that objective existence that the first Creator had not been able to give to it.

This by no means implies that man, who in a certain way has become divinized, can now inflatedly sort of take off from the earth and rise above his humanness. On the contrary, the elevation of consciousness to the rank of a second divine creator of the world is the process in which man becomes fully man (human) for the first time. The statement "In this moment I was the first man" contains also the idea of the full realization of humanness. The creative power that earlier, with the first creation, was stationed yonder, on the side of the transcendent God, has now passed into the hands of man; of course, not of him as person, individual, but of human consciousness as such. There is a crossing over from the one to the other, God and man to some extent exchange their natures and positions, inasmuch as God is now also dependent on man, whereas before only man had been dependent on God, and created man has taken over some of the creation task that before had exclusively been in the hands of God.

It is evident that such a view, which sees in man's becoming the second creator of the world the condition for the full realization of man as human being, has departed from the image of man as naturally existing organism. For Jung, man is not fully man merely by virtue of factually existing or by having been born. The full sense of humanness is a task, an *opus*, and, we have to add, an *opus contra naturam*. The fully realized human existence is the sublated existence of natural *homo sapiens*. Man becomes man in that special knowing that Jung talked about, not through his literal existence in the sense of *Vorhandensein*. So, just as much as Jung in his psychology left myth and nature as the foundation or framework of psychology behind, he also departed from the natural definition of what "human" means.

PART II: THE EXPERIENCE UNDERLYING THE
THEORY OF THE SELF

The two halves, negative and positive, of the first experience are empirical experiences. They can be dated and located, i.e., they are events in empirical time. Jung's experience of the Self, by contrast, is not datable. The experience of the thought of the Self was not an event in time, but itself an experience of and in thought, in the same sense perhaps that Heidegger is speaking, in the title of one of his writings, of "the experience of thought" (*Aus der Erfahrung des Denkens*). Thus it was a background experience informing his mind, not a foreground or literal experience. For this reason, there is not an analogous report about it as about his "loss of myth" and his East African experiences. We have to reconstruct this experience from the finished statements of Jung's about the Self, in order to be able to in turn reconstruct the meaning of those statements from the reconstructed underlying experience. There are many quotations about the Self with which I could begin. I take only a single one. In a letter, Jung wrote:

> For about 1900 years we have been admonished and taught to
> project the self into Christ, and in this very simple way it was
> removed from empirical man—much to the relief of the latter,
> since he was thus spared the experience of the self, that is, the
> *unio oppositorum* [union of opposites].[3]

---

[3] *Letters 2*, pp. 453f., 18 June 1958, to Herbert E. Bowman.

There are two essential statements about the Self in this quotation. The direct one about the Self as union of opposites and the indirect one consisting in Jung's rejection of a projection of the Self upon Christ. I will begin with the union of opposites. It is obvious that with the Self we are in the realm of thought, not in the realm of natural things or images. Jung is concerned with the psychic opposites, just like that. The "opposites" just as much as "unity" and "difference" and "identity" are so-called "concepts of reflection" (*Reflexionsbegriffe*), that is, concepts that do not refer to empirical objects or phenomena given to sense experience, but concepts that refer to abstract relations with which the reflecting mind within itself structures its own experience.

In empirical reality you can see two animals fighting with each other, you can *imagine* the hero slaying the dragon, etc., but you cannot see or imagine psychic opposites. Jung is not speaking about such concrete animals, beings, figures, powers who first of all exist and then in addition *happen* to be in opposition to each other, but might just as well also be in a harmonious relationship. He is speaking about the psychic opposites as such, which is very different indeed from things or aspects that incidentally are in opposition with each other. Although in practical reality the psychic opposites always appear in the form of *concrete* conflicts, this is only a secondary *exemplification* of the psychic opposites. It is not the opposites themselves that Jung is speaking about and that the Self is about. You cannot ask: what are the opposites, because that they are opposites is all that is to be said about them: they are opposites and no more. With the notion of the Self, Jung has left the sphere of sensuality, sensory intuition and imagination, the sphere of contents, and entered the sphere of *abstract* logical or conceptual relations.

This observation is confirmed when we look at the other information about the Self in our quote, Jung's rejection of the projection of the Self upon Christ. This is a very odd use of the concept of projection. Normally we speak of projection when we see in some other real person a content that actually belongs to us, but that we are unconscious of. But for 1900 years, Christ has not been a real empirical person for us, not like this dangerous looking neighbor of mine or my boss, etc., who normally carry our projections. Christ has been an image, an imaginal person. In this sense, he could be called the archetypal image of the Self. Christ thus is the self-manifestation of a psychic content, the epiphany of an imaginal truth, he is a *phainomenon*, but not something empirically real upon which we could project anything. If we applied Jung's use of projection here to Greek religion, we would have to say the Greeks projected the experience of sensuous love upon Aphrodite and thus they were themselves spared this experience. But this would, of course, be nonsense. The Greeks obviously did experience sensuous love in a very pronounced way. Aphrodite is not the carrier of a projection but the divine personification of the archetypal depth *of* the real, human experience of sensuous love. On this point, there is no difference between Aphrodite (or any of the other Gods anywhere) and Christ as image of the Self. The difference is only in what they are images of: Aphrodite, the image of erotic love; Christ, the image of the Self.

Now, if Jung here nevertheless and unfairly sees a projection and criticizes this, this must mean two things. First, there must be a fundamental difference for him between the psychic reality of the Self and all the other psychic contents represented by the polytheistic gods. Jung would never have criticized the fact that people had mythic images and personal divine representations in heaven for all the various aspects of real human experience such as the experience of love. Indeed, in his *Answer to Job* he vehemently insisted that even today woman needs a personal metaphysical representation in heaven. But when he comes to the Self, then all of a sudden one's having such a divine personal representation is for him an illegitimate projection. The fact that he applies two different standards must be due to the special nature and content of the Self archetype, of what the Self is about. The Self is such that what would be natural and even desirable in the case of any other archetypal reality, namely, to have a personal representation, is totally wrong.

Secondly, probably on account of this difference, Jung feels the need to *disrupt*, to cut into, the normal flow of the life of the soul, which, as Hillman especially has shown,[4] naturally tends to personify and to imagine things. By calling the very ordinary and primary soul activity of personifying, in this case the personifying of the Self in the figure of Christ, a projection and, indirectly, a defense against the real

---

[4] See James Hillman, *Re-Visioning Psychology* (New York: Harper & Row, 1975), Chapter One, "Personifying or Imagining Things."

experience of the Self, he prohibits us from giving ourselves over to the image or personal representation. In the case of the Self, he tries to cut us loose from the image, he interdicts *personifying and imagining*. Why? Because, he says, this relieves us, this spares us from having to really experience—and thus to *be*, I would add—the Self ourselves.

What is so special about the Self? I think this comes out in the *name* of this archetype: Self. The Self cannot be personified, cannot be imagined, because then it would be inevitably *objectified*, turned into an object and content of consciousness. But this would mean that it would no longer be what it is supposed to be, Self. Because "Self" refers to the innermost subjectivity of the subject it cannot be represented. It cannot be symbolized. It can only be *experienced*, or to be more exact: it *is* in itself experience, the process of the union of opposites, the process of a logical, dialectical relation. Since it *is* experience (has the nature of a process or experience), it cannot be a content, not a phenomenon, not something *that* we merely happen to be experiencing. The moment it became a content or image, it would cease to be the Self. Now it becomes a bit clearer why Jung considered seeing Christ as the Self to be a projection. The image of Christ sets up some externalized Other and thus indeed moves away from us what should be strictly we ourselves. Any image objectifies, and objectification means establishing otherness or not-self, giving the respective content the *form* of otherness.

With this insight we have unwittingly returned to the earlier topic of the Self as union of opposites. If consciousness establishes some literal or structural Other out there, there cannot be a union of opposites, because then there are Two, two separate entities between whom the opposites will be distributed, each representing one side of the opposition. As long as I relate to Christ, there cannot be a real union of opposites, for even if I love Christ and Christ loves me, the fundamental, metaphysical distance between him and me remains. There may be harmony between us, I may even have mystical experiences of a kind of "sexual" union with Christ, but there can never be a real unity, oneness. And then there cannot be Self, because the Self means that in myself and as myself I *am* both myself *and* my other. I am also the opposite of myself. There *must* not be a literal Other, if I am to become conscious of the fact that I am *myself* my other, *myself* my own opposite and thus divided from myself. And only if I have become conscious of myself as the irreconcilable opposition of myself and my Other, and at the same time conscious of the fact that this opposite Other *is* also *myself*, did the union of opposites occur and did I *ipso facto* advance to the status of Self.

The phrase "union of opposites" is an abbreviation. If one unfolds the complex logical relation implied by this abbreviation, one would have to say: the unity of the unity and the opposition of the opposites. I will take this statement apart into a sequence of several sentences. 1. I am not identical with myself, I am torn apart, I am my own opposite. I am a living contradiction. 2. Nevertheless, this Other who is my own opposite is nobody else than I myself. I am both myself and my opposite. In this sense I am united with my opposite. 3. I am the unity of the first statement about my being a contradiction and of the second statement about being united with my own Other. The realized Self is that status of consciousness that consciously exists as the complexity of this logical relation, but relation not in the sense of a static structure, but as the fluidity of a dialectical movement, as process and performance.

The fact that all this is very difficult to understand shows how far away this is *from*, and how foreign *for*, our ordinary experience and thinking. It also shows that with his experience of the thought of the Self Jung performed a revolution. He broke through the boundaries of the present stage of consciousness in psychology and opened up an entirely new stage of consciousness. His psychology of the Self implies the irrevocable departure from mythic imagination, from personifying, from personal divine representations, from an orientation, in all essential regards, by means of perception, sensory intuition and natural imagery. The Self, because it is really "self," really we (each of us), as subjects, removes us into the abstract sphere of logos, of processes that can only be thought, but not seen, envisioned, imagined any more. The shadow, the anima, etc. are contents and phenomena, objects of consciousness, psychological beings, they can be imagined and personified. Not so the Self. It is not a content. It is the union of opposites (to continue using this abbreviation for the full expression) and as such really only an unrepresentable (*unanschaulich*) internal logical relation and process. The Self cannot *be* a content because then it would be alienated from its very notion. The Self can only be if and to the extent that *I* in fact *become* and *be* it, that is, to the extent that

I have risen to that level of consciousness on which I exist as, *and* am truly aware of myself as, the unity of unity and opposition of the opposites; the self can only be to the extent that I have risen to that level of consciousness on which I experience, and have comprehended, myself as the complex movement of this dialectic.

Now we can understand what is meant when Jung said that the birth of the Self presupposes the death of the ego. Of course, this does not mean that we lose all our ego functions and the capacity to cope in ordinary reality, that we have sort of left this world in order to to be immersed in the transcendental. It means at once something much simpler and yet much more radical, revolutionary. It means that revolution of the *definition* of man in which we as substance, beings, entities go under into that dialectical movement or into the Concept. Ego in this context means that *natural* view of things for which the existing entity is the first reality and for which only thereafter this entity can be said to have certain qualities, a certain essence, to undergo certain processes, to behave in this or that manner, etc. The death of the ego or becoming Self means that psycho-logical revolution in which existing entity on the one hand and essence or concept on the other hand exchange their position and rank, in other words, where I as hard self-identical entity go relentlessly under in my concept or essence, in what I really am.

"What I really am" does not refer to all my concrete empirical characteristics. All *that* is part of my ego-personality and would as such, as something *psychic*, be a subject-matter of human biology. But the Self is not a psychic, but a *psychological* reality and a subject-matter of psychology. "What I really am" refers to me as ultimately being the union of opposites. My essence, what I really am, the *Logic* or *Concept* of "me," becomes the first reality, and the fact of my still being an existing entity is now reduced to being a sublated moment in me as the logical movement that plays between the opposites, in me as the *Concept*. To have become Self means to have become the *existing* Concept. The logic of me as being human, being mind and soul, now holds the predicate "existing," which before belonged to me as substance or entity, and the substance or entity has become a logical moment within the logic of being mind and soul.

I am ego as long as I am defined as an existing being and consequently have as my prime interest my self-preservation—not only literal physical self-preservation, nor only emotional self-preservation, but also *logical* self-preservation, i.e., the preservation of the very *definition* of me as existing entity or being. Becoming Self, by contrast, means that this definition sort of dives into, and drowns in, the logic of the play between the psychic opposites as the now first and dominant reality.

This is what the important alchemical image of the "Immersion in the Bath,"[5] in the water, is about. It is not *I* as person, as ego-personality, that has to be immersed in the water. Then we would still be thinking on the empirical-factual level of psychic behavior, not on the level of soul and psychology. No, my *definition* as entity and substance, as existing being, has to suffer this fate and to die from drowning, that is, it has to be dissolved into the fluidity of logical movement. The immersion of the person in the bath would only be one of two things: either a literal catastrophe (psychosis, death) or an *emotional* experience without real psychological transformation. Emotional experiences have the same status as tourism has in the modern world. There is also a psychological tourism. As tourist you may watch rituals performed for you by exotic tribes, or even be invited to participate in them, but you return home as the same person that you were before. A real transformation is a logical transformation, a transformation in one's self-definition. And this is why it is not me as empirical person, but the definition of myself, or what Kant called the *Menschheit in der Person*, the logical universal *in* the particular, that has to experience the immersion in the bath.

These were the problems that were contained in Jung's experience of the Self and that he was struggling with in his psychology of the Self. But we also have to see that Jung was conceptually not really up to his own experience. He did not make it easy for his audience and readers to see what his thought of the Self was really about. He made many different, often contradictory statements about the Self and individuation, speaking one way to theological critics and the opposite way to scientific critics. Now it is true, certain of those contradictions are due to the contradictory nature of the Self. But not all. Some are due to Jung's own conceptual helplessness and deep ambivalence. And this helplessness and ambivalence in turn are due to his resistance to

---

[5] See C. G. Jung, *The Psychology of Transference*, Chapter 4, *CW* 16 § 453 ff.

do in the logical *form* of his consciousness what the *content* of his experience, the experience of the thought of the Self, demanded. His resistance shows in four main areas or forms: (1) in his methodological stance; (2) theoretically, in what constituted for him the ground of psychology or the ultimate reality; (3) in an essential part of the content of his psychology, i.e., of the Jungian narrative; and (4) in the mode of his thinking.

1. His methodological stance: Here the resistance shows in his vehement refusal to admit that the idea of the Self *is* a thought, *has* the form of a thought. He insisted that it was a fact, an empirical find. His empiricism was a way of shielding himself. By declaring yourself to be interested exclusively in empirical facts, you, as an I, do not take responsibility for what you are saying. You hold back; you (logically!) reserve yourself; you yourself stay out of it vis-à-vis the objective facts. But, of course, psychology demands that the subject truly enter the scene, give itself over to the contents, immerse itself in them, rather than stay aloof as the innocent observer. It is not enough to preach semantically the alchemical immersion in the bath, but syntactically, in your methodological stance, insist on staying outside and remaining dry.

2. The theoretical ground of his psychology: As much as Jung was committed to the soul and, against the spirit of his times, wanted to turn psychology into a psychology *with* soul, nevertheless, in his thought the primacy of the idea of *personality* remained unshaken, so that soul was ultimately relegated to a subordinate position. In spite of his awareness that we are surrounded on all sides by the psyche, when it really counted, Jung fell back on personality as the ultimate substrate of psychological life. His experience of the thought of the Self would have required a reversal in the relationship between personality and soul. However, by anchoring the soul in the concept of personality, he cemented the priority of the existing entity over the concept or logic. His psychology remained personalistic and anthropologistic, and thus psychologistic.

Because Jung clung to the concept of personality as the ultimate psychological substrate, he also believed that one's personal *analysis* could be the locus where the individuation process as the process of the realization of the Self takes place. This is naive. Probably led astray by the fact that the word 'individuation' *seems* to contain a reference to 'individual,' he projected the task of individuation on the individual person, as if each person had *his* individuation, his own private Self. But I don't have *my* Self, *my* personal individuation: to think so would mean to subordinate the Self to the ego and Self-psychology to ego-psychology. The Self is not mine, the individuation not my development, not a process in me. The individuation process is a process that unfolds in the logic of the soul. And it happens not to the individual person, but to the "*Menschheit in der Person*," to the concept or definition of man. And this is why in an empirical reality life-time, if one wants to get a glimpse of the ongoing individuation process, one has to look at what is happening *in the culture at large*, not in the consulting room, and over a long time-span, not during an individual's short life. This process is larger than we. We as individual persons can at best, but inevitably will also have to, *partake* in it one way or another.

The alchemical laboratory in which the Self is realized is history, not me as person, not my analysis as process, not the consulting room as location.

For the empirical individual the (properly understood) process of individuation—precisely because it is a logical and cultural process—goes along with his *de-identification* or *distinction* from the archetype (from archetypal roles, from having to represent the Self or to be the place of its realization, and thus from the inflated importance that expresses itself, e.g., in the idea and feeling that "*I* have to realize the Self," that *my* personal analysis is the place of the individuation process. The human person is released into the modesty, simplicity, and weakness of his or her real humanness and empirical nature). All the mythical garments in which man had hitherto been cloaked can ultimately be taken off. This is what individuation means *practically*: I am just myself, the empirical person that I am, no more, no less, no better, no worse. "The greatest limitation for man is the 'self'; it is manifested in the experience: 'I am *only* that!'"[6]

The Self as union of opposites is definitely not something like our becoming a *mana personality*. If this were the end-product of the individuation process, it would lead to an inflation. On the contrary, the realized Self means the departure from such ideas belonging to

---

[6] *MDR*, p. 325.

the natural imagination, and it means the move into a very humble, simple, earthy form of existence.

3. The content of his psychology, or the Jungian account, narrative, myth: According to Jung, the trinity is incomplete and has to be overcome in favor of the quaternity. He does not realize that the trinity is the union of opposites, *is* the expression for the experience of the Self. By defecting from the trinity, he also deserts the Self and hinders its realization.[7]

4. The mode or style of thinking: Jung clung to the mode of imagining, mythologizing, and symbolizing and passionately refused to advance to thought proper as a psychological mode. Thus, he also considered the mandala, the image of the Old Wise Man, the Holy Grail, the alchemical *lapis*, the images of the tree and of the fish, to mention only a few of a host of others, as *symbols* of the Self. Apart from the fact that it is hard to see why most of these definitely static images[8] should be symbols of the Self, if Self is the process of the union of opposites, we also have to see that Jung in this way promotes the very kind of "projection" of the Self onto something that he himself had adamantly rejected in the passage quoted above, the projection on something that then relieves us of really having to become and be the union of opposites. Whether we "project" the Self onto Christ or onto the mandala, onto the fish or the Old Wise Man, makes no essential difference. It is always out there, *in* the respective image, and away from us.

In all four ways, which of course are interconnected, four forms of the appearance of one and the same self-reservation, Jung obscures the core of his own experience and makes it easy for his readers to misread the message about the Self. It remains to us to free the important insight contained in his experience from the sometimes counterproductive formulations that Jung gave it.

Basically, Jung's fault is that he still tries to construe the Self-psychology on the level of mythological or symbolic images, that is, on the level of contents, although the Self is really nothing else but

---

[7] On Jung's discussion of the Trinity and quaternity, see my essay, "The 'Patriarchal Neglect of the Feminine Principle': A Psychological Fallacy in Jungian Theory," in *Harvest: Journal for Jungian Studies* 1999, vol. 45, no. 1, pp. 7–30.

[8] The mandala may be excepted. It has to be thought of as a stationary image of motion, as the wheel of time.

the call to us *to move from* that level to the level of logic, of logical form and logical movement. We have to understand that the union of opposites, in other words, the oneness of oneness and difference of man and God, is ancient mythological and ritualistic stock, *but that this did not lead in ancient times to a concept of Self* ! The union of opposites is nothing new and nothing special. But the Self, as it appears in Jung's work, is absolutely new, at least in the Western world. And what *is* new and special about the Self is that it requires the transportation of the ancient experience of the "union of opposites" from (to say it with different vocabulary) the sphere of semantics to the sphere of syntax, from myth to *logos*. This revolutionary move is what the Self is about. For only on that new level of consciousness, the level of "syntax" or logical form, can the union of opposites be truly "*self*," i.e., psychologized, in here, in the mind, in the subjectivity, instead of imagined (as in mythology), acted out (as in ritual), or emotionalized (as in mystical or personal experience), the three main ways of externalizing, in other words, of giving the Self the *form* of not-self.

CHAPTER NINE

The Question of Jung's 'Anti-Semitism'
Postscript to Cocks

It is astonishing how persistently and with what undue emphasis such labels as "fascist" or "anti-Semite" continue to be attributed to certain thinkers such as C. G. Jung or Martin Heidegger, and it is deplorable that these labels are for the most part used only to discredit their works *in toto* and to absolve the public from the obligation of a serious and open-minded study of their ideas. Instead of examining the validity and the weight of such charges on the basis and in the context of the entire life and work of these men, one frequently tries conversely, (perversely,) to interpret their thought reductively in terms of their alleged fascist inclinations and thus searches their works merely for any features capable of lending some kind of support to this presupposed bias. This is an approach not altogether unlike the practice of the Nazis themselves, for whom the classifications "Jewish," "communist," etc. made any argumentation on the basis of substance superfluous. Since the charge of anti-Semitism happens to adhere to the name of C. G. Jung, it becomes necessary, even for those who see Jung differently, to examine closely the grounds for this charge and to engage in an unbiased discussion of this entire topic. The preceding article is a valuable contribution to such a discussion.[1] Writing as an historian, Cocks presents facts that speak for themselves. Nevertheless, it seems questionable whether such an emotion-laden issue can be 'settled' by historical evidence alone. Do not the intense emotions connected with this topic indicate that a sensitive spot in the depth of the psyche is stirred, that this topic extends into dimensions far beyond the historical-factual? Indeed, the facts established by the historian themselves raise a number of questions.

For once, even if it seems clear from the material presented by Cocks that Jung's behavior was not motivated by an anti-Semitic bias, there still remains the question of why Jung spoke publicly of the difference between a Jewish and a Germanic psychology, of an Aryan and a Jewish unconscious—and that precisely during those years when anti-Semitism began to change from a mere ideology to a life-threatening political reality. This is probably the main point of departure for these accusations, then as well as today.

Thus, in a review in *Psyche* (1975, pp. 273-85) from a Freudian perspective of Jung's *Briefe*, in which Jung's protestation of his good intentions as president of the General Medical Society for Psychotherapy is accepted as subjective truth, we find the expression of astonishment at "the hardly credible political naiveté" with which Jung fended off "as malicious misunderstanding of his thoroughly scientific interests" the general indignation caused by his having made the distinction between an Aryan and a Jewish unconscious and by his thus having *de facto* joined in "the chorus of the regime conformists of that time." The author of this review, Ilse Grubrich-Simitis, does not blame him so much for the substance of his reflections on racial differences, but rather states that it was above all the *timing* of his remarks that makes them scandalous, the timing which betrayed his un-suspicion and total disregard for the historical situation. Jung viewed the phenomenon of fascism with a frame of mind, "in which historical, truly political categories, even sociological or economic

---

[1] *Editor's Note:* In an article entitled, "C. G. Jung and German Psychotherapy, 1933–1940: A Research Note" (*Spring 1979*, pp. 221–227), the historian Geoffrey Cocks investigated the question of "whether Jung's actions with respect to Germany after Hitler's assumption of power necessarily represent the expression of a fundamental anti-Semitism on his part." In the present "Postscript," Giegerich follows up Cocks's historical approach to this question with a discussion of how a psychological approach to it would have to be conceived.

criteria were totally lacking and which therefore was unsuited for a realistic evaluation of the situation." She concludes her discussion of this aspect by terming Jung's letters of this period "a moving lesson in political psychology."

Jung himself confirms this "political naiveté" of his when he states: "... [A]t bottom I was completely unpolitical" (*Briefe* 1: 280). But whereas Jung's political disinterest will be disposed of by many as a lacuna in his personality or in his approach, it can become a starting point for further inquiry: why did Jung not think in strictly political terms and what does his approach aim at? Here we cannot discuss this question fully, but must confine ourselves to a few general remarks. What strikes the eye is that Jung reacted to the race issue in the same way as he did with respect to the 'schisms' in depth psychology. In both cases, Jung did not believe in simply taking a stand for or against, in advocating one view and combating the other and in thus forcing the question into a deadlock. Jung wanted "to bring the parties together round a conference table, so that they could at last get to know and acknowledge their differences" (*CW* 10 § 1032).

His was a therapeutic approach. The therapist does not settle the conflicts of his patients by calling one side "right" or "good" and the other "wrong" or "bad," but tries to raise the whole question to a level where one is no longer caught by the issue from behind and carried away by one's subjective emotional reactions. In much the same manner, Jung wanted to raise the race problem from the political level, where one has to choose between conformism and non-conformism and where, ultimately, power decides the issue, to a psychological level, where critical reflection and consciousness are possible—as he had already done with the theoretical conflict between Freud and Adler, by viewing it from the typological perspective.

Seen in this light, what appeared as "political naiveté" from a political perspective, reveals itself as nothing less than *psychological faith*: "This naive belief of mine in the human soul may appear, from the Olympian standpoint of a hypertrophied intellect or of partisan blindness, laughable, suspect, unpatriotic, and God knows what" (*CW* 10 § 1022). Jung was not unpolitical or even a-political in the sense that he avoided the political issues of the time and escaped into the realm of "*Innerlichkeit*." He was very much engaged, in Mattoon's sense (*Spring 1978*). He was unpolitical only in that he wanted—in lieu of a dogmatic right/wrong answer—to apply the approach of psychological conflict resolution through critical reflection even to political or ideological conflicts. He did not walk into the trap of literalism, either by joining in the battle on one side or the other, on the one hand, or by avoiding the entire issue as if it were "a taboo area which none may enter on pain of death" (*CW* 10 §1031), on the other; he wanted to *tackle* the hot problem that he found constellated in his time and to see through it.

In other words, he did not restrict psychologizing to the personal problems of private life and revert to a pre-psychological position as soon as ideological, political, or theoretical differences cropped up, but remained a psychologist throughout; and that he did not succeed was not due to a 'lacuna' on his part, but to a lack of psychological faith and of psychological maturity on the part of the public: nobody was ready for the psychological approach, nobody gave it a chance. The general experience of psychotherapy justifies the view that much wind could have been taken out of the sails of the race question if people had been willing to question critically their emotional involvement in it and see it as a collective psychological problem. If one wants to find fault with Jung, then it can only be for his not realizing that he was 'ahead of his time' and for overestimating his contemporaries, who, as history has shown, were capable of reacting only on the level of pro and contra judgments. Here he may really have been naive—but faith in the soul is probably never 'realistic' and 'effective.'

So I would agree with I. Grubrich-Simitis, albeit for opposite reasons, that Jung's letters from the Nazi era can be "a moving lesson in political psychology." They should not be seen as teaching us to be more political-factual or to take a clear stand against whatever appears to be evil or wrong—this would be nothing but a sublimated form of primitive conflict resolution by brute force.

They should, rather, be considered an invitation to all of us truly to let ourselves in for the real issue behind whatever problem or prejudice happens to be constellated, regardless of whether it is reasonable and acceptable or stupid and embarrassing, and thus to proceed from the factual level to one where psychological movement is possible.

This is the actual reason why—valuable as Cocks's research may be—it is not sufficient to answer the question of Jung's alleged anti-

Semitism on the historical-factual level (with yes or no or something in between). For such an answer does not move anything. A true answer can be given only by taking up the task that Jung pointed out and which is still waiting to be done: the task of *entering* the tabooed precinct of racial prejudices, of allowing them to touch us, of making the imponderables of ethnic differences themselves a subject of *psychological* examination and of penetrating them to a point where their *mythic proportions* and our historical and ethnic rootedness become visible. This is, however, a task that demands more in the way of knowledge and psychological insight than most of us are likely to be able to provide, as becomes clear from one of Jung's letters of April 1957 on the ethnic background of Freud's thinking:

> For a real understanding of the Jewish component in Freud's outlook a thorough knowledge would be needed of the specifically Jewish assumptions in regard to history, culture, and religion. Since Freud calls for an extremely serious assessment on all these levels, one would have to take a deep plunge into the history of the Jewish mind. This would carry us beyond Jewish orthodoxy into the subterranean workings of Hasidism (e.g., the sects of Sabbatai Zwi), and then into the intricacies of the Kabbalah, which still remains unexplored psychologically. The Mediterranean man, to whom the Jews also belong, is not exclusively characterized and moulded by Christianity and the Kabbalah, but still carries within him a living heritage of paganism which could not be stamped out by the Christian Reformation. I ... have realized that one must take all these facts into consideration in order to gain a real understanding of psychoanalysis in its Freudian form ....
>
> In view of the blood-bespattered shadow that hangs over the so-called "Aryan understanding of the Jew," any assessment that fell below the level of these—as it may seem to you—high-falutin conditions would be nothing but a regrettable misunderstanding, especially on German soil. (To Edith Schroeder, *Letters* II: pp. 358–59.)

CHAPTER TEN

Hospitality Towards the Gods in an Ungodly Age
Philemon–Faust–Jung

In the last act of Goethe's *Faust II*, two modest old people, Philemon and Baucis, owners of a tiny lot, have to give way to Faust's gigantic project of land reclamation and indeed are killed as a result. We remember Philemon and Baucis from mythology as the only couple housing and hosting the homeless Gods during a godless age. If Faust's existence[1] is equivalent to the removal and destruction of Philemon and Baucis, then the mode of being-in-the-world incorporated by Faust must also be equivalent to the elimination of hospitality towards the Gods. Goethe shows that the core and essence of Faust's existence and, inasmuch as Faust is an allegory[2] of Modern Man, the essence of the modern style of being is inhospitality. In the following, I would like to have a closer look at this inhospitality and what it amounts to.

---

[1] I restrict myself to the Faust of acts IV and V, without discussing the question of the relationship of this Faust to the one (ones) in the earlier acts and especially in *Faust I*.

[2] The traditional view of *Faust II* is that it is decidedly not allegorical but symbolical. In pioneering studies, two authors disprove the basic premise of 150 years of *Faust* scholarship and advance the thesis that this work is an allegory—a thesis that had been long overdue. Heinz Schlaffer, *Faust Zweiter Teil. Die Allegorie des 19. Jahrhunderts* (Stuttgart: Metzler, 1981). Wolfgang Benn, *Hermetik, geschichtliche Erfahrung, Allegorie. Die konstitutive Funktion von Goethes hermetisch beeinflußter Naturphilosophie für die allegorische Natur des Faust II* (Frankfurt a.M.: R.G. Fischer, 1981).

My lead comes from C. G. Jung. In 1923, when Jung built his
Bollingen "tower," he carved the following inscription over the entrance
gate, "*Philemonis sacrum, Fausti poenitentia,*" i.e., "Philemon's sanctuary,
Faust's atonement."[3] An inscription over the gate to one's home is like
a motto under which one's entire life and thought is placed. By placing
his spiritual existence under a motto taken form the world of Goethe's
Faust, Jung shows us that what happened there was of personal
significance for him.

We are wont to see the works of poets and writers only as
"literature" and therefore to approach them only with a literary,
aesthetic, and historical frame of mind. Thus, it might be surprising
to find that Jung by no means had a merely literary relationship to
Goethe's *Faust,* but rather saw in the Faust story a reality, a fateful event
in the history of the soul, and as a consequence, felt it inevitable that
he would have to react and respond personally. What Jung shows us
is that a poetic work is not only for aesthetic appreciation and scholarly
interpretation, but can also make personal demands on our lives. This
happens as soon as and wherever there is an awareness of what Jung
terms psychological reality, as distinct from physical reality on the one
hand, and from ideas in the sense of the subjective and therefore merely
imaginary, unreal fabrications of ego-consciousness on the other.

Such an awareness of psychological reality is nothing but faith
in the *reality* of the psychological, in the *reality* of the soul and its
products. When we read a work of literature from a psychological
rather than a merely scholarly perspective, the world and events
portrayed there cease to be ideas from a historical past that we can
stay detached from and begin to take on the character of a reality
around us, affecting us, as it were, from outside, much as economic
or metereological realities do. And then it may happen that this
reality hits us and cuts into our lives. It is in this sense that Jung's
comments are to be understood, when he writes in a letter from the
year 1942 that one day it dawned on him with a shock and all of a
sudden that he had taken over *Faust* as his inheritance, and as the
advocate and avenger of Philemon and Baucis to boot.[4] Similarly, we
read in his *Memories* that he felt personally affected, and that if Faust,
on account of his hubris and inflation, had caused the murder of

---

[3] *MDR*, p. 222 note, and *Letters I*, p. 49 (to Keyserling, 2 January 1928).
[4] *Letters I*, p. 309 (to Paul Schmitt, 5 January 1942).

Philemon and Baucis, he, Jung, himself felt guilty, almost as if he had had a part in the two old people's death.[5]

I, too, want to look at the Faust-Philemon story with a psychological eye. Therefore, I would like to remind us before we enter into our subject that this is not a matter between that particular historical or imaginary individual Faust and that other particular mythological individual Philemon. Rather, it is *our* story: *we are in it*, and it shapes our lives, demanding of us payment of debts that were incurred long ago.

*   *   *

Goethe does not repeat the classical Philemon story in his play. In fact, at first glance it might look as if the Philemon of the old myth and Goethe's Philemon did not have much more in common than the name. And yet, through covert allusions, Goethe clearly shows that he wants us to be aware of the classical story and thus to be able to see the contrast between the mythical and the modern, Faustian situation. The contrast with the old version of the Philemon story is Goethe's actual theme. Goethe does not want to recreate an old tale in his own way, as was the case when he wrote *Iphigenie*, e.g., so that the Philemon scenes would, to be sure, take some of their material from the tradition, but nevertheless be self-contained as a new version in its own right. No, Goethe's Philemon scenes are obviously set against the background of the myth, so that, when reading them, we are not in one world, a whole world, but in a reflected, broken world, or, if you wish, simultaneously in two worlds. Inasmuch as the old myth is an inherent element of the Philemon scenes in *Faust*, albeit only by way of covert allusion, we have to acquaint ourselves with the classical story of Philemon and Baucis.

This story, the motif of which is widespread and dates back very far into antiquity, has come down to us mainly in the form given to it by Ovid in his *Metamorphoses* at the end of antiquity.[6] I am not interested here in the details with which Ovid embellishes the tale, but only in the meaning of its central theme, hospitality, as it is

[5] *MDR*, p.222.

[6] Ovid, *Metamorphoses* VIII, 611-726. See Manfed Beller, *Philemon und Baucis in der europäischen Literatur*, Heidelberg (Winter) 1967 (with bibliography) and Marie-Louise von Franz, "Der unbekannte Besucher in Märchen und Träumen," *Analyt. Psychol.* 6: 437-449 (1975).

displayed in the plot. Summarized, the story runs like this: The world has become ungodly. Two divine strangers, Jupiter and Mercury, wandering on the earth, do not find any hospitable place of rest, until Philemon and Baucis, living under very modest conditions, accept the two guests into their home and serve them hospitably, not withholding from them anything that their scant household can offer. Baucis is even willing to offer them their only goose, saved for a special occasion as a sacrifice to the Gods. Then it happens that the gods reveal themselves, the simple hut is changed into a temple, and the two old people are made the priests of this sanctuary forever, whereas at the same time a flood consumes the ungodly human race.

The story tells of a metamorphosis. In the beginning, there are two wanderers, probably dirty and in rags and not the least bit divine; and a most simple hut and two modest old people. In the end we have two Gods, a magnificent temple, and two dignified priests. It would be a mistake to see in this sequence of events a magical miracle, the sudden literal change from wretched to splendid. I maintain that the change from the initial situation to the final one does not happen to the objective reality that we are told about; it does not belong to the real time of the object, but belongs to the technique and the conditions of narration and falls into *its* time. The transformation is a shift of the perspective from which one and the same reality is viewed. It is a change that happens to us as we hear the story, or to the teller of the tale as he proceeds, not to the actual hut, the two wanderers or to Philemon and Baucis, about whom he tells us. We, the hearers or readers of the story, are moved from one view of things to another, from a preliminary and superficial view of the world as positive fact to one capable of perceiving the divine essence even in the most simple event.

This would mean that as far as the sphere of actual fact is concerned, the wanderers are at the end the same wretched vagabonds as in the beginning. Likewise, the thatched-roof hut will not have changed. Conversely, however, we must also see that viewed from the perspective of the deeper essence of things, that is, from the perspective to which this story wants to lead us, the hut is a temple not only at the end of the tale, but also from the very beginning—inasmuch as it is Philemon's home, that is to say, the home whose nature it is to receive the Gods.

The story of Philemon and Baucis is thus not a myth proper, not a representation of archetypal happenings *in illo tempore*, but a legend playing once and for all in our worldly reality. It does not begin in heaven, in a mythical or metaphysical background, but, as is expressly stated, in an ungodly, that is to say, profane world. And despite its ending, the story never leaves this secular sphere. It is not a tale of the incursion of existing gods from outside this world into earthly reality, of a visit that the human world has been paid from the beyond. In a certain sense, one might even be allowed to call this an atheistic story. At any rate, it is very much down to earth and free of any other-worldly mystification. For there are no Gods here that would be different and separate from our ordinary human reality. Rather, what this story is actually about is how within common reality and precisely out of it, the divine blossoms out, if I may say so, or how everyday reality blossoms into divine beauty. From within two homeless wanderers in rags and two poor old people in a modest hut, a brilliance is slowly or suddenly seen to shine forth, without there being a miraculous change of the factual living conditions.

On the face of it, what factually happened is very simple and ordinary. Two strangers have been received into a home and entertained. The hosts and the guests obviously hit it off well, and so the goose reserved for a special occasion is remembered and served, because Philemon and Baucis realize that in this very moment the special occasion has indeed arrived. That is all. There is nothing spectacular, nothing mystical or magical. Just a human encounter, the consumption of food and drink and a fruitful conversation, all this, however, within an atmosphere of true hospitality.

The revelation of the Gods that the story reports is nothing more than that this very natural moment of hospitality finds its fulfillment and completion. The Gods here are not supernatural beings but merely the embodiment of the inner essence of this particular present. For why is it Jupiter and Mercury who wander on the earth and not any other of the many Gods? Jupiter is Zeus *Xenios*, the God of hospitality, in other words, the very God of this moment. And the presence of Mercury, the God of commerce and interpretation, of exchange and communication, is indicative of the fact that this evening must have led to a true meeting of minds between the hosts and their guests. Jupiter and Mercury are none other than the divine face of this very natural situation, a kind of "*Augenblicksgötter*" (but in a sense different from that of Usener).

Philemon and Baucis, with a total devotion to what this moment of having strangers asking for a place to stay demanded of them, willingly spent or even wasted the little they had on this moment, without reserve, without worrying about what to eat the next day. Because they lovingly surrendered in this way to the present and allowed what they had to be consumed, the present could be consummated in return and flow over and reveal its own immanent archetypal or divine face. The moment of hospitality began to shine or to speak. By contrast, one could also imagine—and we will soon encounter an example of this—a situation of factual hospitality that nevertheless remains mute and without luster, without releasing its own essence.

It seems to be love that makes the difference. It is significant that the name Philemon means "the loving or hospitable one." Similarly, Baucis is the tender or affectionate one. And again, the goose that Baucis offers to the Gods is Aphrodite's bird. Love makes it possible for the hosts to surrender and to splurge instead of keeping and holding on anxiously to what they have or even greedily hungering for more. By letting go, by freely sacrificing the goose to their guests, Philemon and Baucis feed the moment with love and with the rich fat and round wholeness of this bird. This feeding, this nurturing the here and now with the "goose" is what releases the image of the present moment, which would otherwise remain hidden.

Of course, it is not only a situation of hospitality that can flow over into its image.[7] Any moment to which we abandon ourselves with this loving devotion will find its fulfillment. The Gods of the polytheistic Pantheon are the faces or images of all the various (arche-)typical, truly consummated moments.

Why then does our story choose a moment of hospitality as an instance of fulfillment that could just as well be shown in any number of other situations? This is not an arbitrary choice. The moment of hospitality is not chosen as one possible example from any number of suitable moments. What our tale wants to show as its deeper meaning

---

[7] I have discussed the idea of a moment's "flowing over" into its image in my "Buße für Philemon: Vertiefung in das verdorbene Gast-Spiel der Götter," *Eranos 51-1982* (Frankfurt/Main: Insel, 1983), 189-242.

is that it is hospitality to whatever present moment may knock at our door that allows that moment to reveal its divine iance. Since the theme of the story is hospitality in the sense of abandoning ourselves to the present, the plot of the story also has to involve guest and host and Zeus *Xenios*. But the actual hospitality intended here is not literal hospitality—spending a lot on parties, having an open house for all and sundry; nor is it the Christian ethic of "love of thy neighbor." It is the devotion to the present and its hidden presence, its face and voice; it is the reception and the feeding of the image.

So, the change that this story of hospitality is about is the move from positive fact to image, the move from a mentality that reads events as narrative (a series of successive developments in time leading to an end-result) to one that views the same events imaginally, i.e., as simultaneous facets of one image. This story is a narrative, but a narrative whose very action and plot is nothing less than the overcoming of the narrative mode. Instead of itself being a myth, it is the story of a first transition, a *rite de passage*, into myth, out of an ungodly view of things and into an imagistic mode of existence.

The inference we can draw from this is that if we live life as narrative, as development, as a heroic, the Gods cannot be present; even more, we would constantly and by necessity be closing our door to them and turning them away. For, living in the narrative mode, we would always be waiting for the spectacular ending of our life story or for a peak experience in the succession of events, for the miraculous literal appearance of the Gods, and we would, therefore, not be able to recognize the Gods already present in the ordinary, lowly guise of the here and now. Conversely, only when life is seen as image does it become possible to see and receive the Gods, because only then are we not hastening expectantly to every next moment, but can consummate the present. And only then does Philemon ('the loving one') live in us. Could this mean that the essence of love is the perception and reception of the image (of whatever thing or person is loved) and, on the other hand, that seeing the image, seeing imagistically automatically implies loving?

At first sight, Philemon's lack of concern about the next day seems to carry the same message as Christ's dictum: "Take no thought for the morrow," "Take no thought for your life, What shall we eat? ...

Behold the fowl of the air: for they sow not, nor do they reap ..."
(Matt. 6:31, 25f.). In fact, however, the two kinds of carefreeness are
diametrically opposed. In Christianity, it is God who is the host, God
who makes a great supper and bids many to come (Luke 14:16ff.).
Christian man, therefore, must not take thought for the morrow,
because he knows that the heavenly Father feedeth him, nay, *has long
ago* provided for him once and for all. Being the invited guest and
resting in Abraham's bosom (Luke 16:22), he is screened from the
unmitigated impact of the events of life. No present will knock at his
door, addressing itself precisely to *him* with the freshness, full force,
and immediacy of an original presence or visitation. Events do not of
themselves mean him, but are meant for him as trials or gifts of grace
("presents"!), i.e., as the Father's educational means to an ulterior end.
Everything that happens is suspended in the all-encompassing
relationship of the heavenly Father to his child. Not even the ultimate
event in life, death, has a sting.

Thus, there can be no truly "new" events necessitating
fundamental changes of attitude, such as there are for Philemon, for
whom every moment might bring the arrival of a new, fully different
guest. As there is only one God in Christianity, so there is only one
single event (i.e., the Advent): the coming of the Lord. But even this
single event does not have the nature of a true advent (a divine guest's
asking to be received by man), but is the "advent" of God's *invitation*
to man to *come to him*. If the Christian advent is thus the negation of
a true advent, we can understand why the coming of the Lord cannot
have a place in the here and now of real life, but must—in order to
circumvent the present (and presence)—necessarily be split in two:
into an event of the pre-present, or past (first coming), and one of the
post-present, or future (second coming), a matter of remembrance and
hope. The present remains empty.

Because Time is thus deprived of the possibility to be a "present"
and having been subjected to the rule of the "past" and the "future,"
we see why in the Christian West real life by necessity had to become
at once "historical" (a positivistic causal development) on the one hand
and "utopian" (the pilgrim's, the scientist's, the technologist's progress
towards the promised land) on the other. Now every moment
essentially *is* nothing else but the *no*-longer of its antecedent causes
and the promise of a *not*-yet. And consequently, it is nothing (*nihil*)

in itself, nothing containing a depth and an image of its own that could
be loved. Here it is no longer man, but God alone who is the
'Philemon,' 'the loving one': "For God so loved the world ..." (John
3:16). God has absorbed all love into himself, so much so, that man
no longer has any capacity to love of his own and that, as a result,
"love" needs to be imposed on him as a moral obligation (Matt. 22:37–
39: "Thou shalt love the Lord, thy God ... Thou shalt love thy
neighbour as thyself")—which of course means the sapping of the very
notion of love.

God as infinite love—this is a complete reversal of our Philemon
myth and entails the end of man's hospitality towards the God(s).
Indeed, inhospitality is expressly built into the Christian myth as an
inherent element in nothing less than God's plan of salvation through
Christ's Crucifixion: "He came unto his own, and his own received
him not" (John 1:11). Christian man is, so to speak, defined as
Inhospitable Man, in the sense that accepting God's invitation to the
great supper is identical with the admission of one's own
emptyhandedness before God, the admission that man has absolutely
nothing to give and therefore can and must receive everything out of
the hands of the Lord.

*   *   *

As I said earlier, Goethe does not recreate the Philemon story in
his *Faust*, his Philemon scenes are completely new and independent,
but we are, nevertheless, time and again referred back to the old story
through parallel and contrasting features. Above all, however, Goethe
takes up its central theme by immediately introducing Philemon and
Baucis as allegories of hospitality and piety. A wanderer appears and
is received kindly. But—and this is the special feature of the Philemon
episode in *Faust*—the actual hospitality is here a matter of the past
and of remembrance, not of the present. For the wanderer merely *re*visits
the two old people here, after having formerly, a long time ago been
rescued by them from shipwreck and hospitably accommodated. So
this is not an original moment, virginal and self-contained, but a copy,
almost a kind of imitation, that will have to be measured against the
former original.

Apparently, within the Faustian situation of modern man, an
unbroken present of hospitality is no longer possible. The present

has broken apart into an earlier and a today and thus it does not allow for man's being entirely absorbed by the present moment. So it is not astonishing that the moment of hospitality cannot find its fulfillment and consummation here. This is made very clear. Baucis asks her guest, "Not a word? No morsel raising, / That your famished mouth may eat?"[8] No food is consumed, the stranger remains silent, and thus the entire situation remains mute and without luster. This time, the wanderer is not revealed as a God, he remains only this empirical individual. The true guest does not present himself. Philemon and Baucis are able to be hosts only in the literal sense; the actual philemonic hospitality, which would accommodate the moment itself with its imaginal depth and thus allow it to flow over into its divine shine, is no longer possible. The hosts have become historical to themselves, and in the guest whom they accommodate they do not receive the present moment, but essentially the *former* guest.

What is it that makes the guest speechless, prevents consumption and consummation, and splits the present into the historical "formerly" of an original fulfilled hospitality and the "now" of a pale, empty repetition? It is the influence of Faust, the fact that *this* present is the presence of Faust and not that of the Gods, i.e. of true hospitality. Already here the true Philemon is dead: he is his own past, and if in *Faust* he perishes only later, then this is not a new development, but only the allegorical visualization of what is true from the onset. At bottom, however, the two old people remain the accomplished hosts of the present even here, precisely because they are *onetime* hosts and give way through their death; for it is only by giving way that *this* present, which after all is the present of the *in*hospitable (i.e. the historical, technical) relation to reality, can be accommodated. Since Philemon and Baucis remain the true hosts to the moment, even if this moment is the moment of their negation, their hospitality and this moment can find fulfillment only in their death. And thus it is the flames in which they perish that bring the only shine and brilliance into these oppressing scenes.

---

[8] I use the *Faust* text in the "Hamburger Ausgabe" and quote from the translation *Faust Part Two* by Philip Wayne (Harmondsworth: Penguin Classics, 1959). References are to the pages of the translation and the lines as in the "Hamburger Ausgabe." This present quotation: p. 253, lines 11107f.

*   *   *

The Faust-Philemon story is a story of mirroring. The old tale of Philemon is reflected in the mirror of a modern Faustian reality. And Goethe shows what *this* reflection amounts to. It amounts to the destruction of Philemon, i.e., of mirroring, of receiving the image, as such. It is as if the waterlike surface of things and moments is no longer allowed to reflect the inner divine essence, as had been the case during Philemon's time. Man now reaches through the surface for what is "behind" it to find something that can be put to practical use, and he thus disturbs the reflecting surface, so that the mirror image is shattered. What remains is, on the one hand, the world of positive fact and, on the other, the world of antiques and museum pieces, which can certainly be well preserved, collected, and auctioned off for thousands of dollars apiece, but will never again bring forth the shine of a divine face.

However, the destruction of mirroring as such must not be taken literalistically. It is a death not in the sense of total disappearance. For Philemon would then not have had to appear at all in *Faust*. But he does, only, however, as the presence of his own past. So it is a transformation in the nature of reflection itself. Reflection now means the presence of the bygone and not the presence of a presence. Reflection not as immediacy, but mediated—media. The Faustian world is the world of historicism, *Bildung*, tourism, of picture taking and television.[9]

Goethe captures Faust's nature when he shows his attitude to the sea and its tide. It annoys Faust deeply that the sea comes time and again to wash the land.

> My eyes were turned towards the open sea:
> Its towering swell against the heaven it bore,
> Then, shaking out its waves exultantly,
> Came charging up the level stretch of shore.
> This grieved me, that a haughty arrogant flood
> Can cast free spirit, rising every right,
> Through passion of the wildly kindled blood,
> Into a trough of feeling's vexed despite.[10]

---

[9] Schlaffer (*op.cit.*), who interprets *Faust II* on the basis of Karl Marx, *Das Kapital*, thoroughly examines this aspect of historicism and *Bildung*.

[10] p. 220, line 10198.

> (*Mein Auge war aufs hohe Meer gezogen;*
> *Es schwoll empor, sich in sich selbst zu türmen,*
> *Dann ließ es nach und schüttete die Wogen,*
> *Des flachen Ufers Breite zu bestürmen.*
> *Und das verdroß mich; wie der Übermut*
> *Den freien Geist, der alle Rechte schätzt,*
> *Durch leidenschaftlich aufgeregtes Blut*
> *Ins Mißbehagen des Gefühls versetzt.*)

"This grieved me ...." This betrays the stance that Faust takes toward whatever may arrive. His annoyance is directed toward advent as such. And in the ocean, Faust sees primarily that which comes to assail the land. Arrival is from the very beginning interpreted negatively as assault. We have to remember here that Goethe had Philemon's original guest come from the sea, indeed, be washed ashore by the sea. So the sea is clearly represented as that which brings the arrival of the guest, as in fact in mythology, many a God has his epiphany from the sea. Faust's response to the arrival of the sea is not hospitable accommodation, but the plan "to exclude the lordly ocean from the shore."[11] And later he will greet a guest who has entered his room, *Sorge* (Care, Worry), with the word "Begone!"[12] and, as a third example, he wants Philemon and Baucis to make way for him and demands of Mephisto to rid him of them. It is not, as Faust claims, that we have no access to the beyond.

> And what's beyond is barred from human ken;
> Fool, fool is he who blinks at clouds on high,
> Inventing his own image in the sky."[13]

> (*Nach drüben ist die Aussicht uns verrannt;*
> *Tor, wer dorthin die Augen blinzelnd richtet,*
> *Sich über Wolken seinesgleichen dichtet!*)

Faust is all wrong. It is not the yonder that withdraws and shuts itself off. On the contrary, the yonder is that which has already come and wants to be received. It is there all the time, knocking at our door or washing against our shore. Plotinus knew better. How did he see

---

[11] p. 221, line 10229 ("*Das herrische Meer vom Ufer auszuschließen*").
[12] line 11422 (my transl.; "*Entferne dich!*").
[13] p. 265, line 11442 ff.

it? "They must come to me, not I to them."[14] It is Faust himself who excludes its arrival by erecting his monumental dams.

But, of course, Faust never wanted access to the beyond, if this meant hosting a guest coming autonomously and of his own accord. The beyond would only have been interesting to him if he could have conquered it. What he is after is possession of the world, *Weltbesitz*,[15] and exclusion of any other autonomous power. He does not merely want more, not even everything, he wants totality. This is why Philemon and Baucis have to disappear. And this all the more so, since they, as the accomplished hosts, represent the opposite principle, with whom there can be absolutely no coexistence. The murder of Philemon is not an immoral action on the part of Faust, but merely the allegorical expression of the objective, almost ontological relation between hospitality and its opposite. Where inhospitality governs, there hospitality begone.

This shows at the same time that inhospitality presupposes the existence of Philemon's world. Hospitality comes first ontologically. Inhospitality (positivism) is nothing in itself, but, being ontologically empty, feeds off the mythic. It is nothing but the continuous destruction, consumption, and elimination of the images—of "Philemon" and the "sea," this continuous negation is its *essence*.[16] Here we have a real *privatio boni*. Faust is the depriving, robbing one. So his name (fist) is not without deeper significance, just as were the names of Philemon and Baucis. Embodying the principle of literal activism—as opposed to Philemon's receptive spirit, he is characterized by the empty fist that needs to grab in order to be.

What especially annoys Faust about the tidal waves is the useless waste of energy, this free spending of strength. Whereas Philemon and Baucis used up everything they had for some strangers without concern about the next day, Faust wants everything employed for and subjected to a practical purpose. Faust says, while watching the sea:

> There wave on wave, by hidden power heaved,
> Reigns and recedes, and nothing is achieved.

---

[14] Porphyrius, *Life of Plotinus*, 33-38.
[15] line 11242.
[16] For more on this "negation" in the light of the history of the Western mind see my paper cited in note 7 above.

> This thing can sadden me to desperation,
> Wild elements in aimless perturbation!
> To soar beyond itself aspired my soul:
> Here would I strive, and this would I control.[17]

> (*Da herrschet Well' auf Welle kraftbegeistet,*
> *Zieht sich zurück, und es ist nichts geleistet,*
> *Was zur Verzweiflung mich beängstigen könnte!*
> *Zwecklose Kraft unbändiger Elemente!*
> *Da wagt mein Geist, sich selbst zu überfliegen;*
> *Hier möcht' ich kämpfen, dies möcht' ich besiegen.*)

Faust's attempt to undo the autonomous rhythms of the present has the natural consequence that the moment is fundamentally depleted. No moment can find consummation. Faust is and must be unsatisfied at every instant ("*Er, unbefriedigt jeden Augenblick!*"[18]). Despite his riches, there is always something he still does not have.

> Thus 'tis a pang of deadly stealth
> To feel what's missing in our wealth.[19]

> (*So sind am härtsten wir gequält,*
> *Im Reichtum fühlend, was uns fehlt.*)

Hostile to whatever *is* ("Accursèd is that here!"[20]), he has to look out for something else, and supposedly better, never seeing in the present moment exactly that very special occasion for which the goose was saved.

> Faced with bliss or faced with sorrow,
> He defers it to the morrow,
> Always on the future waiting,
> Nothing ever consummating.[21]

> (*Sei es Wonne, sei es Plage,*
> *Schiebt er's zu dem andern Tage,*
> *Ist der Zukunft nur gewärtig,*
> *Und so wird er niemals fertig.*)

---

[17] p. 221, line 10216 ff. (Act IV).
[18] line 11452.
[19] p. 258, line 11251f.
[20] p. 257, line 11233.
[21] p. 265f., line 11463 ff.

The other way around, not being able to receive what arrives in each present, it becomes absolutely necessary for Faust to strive of his own accord for the yonder or to be constantly on the lookout for some fulfillment to come in the future (just as, conversely, the orientation toward the future/beyond deprives the moment of its own substance). Faust lives out of a deep resentment, his overriding emotions and mood in the last act are envy, grudge, anger, and annoyance. His glance is gloomy. As he is governed by an orientation toward the future, it is not surprising that Goethe has the allegorical figure of this attitude appear in person: *Sorge*, the spirit of care, worry, anxiousness.

Sorge brings blindness to old Faust. However, blindness is here neither a contingent impairment of old age nor a punishment or after-effect, but Faust's (or modern man's) essence. The end of his life merely brings out in the open allegorically what Faust has been all along. To be governed by the spirit of futurity is to be blind: if the exclusive present that modern man lives in is one of Worry for the future, then the present (gift) of *this* present to man is blindness for what is, as we have seen, the incapability of seeing the present as the moment of arrival—as precisely that special occasion for which the goose was saved.

The hostility to any present turns even against itself. This is shown by Faust's closing his eyes to the one visitor coming specifically to him from without his own present as the embodiment of his mode of existence. Although he has obviously been long in the hands of *Sorge* as his Mistress, he refuses to acknowledge her power.

> But you, O Care, in stealing action hid,
> Creep with a power I will acknowledge never.[22]
>
> (*Doch deine Macht, o Sorge, schleichend groß,
> Ich werde sie nicht anerkennen.*)

He does not realize that *Sorge* demonstrates her power precisely by making you believe you can escape her, such as through great hopes for the future and fantastic projects to bring about the bliss of generations. Faust still believes *Sorge* to be something alien to and outside of him that can be denied entrance. He does not see that she has already come in, is already his. This is why Faust is truly blind, deluded also about the very power that has motivated him all along.

---

[22] p. 266, line 11493 f.

However, this is not his "mistake," but a necessary consequence of being in *Sorge*: it is the very nature of Worry to exist only *as* the attempt to escape from herself, by means of great hopes for the future, and it is the nature of this ontological blindness not to see its own blindness. Thus Faust, having just become blind, says,

> Deep falls the night, in gloom precipitate;
> What then? Clear light within my mind shines still.[23]

> (*Die Nacht scheint tiefer tief hereinzudringen,*
> *Allein im Innern leuchtet helles Licht.*)

His subjective inner vision of a Utopia—the very thing that blinds Faust to what really is here and now—is glorified as the true light.

This remains true down to his death. The anticipation of the future prevents a fulfilled present, even during his moment of dying.

> Foreknowledge comes, and fills me with such bliss,
> I take my joy, my highest moment this.[24]

> (*Im Vorgefühl von solchem hohen Glück*
> *Genieß' ich jetzt den höchsten Augenblick.*)

These final words of Faust's make the emptiness of his highest moment obvious: it has no content of its own, no present, only foreknowledge, anticipation of an imagined future. As he had lived, even so he dies—on credit.

This is underlined all the more by the fact that Goethe makes it clear to us that Faust is hopelessly deluded, his hopes for the future being a vain illusion. Hearing during his death scene the noises of his workers, he believes that they are working on his gigantic land reclamation project, which is to bring lasting bliss to future mankind.

> I work that millions may possess this space,
> If not secure, a free and active race.
> Here man and beast, in green and fertile fields,
> Will know the joys that new-won region yields,
> Will settle on the firm slopes of a hill
> Raised by a bold and zealous people's skill.

---

[23] p. 267, line 11499 f.
[24] p 270, line 11585 f.

A paradise our closed-in land provides,
Though to its margin rage the lustering tides;
When they eat through, in fierce devouring flood,
All swiftly join to make the damage good.[25]

(*Eröffn' ich Räume vielen Millionen,*
Nicht sicher zwar, doch tätig-frei zu wohnen.
Grün das Gefilde, fruchtbar; Mensch und Herde
Sogleich behaglich auf der neusten Erde,
Gleich angesiedelt an des Hügels Kraft,
Die aufgewälzt kühn-emsige Völkerschaft.
Im Innern hier ein paradiesisch Land,
Da rase draußen Flut bis auf zum Rand,
Und wie sie nascht, gewaltsam einzuschießen,
Gemeindrang eilt, die Lücke zu verschließen.)

The depth psychologist cannot help but be reminded here of a famous metaphor in a passage by Freud, in which he describes the purpose of psychoanalysis. "For their object is to strengthen the ego, to make it more independent of the super-ego, to widen its field of vision, and so to extend its organization that it can take over new portions of the id. Where id was, there shall ego be. It is reclamation work, like the draining of the Zuyder Zee."[26]

But Faust has been blinded by *Sorge*, so that he does not see what is actually going on. We, the readers, know better, for Mephistopheles, the voice of truth as so often, informs us about what really is going on. The noise is from the Lemures who are by no means working on Faust's irrigation ditch (*Graben*), but rather on his grave (*Grab*).[27] Goethe, in this fantastic, uncanny scene, gives voice to modern man's humanistic vision of a future paradise, of social progress, or of what the Marxist philosopher Ernst Bloch would call the "principle of hope," the "anticipation of the not-yet" and the "concrete utopia." But at the same time, Goethe portrays this very vision as stemming from utter blindness and delusion. We learn from Mephistopheles' running counterpoint commentary that there will by no means be a future paradise. Goethe, much rather, lets us know

---

[25] p. 269, line 11563–11572.
[26] Sigmund Freud, *New Introductory Lectures on Psycho-Analysis*, ed. Ernest Jones, trans. W. J. H. Sprott (London: Hogarth Press, 1957), no. 24, p. 106.
[27] line 11558.

what this future, brought about by inhospitable man, is really
heading for: destruction, annihilation.

> And yet you work for us alone:
> Your dykes and quays prepare a revel
> For Neptune, the old water-devil,
> His pleasure do you serve, my friend.
> Now, damned and lost, hope leaves your side–
> We are with elements allied,
> And ruin will follow in the end.[28]

> (*Du bist doch nur für uns bemüht*
> *Mit deinen Dämmen, deinen Buhnen;*
> *Denn du bereitest schon Neptunen,*
> *Dem Wasserteufel, großen Schmaus.*
> *In jeder Art seid ihr verloren; –*
> *Die Elemente sind mit uns verschworen,*
> *Und auf Vernichtung läuft's hinaus.*)

"*Und auf Vernichtung läuft's hinaus.*" What else could an attitude
whose essence it is to be *against* that which *is* be headed for? But in
the light of what we learned from Philemon, we may realize that it is
not only the actual event in the end that is the disaster, but already
the narrative mode, this ever jumping to the next moment and waiting
for something great to happen or to be accomplished. To be "out for"
the great utopia means in itself to be heading for annihilation.

But just as Faust strives for a "closed-in land," no longer open to
the waves of the sea, and just as his blindness shuts him off in his own
delusional inner world ("Deep falls the night, in gloom precipitate;/
What then? Clear light within my mind shines still"[29]—*we* know
how "clear" this light is!), so he no longer communicates with
Mephistopheles, nor even hears what the latter has to say. Rather,
Faust and Mephistopheles, ego-consciousness and the unconscious
personality, now speak in separate parallel or interspersed
monologues, with the only difference that Faust is totally locked in
his private fantasy (his *ídios kósmos*), whereas Mephistopheles, very
much aware of what Faust is saying, provides his commentary from
the other side. By having the formal appearance of a dialogue, while

---

[28] p. 268 (last line of translation modified), line 11544 ff.
[29] p. 267, line 11499f.

at the same time being the opposite of a dialogue, this scene makes Faust's alienation and the disintegration of the "total personality" all the more painfully obvious.

In *Faust II* Goethe analyzed prophetically the decidedly dissociated ontological state of the modern technological world (or the dissociated psychological state of modern man's consciousness) and its impending consequences, of which we now, towards the end of the 20th century, are slowly beginning to become collectively aware: the threat of the destruction of our natural world. And we may realize that Goethe's 5th act is a kind of retelling of the ancient Philemon myth *from the other side*, the one that Ovid merely mentions but does not focus on: a retelling from the perspective of the ungodly race, whose destination, it seems, is to be consumed in the flood, in Neptune's revel. Goethe makes it very clear: it is the erection of dykes against the advent of the elemental tidal waves (the erection of what Freud later was to call the "unshakeable bulwark against the black tide of mud of Occultism"[30]) that is the very cause of the ultimate destruction through the elemental flood. It is the counter-phobic defense, this whole paranoid system of dykes and ditches *designed* by blind Faust to bring a future world *free from* the Other, that in truth unwittingly draws near the very powers it fears. We are reminded of the nuclear weapons, originally intended to bring about eternal peace, that nevertheless threaten us with a total apocalypse.

It is very moving to see seventy-, eighty-year-old Goethe, with total honesty and obedience toward that which is, poetically create this Faustian world of idealistic striving and admit its dissociated, self-defeating structure, its self-centered hostility towards the "earth" and the Gods. For this admission also meant the definitive, even though not express renunciation of his own classical *"symbolische Weltanschauung,"* a *Weltanschauung* that Goethe after all had with so much effort tried to acquire for himself and had for so many years tried to defend against the adverse forces of his age and the truths of modernism.[31] His own view, even though seemingly much closer to Philemon's than to that of the Faust of the last two acts due to its neo-Platonic cast, in truth nevertheless belongs on the side of Faust,

---

[30] *MDR*, p. 147.
[31] Andrew O. Jászi, *Entzweiung und Vereinigung. Goethes symbolische Weltanschauung* (Heidelberg: Stiehm, 1973).

inasmuch as it is a defense against the tidal waves of his time and the opposite of a reception of the guest calling on him. In *Faust*, however, Goethe portrayed what he had feared so deeply, not only in its external factual appearance, but penetrating with an astounding clear-sightedness (and foresight!) to its inner image, its imaginal motive forces, thereby finally letting it be, receiving it hospitably.

*   *   *

Returning to Jung now, after having seen what the Faustian mode of being-in-the-world is heading for, we may understand better why he thought it necessary to provide a sanctuary for Philemon and a place of atonement for Faust. Bollingen could be this sanctuary, for it was the place whose specific purpose it was to give room to visitations.

> At Bollingen I am in the midst of my true life, I am most deeply myself. Here I am, as it were, the "age old son of the mother." That is how alchemy puts it, very wisely, for the "old man," the "ancient," whom I had already experienced as a child, is personality No. 2, who has always been and always will be. ... In my fantasies he took the form of Philemon, and he comes to life again at Bollingen. ... here is a space for the spaceless kingdom of the world's and psyche's hinterland.[32]

As opposed to his Küsnacht dwelling, where Jung functioned in his professional capacity and received patients, visitors, and letters from all over the world—literal guests, Bollingen was his place of silence and solitude where he could receive the images, thoughts, and reveries, the waves of the lake, the "animals that come and go,"[33] and where he could house the ancestor spirits in hearth and cooking pot. Here, pumping his own water, chopping wood, lighting the old lamps, cooking his own meals, Jung lived in the modesty and simplicity that is reminiscent of the lifestyle and living conditions of the old couple Philemon and Baucis, both in the ancient tale and in *Faust*, and very far removed from any heroic endeavors, whether they be a Faustian land reclamation and conquest of the world or his own work as a scholar and writer ("Here the torment of creation is lessened"[34]).

---

[32] *MDR*, p. 214.
[33] *Ibid.*
[34] *Ibid.*

There is, of course, one additional link connecting Jung to Philemon and making Philemon important for Jung. During his period of active imagination in the years 1913 ff., there appeared to Jung a figure that Jung called Philemon. This Philemon at first glance seems to have no similarity to either Ovid's or Goethe's Philemon. He was a pagan and belonged into an Egyptian-Hellenistic world with a Gnostic cast. But on a deeper level, it is very easy to see why Jung called this fantasy figure by the same name as the figure of the ancient tale. It was this Philemon who taught Jung that there are things in the soul that he does not make, but that make themselves and have a life of their own, just like animals in the woods or people in a room or birds in the air. So this Philemon was the psychagogue who taught Jung psychological objectivity, the *Wirklichkeit der Seele* (the "reality of the soul").[35]

Granting fantasy images the dignity of an objective reality is nothing else but the very act of receiving them hospitably. The kind of reception that we are concerned with here does not mean that we (the ego) "are for" or "say yes to" or "accept" everything. It has nothing to do with an ego action or attitude; what *we* think about them and whether we are for or against them is not all that important, because it is decidedly secondary. Rather, reception means housing the fantasy images in our psychological "theory" and thus in our ontology by giving them the place of honor and the status of objectively real *animalia* and *daimones*. The Gods do not want our siding with or opting for them, not our "developing" them in ourselves or searching for them according to a conception of the individuation process in terms of a heroic quest or of a journey through the Christian night—this is what the ego may think, in order to boost its importance; they want something else, something at the same time more simple and more fundamental, more radical. *They want to be ontologically acknowledged and respected.*

Seen in this light, it was not only Bollingen that provided a sanctuary for Philemon in Jung's world but also his psychology. By *naming* the persons of the soul—Anima, Old Wise Man, Great Mother, Philemon, Elias, Salome—and by developing his theory of archetypes and the idea of the reality of the psyche, Jung provided just this ontological recognition of the objectivity of the *daimones*.

---

[35] Cf. *MDR*, p. 176.

Here one might object that my playing down the importance of our being for or against the Gods and my stressing theory and names instead reduce the theme of hospitality to a mere question of terminology and theoretical constructs, leaving out (or even devaluing) the realm of real life and felt experience. This is a possible way of looking at it. But I would move in the opposite direction. Instead of viewing the shift in emphasis (from our quest and affirmation to ontology and theory) as a reduction to "mere theory," I would prefer it if this shift were seen as an expansion and revaluation of our conventional idea of theory and as the recovery of a deeper dimension of theory: theorizing and naming as an authentic *ritual* activity, which brings about decisive and very real change. For what does Jung's addition of the construct "archetype" to psychological theory mean? Now that the *daimones* are moored in theory, there is no basis for reducing them to "nothing but fantasy" any more, no possibility for building dykes against the tidal waves in order to create a *free* "closed-in land" of purely human measure and no way to make theory a "bulwark against the tide of mud of occultism"—for the tidal waves are already, and irrevocably so, at *this* side of any potential dam. Now Faust's final vision and hope that when the blustering tides "eat through [the dykes], in fierce devouring flood, / All swiftly join to make the damage good" makes no sense any more. The damage—if it is a damage—can no longer be made good. Jung's theory of archetypes has already opened the door: the stranger[36] (*hostis* to the Faust, *hospes* to the Philemon in us) is already inside the house.

---

[36] "The strange guest" was also a figure in Jung's active imaginations (see *Briefe III*, letter to Sir Herbert Read, 2.IX.1960, p.338, note 6.) In this letter (*Letters 2*, pp. 590f.), we also find the following sentences: "Who is the awe-inspiring guest who knocks at our door portentously?" "All his [the artist's] love and passion (his 'values') flow toward the coming guest to proclaim his arrival."

CHAPTER ELEVEN

Rupture, or: Psychology and Religion

T he subtitle I have chosen for this paper within the limits of the general topic "Religion and Human Sciences in the Contemporary World" may give rise to the expectation that a report follows on the empirical findings of psychology concerning the problem of religion in the human psyche of modern man and on the position psychology takes in this regard. But I cannot simply go ahead and turn to our subject matter. For the word 'psychology,' when placed in the phrase 'psychology and religion' and when seen in the context of the general theme of this symposium, contains some difficulties we should not ignore. So, rather than proceeding to what psychology has to say *about* religion, let us turn psychology back on itself. But it may turn out that such a reflection will also lead to an answer to the question raised by the theme of our symposium, a more adequate one than if we were to proceed directly with psychology's findings about, and its views on, religion.

The first problem is the embarrassing fact that, strictly speaking, there is no such thing as psychology in the singular, but only a multitude of psychologies of often very different, if not mutually exclusive, convictions. We have no difficulties with the fact that there are many religions or, within one religion, many denominations. But

Editor's Note: About twelve scholars from various disciplines, about half of them from Japan and the other half from other countries, had been invited to discuss together the theme of "Religion and Human Science in the Contemporary World" at the Sixth Kyoto Zen Symposium, which took place from March 8 to March 13, 1988 at Hotel Rantei in Kyoto, Japan. The paper on "Rupture" was Giegerich's contribution to this Symposium.

the plural 'psychologies' is hard to accept. Psychology's division into many different schools, or denominations, detracts from its standing as a science. It seems to turn psychology into a kind of religion itself, a number of sects with corresponding practices. This would mean that we could not legitimately speak of psychology *and* religion at all, as if they were two completely different categories. Both would, so to speak, belong on the same side of the 'and.' We would be dealing with an intrareligious difference, not with a difference between religion and something else. I cannot go into this problem here,[1] but merely list it as a first indication both of the strange relationship between psychology and religion and of the fact that psychology obviously does not fit in the conventional idea of a human science. I will restrict myself to the qualification that when I speak of psychology, I mean psychology as understood in the Jungian tradition: analytical psychology, and more specifically archetypal psychology in the sense of James Hillman.

Secondly, it will be noted that the phrase 'in our contemporary world' contained in the general topic has been dropped from my heading. My title sounds as if I raise the question of the atemporal relationship between psychology and religion. But this is only seemingly so. Psychology is not only historically speaking a very new science (as depth psychology it is a child of this century), but it is also intrinsically linked to our contemporary world. From the very beginning, analytical psychology (as well as Freudian psychoanalysis, for that matter) has at bottom been nothing less than an attempt to give an answer to modern man's predicament, to 'neurosis,' as it was termed. To be sure, neurosis was discovered as a kind of malfunction or disorder within the individual, and this personalistic perspective has remained the framework for many psychologists. But without always being conscious and explicit about it, depth psychology has, from the very beginning, viewed neurosis within a wider cultural context and in the light of the Western mythological and religious tradition, for which the 'Oedipus complex' is the most famous example. What guided psychoanalytic thought factually but more or less unconsciously all along, was raised into consciousness and given a systematic expression in Jung's theory of a collective unconscious and an objective, transpersonal psyche. Now, after more than 80 years of

---

[1] Wolfgang Giegerich, "Jungian Psychology: A Baseless Enterprise: Reflections on Our Identity as Jungians," see Chapter Seven in this volume.

psychoanalysis, we can say: psychology has been an attempt to give an account of and raise into consciousness what had dropped out, been lost, or repressed on the way to modernism. Jung said it quite explicitly: "My problem [as a psychologist and in contradistinction to other psychological schools] is to wrestle with the big monster of the historical past, the great snake of the centuries, the burden of the human mind, the problem of Christianity."[2] Jung understood that "without history there can be no psychology, and certainly no psychology of the unconscious."[3]

By giving psychology this task of wrestling with the big monster of our past, Jung did two things to psychology (as understood here). (1) He defined psychology as being always therapeutic psychology, even where it is theoretical and deals with the large issues of our tradition and our age. When conceived as a big monster or as the snake of the centuries, history is no longer the neutral scientific object that it is for the historian. It is a vis-à-vis, almost an animal to wrestle with, something that involves us on a personal, existential level, the level of a therapeutic engagement. (2) Therapy is no longer restricted to the confines of personal problems and personal biography, but is, even where it is the therapy of the individual and his personal problems, always also a therapy of our collective history. It always adresses itself and answers to our concrete historical situation. Psychology is no longer viewed as an anthropological science in search of atemporal truths, but is always relative to a specific historical situation.

True, there have been attempts (one notable example: Malinowski) to prove the timeless and transcultural validity of, e.g., the Oedipus complex, in other words, attempts to turn psychology into the study of the timeless structure and workings of the psyche, ultimately the study of the abstract 'condition humaine' as if psychology were a kind of anthropology and could conceive of itself as something like physics, which understands itself as the study of the timeless organisation of the universe, or like biology, which is seen as the science of the timeless structure and functioning of the living organism. But this interest in timeless essences in the tradition of Western Platonism is not really in keeping with psychology's central vision and vocation. Psychology is called to leave the heights and purity of neutral, intersubjective studies

---

[2] *CW* 18 § 279.
[3] *MDR*, pp. 205f.

and go down into our *real* mess, into what Jung once called the slime and mud at the bottom of the human soul,[4] without however forgetting that the "real mess" is not personal, individualistic, private, but comprises in itself the specific collective situation, which in turn preserves within itself all previous history.

So it would have been more than superfluous to retain the phrase 'in our contemporary world' in my title. It would have been misleading, suggesting that psychology could be *applied*, like an abstract, neutral theory, to our contemporary world, whereas the (therapeutic) involvement with the here and now is *inherent* in the very notion of psychology. Psychology is always speaking about our real (contemporary) situation, even where it overtly may be speaking about ancient mythology or medieval alchemy, etc. It has 'our contemporary world' *inside itself* as its moment (in Hegel's sense), not out there as an object of study that it may turn to or not. In fact, this sense of 'inside of itself,' this intrinsic interiority of its subject matter, whatever it may be, is what constitutes the psychological mode of thinking or what renders psychology psychological.

It is no mere accident of history that psychology was one of the very last 'sciences' to have originated. It could emerge only once all the major sciences had been firmly established, and modernity had come to its fruition through or along with them. For psychology must not be understood as just one of the sciences, differing from them only in having a different subject. Its emergence does not only mean the discovery of a new field or subject of investigation, of a new *Fach* (specialized discipline) beside all the other specializations. Psychology must, rather, be comprehended as the conquest of an altogether new level of reflection beyond that of the sciences, as something like the 'conscience' (in a non-moral sense) of the sciences, as the discipline whose business it is to reflect the changes brought about by the sciences to the psyche, i.e., to our being-in-the-world, and to raise into consciousness, *within* the modern world, the gains and losses brought *by* this modern world as a whole. Because psychology has the job of understanding, it must stand under, on a lower, deeper level than the sciences. It goes to the ground out of which the sciences came forth, the psyche.

---

[4] *Letters 2*, p. 557, to Anonymous, 7 May 1960.

In the quote from Jung where he speaks about the great snake of the centuries, he also named the 'problem of Christianity' as one possible way of formulating what he is concerned with as a psychologist. Again we note that psychology does not have to be applied to religion, here Christianity, but that for Jung at least, Christianity and the problems it involves for our being-in-the-world are, to begin with, what psychology is about. Religion, too, is *inside psychology*, not out there. And thus, strictly speaking, there is no, cannot be, any 'and' between psychology and religion, because the religious problem is psychology's very own problem and not only the problem *of* this or that religion (or *of* religion at large) out there. The psychologist who would follow Jung can neither study religion from the outside as a neutral object, nor, like a believer in one of the religions, approach religion from the basis of confessional involvement. He approaches religion as his, as the soul's very own burden and predicament—to quote Jung: "as the historical burdens Christianity has heaped upon us."[5]

Religion as a burden—what does this mean? One might think that it expresses a negative, critical stance toward religion—religion experienced as the guilty party, and therefore something to be gotten rid of or to be fought against. But what is meant here is almost the opposite. Religion here is *accepted* as our own burden, as our very own problem to struggle with. Religion as a burden is in me, is myself, not my opponent out there. I tried to suggest above that psychology is not on the same level as the sciences; it stands under the plane on which the sciences are located. The same seems to be true for psychology's relation to religion. Both the believers or theologians and the critics of religion (such as Voltaire, Marx, Nietzsche) experience religion, logically speaking, on the same level. The only difference is that the ones say Yes to religion and are for it, whereas the others say No to it and are against it. The level of consciousness is the same. The fact, however, that Jung saw in religion a great burden from which he *suffered* is the sign that he experienced it on an entirely *new level* of consciousness.

What I am trying to suggest here is that psychology does not, just like that, fit in the general theme of this symposium as it has been

---

[5] *CW* 18 § 279.

formulated because it holds a very peculiar position both with respect to the human sciences and with respect to religion. Psychology bursts the concepts contained in the formulation of this topic, and to be what bursts these concepts (and the frame of mind that they involve as well) is what psychology is about. Let me put it in Hegelian terms. Before I do this however, we have to realize that Jung, like the other pioneers of psychology, started out from the daily practice of psychotherapy and not from a well-worked-out theory. The theoretical ideas came (not only historically, but also) logically(!) *after* practical experience. Formulated theory is thus logically not always quite up to the logic inherent in the discoveries and concerns of the psychologists themselves, especially so, since Jung, oddly enough, prided himself on being an empiricist, apparently not realizing what a disservice he was doing to his own work. Very often, revolutionary ideas were expressed in terms of categories of thought that belong to quite conventional, outdated modes of thinking, truly new wine was put into old containers—because the empiricist bias prevented the logical clarification of the new ideas. So when I want to express the logical status of psychology in Hegelian terms, I refer to the status actually inherent in the main thrust of the psychological realities themselves that showed themselves to Jung, but I am not immediately concerned with the status that suggests itself from the terms and categories Jung used to formulate his psychological discoveries theoretically.

Psychology is the discipline whose job it is to transgress from the logical status of 'essence' (*Wesen*) to the status of *Begriff* (Concept or Notion) in the Hegelian sense.[6] Both science and religion (at least in the West) reside in the status of 'essence,' in what Nietzsche analysed to be the Platonism of our tradition and what Heidegger showed to be the metaphysical fetters of Western thought. When one reflects on what individual Jungian analysis, especially the so-called individuation process, ultimately is and means for the individual (what it is to bring about), and when one reflects on what the emergence of the phenomenon of psychoanalysis (both in the sense of the individuation process and of an intellectual reality) ultimately is and means for our age, one can say on both counts that it means nothing less than the

---

[6] I am greatly indebted to Bruno Liebrucks, *Sprache und Bewußtsein*, 7 vols., Akademische Verlagsgesellschaft, Frankfurt (later Verlag Peter Lang, Bern *et. al.*) 1964-1979 for my understanding of Hegel's logic.

fall from one level of consciousness to another, the fall from one logical status onto a lower (or higher) one. This is what I mean by the peculiar position of psychology with respect to both the sciences and religion.

We must realize that religion as we know it is not just the body of teachings, emotions, practices that make up its substance, but also the logical status or level of consciousness that it represents. Likewise, the sciences, and this applies to the human as well as to the natural sciences, are not only the system of knowledge and methods which comprise them; they are also the logical status which the modern sciences embody.

Jung at bottom had a clear knowledge that psychology had dropped to a different level and thus was no longer in the same logical status as the sciences. Reflecting on the standing of psychology as a science, Jung said, "It [psychology] must sublate itself as a science [*sich aufheben*], and precisely by doing so it reaches its scientific goal" (*CW* 8 § 429, transl. modif.). This sentence together with its context states nothing else but that psychology as a "science" is, in true Hegelian terms, the dialectical sublation (*Aufhebung*) of science. Psychology is neither science nor its undialectical opposite, an unscientific faith, a *Weltanschauung*, or what have you. It is the *concrete* negation, the determinate naught (*bestimmte Nichts*), of science. In the same vein, we must also state that psychology is neither religion (or its secular equivalent: a *Weltanschauung*, ideology) nor the undialectical opposite of religion, a neutral irreligious science. It is "sublated religion," *aufgehobene Religion*, just as it is "sublated science," no longer subject to the contradiction of science versus religion, but, by having overcome it, containing this contradiction in itself.

Even if I could not, in the space available here, explain adequately why and how psychology is the dialectical sublation of science and religion, i.e., of the entire logical status to which they both belong, two things are clear: (1) a psychology that has to be viewed this way must be an embarrassment to the prevailing mind; it does not fit into any of the categories we are accustomed to; (2) with respect to the question of religion in our contemporary world, a psychology that has to be understood as sublated religion and science transports us into a radically new situation that makes everything look very different.

Take for example nihilism and secularization, those two forces usually seen as the predicament in which religion finds itself in our age. I think that the idea of nihilism is a trap into which Nietzsche and those who followed him have walked. The problem we are faced with is not nihilism; our problem is the *interpretation* of our situation as nihilism. This interpretation is a defense against the decisive rupture from one level of consciousness to another, deeper or higher one that has long taken place. It is the attempt to account for an undeniable and radical, earth-shaking change without *suffering* it as *our* logical and psychological transformation, as *our* death and resurrection, i.e., the death and resurrection of our consciousness. By diagnosing "nihilism" or "secularization," we can keep the change out there, as a death of religion in the objective conditions in society, while rescuing the continuity of *our* mind, our ideals, expectations—our *notion* of religion. We keep the *status quo* of our mind intact and ourselves innocent ('unharmed') by blaming history out there for having led to a gradual voiding of all meaning. By admitting that nihilism is prevailing in our time, we manage to hold fast to the very categories and values as the dominants informing our *thinking* that overtly we admit having lost their validity in our *objective situation*. It is only a token admission. A real admission would amount to a sacrifice of our cherished ideas and ideals, values and categories. It would amount to "losing our minds."

Jung wrote something to the effect that our consciousness only imagines losing its Gods, whereas in reality we have merely been removed from the place where we can experience them.[7]

We have indeed been removed from the locus of traditional religions. "Truth" has emigrated to a new continent, as it were, whereas our consciousness retains the categories acquired on and suited to the old continent. What is this new continent? Prof. Nishitani has stressed one most important aspect of it: the universality or the planetary scope of the modern world. Another important aspect is the fact that today we live with the knowledge that we could literally annihilate the inhabited earth. This means psychologically that in a certain sense we are no longer irrevocably embedded in nature, but somehow above it, whether we like it and know it or not. It is the external expression of the fact that the natural world has logically been overcome, sublated, reduced to a moment in our consciousness. The natural world as a whole no longer is the sphere in which we (logically and psychologically) dwell and which

---

[7] I am here combining two passages from Jung, *Letters 2*, pp. 594 (to Serrano, 14 September 1960) and 612 (to von Koenig-Flachsfeld, 30 November 1960).

surrounds us fundamentally. It has been reduced to a 'thing' or content in the (as yet unknown, but already *real*) new sphere of our existence.

A third aspect of the "new continent" on which our existence now takes place is the perhaps still more serious fact that logically and ontologically (even if not ontically), the natural, sensual world has already been annihilated. "Truth" no longer resides on the level of things with a concrete and visible shape, but on the level of subatomic and subcellular particles. We *know* that we cannot believe our eyes, trust our senses; we know that what we *see* to be solid things *is* in reality empty space interdispersed with particles in, so to speak, cosmic distance from each other. Things have become phony, ghostlike, even if we do not admit it. We no longer need the Christian teaching of "I have overcome the world," nor the Zen idea of "no image," nor religious methods to free us from the sensual world and allow us to achieve "emptiness"—because what religions once presented as a promise or goal to strive for, or as an inner truth, has long become an accomplished fact, a quasi-"empirical" reality out there in the things themselves. Religion (whose striving for spiritual liberation from the literal world happened only in man's subjective interiority) has been overtaken by objective, indeed physical, reality, so that the central efforts and aspirations of religion lag behind the actual state of affairs. No need to preach to us not to save things that moths and rust destroy (Matt. 6:19), for in a throw-away society this is already the objective logic inherent in the *things* we use. Nothing we collect to "lay up riches" can make us rich any more, because even the most expensive things, such as a $30-million painting, have ontologically become cheap, as is evident precisely from the inflated price.

There has been a fundamental change. The 'same' sun that man saw 3,000 years ago is no longer the same. We can no longer *legitimately* speak of a sunrise, as in mythic times, let alone *see* the God or the Goddess in it. The 'sunrise' is at best a subjective *Erlebnis* in our "*Lebenswelt*" (Husserl), which however is a privatized world without objective validity.

The rupture that has taken place seems to consist in the fact that the world to which the known religions were answers has, as it were, moved out from under them. We are now confronted with a logically entirely new world, to which religion no longer corresponds. The "question" that the world, while constituted as the "natural world," posed in its entirety, i.e., as the sphere in which man psychologically lived, has been answered exhaustively over the last 2,500 years. Now a changed world, one that exists on the post-natural subatomic level, represents a totally new "question." The "conversation" between the world and man, of which the arts, religion, philosophy, the political organization, and culture in general are the record, has moved on to the next question, as it were. Have the traditional religions not been objectively brought into a similar situation as that of the horse-drawn carriages of old? They too are still popular in places of tourism, but only as something definitively obsolete. And only *because* they are obsolete can they fulfill our nostalgic longing. I don't think that the religions (as personal faith, as literal practices) are threatened today; on the contrary, they enjoy increasing popularity. What is threatened, however, is that logical status or level of consciousness of which religion is an embodiment. However, it seems wrong to speak of a threat, since the destruction or overcoming of the logic, *as* which religion *is*, is already a *fait accompli*. This logic has been rendered something of the past by the objective course of history, whereas the products of this logic, the literal religions, extend into our age and are even preserved, much like medieval paintings and other relics of the past are preserved, even after the world in which they belong has irrevocably disappeared.

Now, at the end of the 20th century, as we learn more about early history and gain more objective distance to our own tradition, we slowly come into a position that allows us to see that religion as such may have been only an *interlude* in the history of man, in contrast to one of the eternals of human existence. By saying this, I do not want to advocate any kind of atheistic, agnostic, nihilistic position. Rather, I think in terms of Heino Gehrts's historical vision. Gehrts distinguishes four fundamentally different stages of cultural development, those of the shamanistic, the ritualistic, the religious, and the scientific (or technological) cultures.[8] Shamanism and the practices and beliefs of ritualistic cultures and the so-called high religions are not lumped together under the general heading of "religion." Rather, according to this view, a most fundamental hiatus,

---

[8] Cf., e.g., Heino Gehrts, "Vom Weltenbaum zum brennenden Baum. Die kulturellen Entwicklungsstufen im Geborgenheitserlebnis", GORGO 13, 1987, pp. 41-66 or *idem*, *Von der Wirklichkeit der Märchen* (Regensburg: Erich Röth Verlag, 1992), especially the introduction and chapter 1.

indeed a watershed, separates the first two cultures from the religious one, a much more radical hiatus than is to be found between the shamanistic and the ritualistic cultures or between the religious and the scientific cultures. Religion is relative to one stage of cultural development only. It did not exist 3,000 years ago. It may not exist in the future.

This vision is very helpful. It makes it easier for us to let go (not just of the specific contents, but of the very notion) of religion without having to fear that then we must succumb to nihilism. In fact, we can see that the problem of nihilism arises only for him who may be willing to resign himself to the "death of God [or of other contents of religion]," but only to cling all the more, in his secret expectations or as his hidden demand, to the idea of religion. We can understand that more than the sacrifice of the contents of religion and less than our reconciliation with absolute nihilism is demanded of us. Today it is merely a question of the rupture from one stage to another. Just as shamanism and the ritualistic mode of being-in-the-world were superseded by religion, now religion seems to be in the process of being superseded by something new, of which we as yet have no idea.

'Religion' is only the answer to or correlate of that world that was constellated as the *natural* world, the world as experienced by "common, natural consciousness" in the modern sense of 'natural.' This is not *the* world. It, too, did not always exist and, as we already pointed out, it has, ontologically speaking, begun to cease to exist for us. The world during the shamanistic age was a very different one, and this is why man's answer to the world at that time was not religion but shamanism.

I would therefore not ask what we can expect from religion and what concrete measures need to be taken to realize our expectations. I would not think about how to rescue our various religious traditions and bring them over into the changed world of today. For any such attempt would in my eyes only amount to an attempt to rescue the logical status or level of consciousness that we are subjectively living in and comfortably accustomed to and to freeze us psychologically in the past, while objectively we have for long been living in a reality characterized by a new logical status. The rupture in the objective world out there necessitates a corresponding rupture in us, and in us not as persons, but as the logic or psychology as which we live. It is not enough to try to adapt our religions to our new situation, it is not them that have to be adjusted. It is us. And this is why I think the answer to the problem of religion in our contemporary world is "psychology"—not psychology as a particular science, as this or that school of thought, but psychology as a move to be made, the move of turning the question of religion back onto ourselves, onto that which is closest to us: our status of consciousness; in other words, psychology as the realization of the unavoidable necessity of the death to be died by our frame of mind.

As long as we cling to our religions, we blind ourselves to the divine that would show itself in utterly new and unimagined shape from within our real world. We would monotonously repeat the same old answer, even after a new question has been asked. We *are* removed from the place at which we would be able to see, as Jung said, but of course not because *we* have moved away, but rather because we stubbornly stationed ourselves at the old locus of truth and did not go along, in our subjective consciousness, with the move made by our objective consciousness, the "implicit" (*ansichseiende*) psychology or logic inherent in our modern world itself.

Maybe the time has come to apply the Christian "Blessed are the poor in spirit" to Christianity itself, to religion as such; and to apply the emptiness that was hitherto sought *within* Zen to Zen itself as a whole. We have to learn (not to strive for emptiness, but) to live with and in the emptiness that already prevails. We don't need (actively) to sacrifice our religions, nor the notion and status of religion as such. The sacrifice in question here is one that has already been objectively inflicted upon us. We only need to own it, to allow it to *be*. Religiously and metaphysically, we stand with empty hands. This is what Jung saw too. He compared us to beggars who, by borrowing exotic religious ideas from other cultures that are not our own, try to pose as theater kings. And he said, "... [S]o spiritual poverty seeks to renounce the false riches of the spirit in order to withdraw not only from the sorry remnants ... of a great past, but also from all the allurements of the odorous East; in order to, finally, turn within to one's inner self, where, in the cold light of consciousness, the blank barrenness of the world reaches to the very stars."[9]

---

[9] C. G. Jung, *CW* 9i § 29, transl. modif.

We have to learn to *suffer* our hands to be empty, in the fullest sense of the word suffer. No image. No symbols. No meaning. No Gods: No religion.

For is it not the empty hand, and the empty hand alone, that can be filled? As long as we cling to our religious traditions, we pretend to be in possession of something. We thereby prevent the advent of what can come, if at all, only as the free gift of the real world to him who is ready to receive because he has nothing whatsoever of his own accord, as the gift to him who no longer, with a modesty that is disguised arrogance, denounces our poverty as nihilism, but comprehends it as the presence of the unknown future.

CHAPTER TWELVE

Deliverance from the Stream of Events
Okeanos and the Circulation of the Blood

In his book *H₂O and the Waters of Forgetfulness*, Ivan Illich discusses the history of the imagination of water as stuff. Water has not always been H_2O, as we might assume, being used to our scientific thinking. That it came to be H_2O, after once having been mythical water, has a long history.

An essential element of this history is, according to Illich, the invention of the circulation of blood by William Harvey (1628). For it was blood that for the first time gave rise to the idea that a stuff circulates within itself, an idea that in the long run became essential also for city planning. As Illich shows, the idea that we now take for granted, that water, just as it is piped into the city, must leave the city by its sewers is very modern. I quote a longer passage from Illich's text:

> The modern idea of a 'stuff' that follows its destined path, streaming forever back to its source, was still foreign to Renaissance thought. The concept of 'circulation' and not only its embodiment in the blood represents a profound break with the past. The newness of the idea of circulation is perhaps as crucial for the transformation of the imagination as was Kepler's decision to replace the translucent spheres carrying a luminous planet (in which Copernicus still believed) with the new elliptical orbits traveled by rocky globes. Circulation is as new and as fundamental an idea as gravitation, preservation of energy,

evolution, or sexuality. But neither the radical newness of the idea of circulating 'stuff' nor its impact on the constitution of modern space has been studied with the same attention that was given to Kepler's laws or to the ideas of Newton, Helmholtz, Darwin, or Freud.

Bodies had always been able to circle around a center. The abstract concept of circular motion had lent itself to influential metaphors. The presence of the center 'altogether at once' at each point of its circle's periphery had been a symbol for God, soul, and eternity. Time too was thought by many schools to pass in circles. The phoenix was the symbol of renewal by fire; Plato described cyclical renewal as a periodic flood. Souls were able to be born and reborn again. But the connection between 'waters' and what we call circulation had not been made. Before Harvey the 'circulation' of a liquid meant what we call 'evaporation': the separation of a 'spirit' from a 'water,' for instance the distillation of liquor from wine, or the process of 'spiritualization' by which blood was assumed to pass through the septum (we now consider impenetrable) from the left to the right of the brain. The idea of a material that flows forever back to its own source constitutes a major innovation in the perception of water, a transubstantiation of its 'stuff.'

The first liquid to which 'circulation' was ascribed was the blood ....[1]

The radical change in the imagination with the beginning of the modern age emphasized by Illich cannot be underscored too much. This change indeed has the character of a revolution. It means an ontological transformation: a change of man and his world in their *Being*. It is not merely a shift in scientific theories: the world itself and we along with it have truly become different through this seemingly only intellectual revolution.

But as regards the invention of the circulation of blood by Harvey in the 17th century, it seems to me that the radical newness is not exactly where Illich is placing it. It is not really completely new that a stuff, and water at that, circulates in itself and returns into its source.

---

[1] Ivan Illich, *H₂O and the Waters of Forgetfulness*: Reflections on the Historicity of "Stuff" (Dallas: The Dallas Institute of Humanities and Culture, 1985), chapter "Harvey Invents Circulation." On Harvey and the discovery of the blood circulation from a psychological, imaginal perspective see the essential study by James Hillman, "The Thought of the Heart," *Eranos 48–1979* (Frankfurt: Insel, 1981), pp. 133–82.

Therefore, the undisputed revolutionary novelty of the discovery of the circulation of blood seems to me to be of a different nature.

For the idea of a stream of water circulating in itself and returning into its beginning belongs to the oldest and universal stock of mythical imaginings. It is the idea of an ocean completely surrounding the flat disc of the earth: Okeanos. Okeanos originally was not a sea proper, but a river, and accordingly masculine, and was referred to as "Father Okeanos" in contrast to the depth-psychological equation of sea = the unconscious = mother. He is called by Homer "the origin of the Gods," "the generation of all" because with his inexhaustible procreative power he had begotten everything with Tethys, the "mother," the receptive primal water goddess.[2] Similarly, the Egyptian primal ocean Nun, who, as "World Encircler," surrounded the earth, was termed "Father of the Gods."[3] There is even an extant early pictorial representation of the primal stream surrounding the earth. A New-Babylonian map of the earth from the early 6th century B.C., which however dates back to an original from the 8th or 9th century B.C. and is presumably the oldest map of the world at large, shows the primal ocean, here called "Bitter River," flowing around the circular disc of the earth.[4]

Kerényi says of the Greek primal ocean, "However, Okeanos was not an ordinary river god, since his stream was not an ordinary stream. Even after everything originated from him, he still flows *in a circle* at the outermost edge of the world, *streaming back into himself.* The rivers, springs and wells, the entire sea, they all continuously originate from his wide, strong stream. When the world was already under the rule of Zeus, he alone was allowed to remain in his old place, which actually is no place, but mere streaming, border and separation from the beyond,"[5] just as according to Hornung the Egyptian Nun is the "world-encompassing border between world and non-world, between Being and Non-Being."[6] Okeanos is pure "circular streaming."[7]

---

[2] Karl Kerényi, *Die Mythologie der Griechen*, vol. I (München: Deutscher Taschenbuch Verlag, 1979), p. 19. My translation.

[3] Erik Hornung, *Der Eine und die Vielen* (Darmstadt: Wiss. Buchgesellschaft, 1971), esp. pp. 154 and 276 f.

[4] Hermann Bengtson and Vladimir Milojcic, *Großer Historischer Weltatlas, Erläuterungen I. Teil* (München: Bayerischer Schulbuch-Verlag, 1954), col. 58.

[5] Kerényi, *ibid.*, my italics and translation.

[6] Hornung, *op. cit.*, p. 154.

[7] Kerényi, *ibid.*

Even in Plato, that is to say, outside the ancient mythological world, we find, in a philosophical myth describing the structure of the world and underworld, the following statement about the rivers: "Indeed, there are some that move in circles, wind themselves around the earth one or several times like serpents and then ... pour back again. ... Thus there are quite a few ... streams, ... of which the largest and the one flowing all around as the outermost is so-called Okeanos."[8]

Here we have in all clarity the conception of a water continuously streaming back into its source, in unending circulation. Even the etymological meaning of the word Okeanos, derived from Semitic, is supposed to be "circling."[9] Thus, the application of the idea of circulation to a liquid stuff cannot be what is novel about Harvey's discovery of the circulation of blood and what brought about an ontological change in modern man and his world. Harvey's discovery, much rather, follows a very old mythical conception, an archetypal idea, and is, with respect to its content and form, downright conventional.

What nevertheless makes Harvey's invention undoubtedly revolutionary must be something else. What this is becomes apparent if we compare the two ideas: on the one hand, the idea of a world stream, enclosing at the outermost edge of the earth and as the border between Being and Non-Being, world and non-world, everything that is and happens—on the other hand, a river circulating *in* man. This contrast must be supplemented by the complementary facts that at the time when Okeanos encompassed the earth, there didn't exist a circulating (blood-) stream in man, and that at the time when the circulation of the blood was discovered, Okeanos no longer flowed around the circular earth. The earth had by that time long turned into a globe, and at the latest, with the expeditions of Columbus (1492), Vasco da Gama (1498) and Ferdinand Magellan (who was the first to sail *around* the world, 1519-1522), the river encircling, and marking the border of, the earth disc had been breached, so that the idea of an Okeanos had psychologically become obsolete. The breach through the enclosure into the open, into the infinite, had been sealed. Once and for all, Okeanos was reduced to

---

[8] Platon, Phaidon, 112 d and e.
[9] See Weizsäcker, "Okeanos" in W. H. Roscher, *Ausführliches Lexikon der griechischen und römischen Mythologie,* 816.

a mere ocean, which, even though immense, no longer separates world and non-world. At its other bank one is no longer in danger of falling into nothingness; to the contrary, other continents just like the familiar ones open there before us, the "New World" (i.e., still truly "world"!) in contrast to what only then began to be termed the "old world." And even beyond the earth there is no nought, but the vastness of an infinite number of additional worlds.

The almost literally world-shaking quality of this change becomes evident through this comparison: what psychologically or imaginally happened through the discovery of the ciculation of blood (or what is reflected in it) is the transposition of the archetypal idea of the primal stream from out in the world into the interior of man. In the mythical age, this archetypal idea was projected into cosmic reality; now, in the scientific age, the same idea is experienced as projected onto the inside of the human body: the coursing of the blood in our veins has become the new carrier of the ancient mythical idea. Man has so to speak incorporated, interiorized Okeanos, thus freeing the world around himself from the primal river encircling it. But perhaps it would be more fitting to say that man is the victim of this process of transposition of Okeanos. With reference to a mythological motif not too far removed from ours, the motif of the four rivers (e.g., the four rivers of paradise, Gen. 2:10–14, the four rivers flowing from Mount Meru in Indian mythology, the Germanic four rivers originating from the spring Hvergelmir, etc.), David Miller formulated a similar observation: "When the mythological symbol-system dropped away in favor of a more sophisticated view of the cosmos, the rivers went underground into the human body,"[10] namely in the form of the four humors of the body in the Medieval doctrine of the temperaments.

Modern biology concretistically "acts out" this very same imaginal process of the incorporation of the ocean that Miller and I are trying critically to reflect. It has the same idea, but projects it into the literal organism and its environment. It *believes* in the interiorization of the sea through discovering a similarity in the composition of the ions in sea water and in blood (a fact of which A. J. Ziegler kindly reminded me) and by imagining, accordingly, blood as the sea taken inside the organism. Biologically, therefore, we say that man has not really become

---

[10] David L. Miller, "Achelous and the Butterfly: Toward an Archetypal Psychology of Humor," in *Spring 1973*, pp. 1–23, at p. 8.

independent of the ocean as the original element of life; rather, he carries the sea, "in" whose medium he still lives in the inside of his body, around with him, in the reduced form of the blood system. Biology, by scientifically demonstrating the idea of the interiorization of the sea to be a literal fact, fulfills psychologically the task of completing the process of this interiorization. Now the interiorization is an avowed theory, whereas with Harvey this interiorization, even if it had already become a fact, remained implicit and unconscious. If it is "scientifically proven" and an objective fact, independent of our thinking and rooted in the reality of our physical nature, that the circulating blood is our own inner "ocean," then the psychological undoing of the original nature of Okeanos as the stream *all around* us has become absolute: reified, physical.

This transformation in the history of the soul is truly tremendous, because it amounts to an inversion of Being, a turning inside out (or rather, outside in).[11] Formerly, man existentially stood in the middle of the earth, surrounded by the primal stream, and knew himself to be encircled by it on all sides; today he carries the stream of pulsating life in himself! It is obvious that this fact gave man an enormous charge or boost. For it is, as far as the objective psyche is concerned, of no small importance whether man lives with the image of the river of life surrounding everything earthly and thus also his own existence, or whether he lives with the image of the stream of life circulating in his own body. Each of the two possibilities results in a fundamentally different mode of being-in-the-world, in a different relation to himself and to the things on the earth, in an essentially different orientation outwards to the visible and tangible world and upward from the sublunar reality to the superlunar celestial sphere. Each frees the world in different ways and at the same time sets different limits.

In order to learn what existence in a world surrounded by Okeanos means, we must enter more closely into the mythical imagination of this complex of reality. For the Greek world, I rely largely on the material

---

[11] The process of the "inversion of Being" is briefly discussed in my paper "Saving the Nuclear Bomb," in Valerie Andrews, Robert Bosnak, Karen Walter Goodwin (eds.), *Facing Apocalypse* (Dallas: Spring Publications, 1987), pp. 96–108, and at greater lengths in my two volumes on the *Psychoanalyse der Atombombe* (*Die Atombombe als seelische Wirklichkeit. Ein Versuch über den Geist des christlichen Abendlandes* (Zürich: Schweizer Spiegel Verlag, Raben-Reihe, 1988) and *Drachenkampf oder Initiation ins Nuklearzeitalter*, *ibid.* 1989).

gathered by Onians.[12] Okeanos was not limited to his manifestation as a river of water. He was more specifically imagined as a serpent girding the world as a solid belt. We already know this serpent from the Egyptian "World Encircler" cited above from Hornung, who was a serpent, as was the Germanic Midgard serpent which (according to *Gylfaginning* 34) lies in the sea around all countries and bites its own tail. Porphyry comments on a passage from Homer (where mention is made of an assembly of all Gods to which only one God, Okeanos, was not able to come) that Okeanos had to hold things together. Okeanos, thus, does not merely mark the border between world and non-world in a static, geographic sense; he is, rather, an active and dynamic force to be compared perhaps to the iron tire around a wooden wheel of spokes: the girdle binding and holding together that which it surrounds. That is why he cannot leave, having a function on which the existence of the world depends. As late as Seneca, we still hear of the *"vinculum terrarum Oceanus."* That he has the task of holding the earth together helps us to understand that in another culture, in the shamanistic world of Siberia, the archetypal conception corresponding to the world ocean is not experienced in the image of stream and serpent, but as the unshakeable, solid belt of a mountain range (the Altai Mountains).

To be surrounded by Okeanos meant to be bound. And yet, this belt was also dynamic: pure streaming, the stream of events. The connection between streaming and binding in the idea of Okeanos is made by an Orphic association. In an Orphic creation myth, the world egg is generated by a serpent which arose out of water and slime; and this serpent was called Chronos, a word usually translated with 'time.' Okeanos as the world stream, the serpent as bond, and time all belong together in the same archetypal complex of images, as is confirmed by testimonials from other cultures. Thus, the Bantu, e.g., believe "that time is a stream returning into its own source,"[13] and the Egyptians imagined time most of all in the shape of a

---

[12] Richard Broxton Onians, *The Origins of European Thought about the Body, the Mind, the Soul, the World, Time, and Fate,* reprint of the 1951 Cambridge University Press edition, New York: Arno Press, 1973, esp. pp. 249 ff., 316 ff., 411 ff., 443 ff.

[13] *My People, The Incredible Writings of Credo Vusa'mazulu Mutwa* (Harmondsworth: Penguin, 1971), p. 54, quoted from Heino Gehrts, "Initiation," in *GORGO 8*, 1985, p. 11.

[14] See Erik Hornung, "Die Entdeckung des Unbewußten in Altägypten," *GORGO 9*, 1985, p. 63.

serpent.[14] In Greek thought, time and serpent and stream expressly come together once more in the figure of Aion. Aion is, on the one hand, the procreative life-fluid which, as spinal marrow and identified with *psyché*, was likewise envisioned as a serpent (cf. the Kundalini serpent in Indian thinking). On the other hand, Aion was a compelling destiny, a daimon controlling life, from which resulted the meaning of 'lifetime,' 'period of time' ('eon'), and 'eternity.' For Herclitus, Aion is the power controlling the changes of the world. As daimon he is represented as a winged lion-headed, but otherwise human, figure encoiled by a serpent. According to the Orphics, Chronos was mated to Ananke[15] (Necessity), which also lies around the universe, as the Pythagoreans believed.

Time as a circulating stream, therefore, did not originally have the meaning that we connect with the expressions "cyclical idea of history" or "eternal recurrence" in contrast to a linear conception of time. It is not a question of a continuous repetition, but rather of human existence being ontologically imprisoned, as it were, in earthly life as a whole, and in each moment in particular. Whatever passes, whatever the stream of events brings forth, is compelling and inescapable. Ananke nails human existence down to the here and now. Each present is its own Alpha and Omega, just as in ritual cultures the creation of the world was not a one-time event at the beginning of time, but the essential beginning of *each* new time. Here, there is no future into which man can escape from the real present, nor a past to which one can look back as to the good old days, in which everything was supposed to have been better. The serpent as inexorable daimon encoils me and holds me fast in my present. The bond encircling all Being compels me ever deeper into each present reality, it forces me to exhaust this reality in its full intensity. No exit. No escape. Here I can never play a hope for the future against my present real fate, because the serpent of time encloses me hermetically in the experience of this destiny. If this destiny is to have a meaning, then this meaning must be born out of the heart of this very destiny and within the unsurpassable borders set by Necessity; it can be revealed only by my 'stewing' in whatever happens. Never could it lie in a subsequent event, in a future

---

[15] On Ananke see James Hillman, "On the Necessity of Abnormal Psychology—Ananke and Athene," *Eranos 43–1977* (Leiden: Brill, 1974). Expanded version in: *Facing the Gods*, ed. James Hillman (Irving: Spring, 1980).

or a beyond. If each fateful event does not itself unfold its meaning, then there is no meaning at all.

Thus, Okeanos is the image by which man expressly situates himself ontologically in his finite nature, as mortal in contrast to the immortals. The almost ubiquitous archaic idea of a primal stream or serpent girding the world, a serpent mated to Necessity (at least according to Greek thought), was in no way suggested by empirical experience. It arose from a psychological necessity: the necessity to commit oneself unrelentingly to life on this earth as it really was (and not as it might be wished to be). In numerous symbols of daily life— public as well as private—and in corresponding ritual acts, archaic man felt the need to continuously keep in his view his being bound, on the ontological level, by the serpent encircling every here and now. As such symbols, I mention band, tie, cord, ring, girdle, noose, knot, yoke, wreath, crown, woven fabric, spun yarn.

If the poet laureate received a wreath, the victor a crown, band, or belt, this originally did not mean an honour for a past deed; rather, it was to render visible that bond which was inherent in the deed itself and with which the victor had been invisibly crowned all along by fate, through the very performance of his deed. A victory, an accomplishment was experienced as a band put on man by the Gods or by the Fates, and this band was thought of as a portion of time, a period in his life, a fate spun by the Moira.

As was a victory, so also was kingship a band that made him who was bound by it king. We see that in general each event, each action was considered a binding obligation. If this is the case, then I cannot disown a deed I committed, cannot simply dissociate myself from it ("I did not intend to do it," etc.). The real event commits me to it by virtue of its binding reality. I must acknowledge it, bow to it, must perhaps allow it to teach me about my real nature, in order to live in harmony with my reality and necessity.

The diadem with which the king or victor was crowned also helps us to understand the collar put around the neck of a slave, thereby binding him to slavery. There is no essential difference between the band of a king and that of a slave. Both express the inexorable obligation of a fate. In the slaves, ancient man continuously kept the paradigm of the condition of man concretely before his eyes. Slavery was the objective realization as a social institution of what in essence was the ontological nature of man.[16] This also explains the fact that those who had become slaves basically submitted to and accepted their fate, as Tacitus reports in his *Germania*, where he says that the Teutons play dice with such a recklessness that even after having lost everything, they play, in a last decisive throw, for their freedom and life. The loser goes into slavery without antagonism. Even if he be younger, even if he be stronger, he allows himself to be bound and sold. We understand why: throwing dice is not a ridiculous accidental affair; it brings to light what kind of band fate has long put around the person concerned. Factual slavery is merely the external realization of an existing fateful necessity. To rebel against it would be foolish. An especially impressive example of this behavior and this attitude is found in Indian literature: the dice playing of the hero Yudhisthira in the epic *Mahabharata*.

The mandala (which originally was the circle of Times[17]) can be seen in this light, too, as the image of that which binds us unrelentingly into the stream of events. This understanding would remove the belittlement and sugar-coating that Jung's interpretation of the mandala as the representation of the self has acquired with some Jungians within an ideology of "self development" and "growth" and "wholeness." The self could again be understood as the *reign of the inexorable necessity of my nature over myself*, and wholeness or completeness as the *telos*, the compelling band of each fateful portion of time—not *my* wholeness, but the wholeness of each moment.

The word *telos* takes me to another aspect of the encirclement by the Okeanos serpent. The original meaning of *telos* was, according to Onians, not goal, end, act of completion. Rather, it meant the band spun by fate, the band that brings forth the fulfillment of a qualitative portion of time and which has its visible embodiment in the diadem. In the world girt by a solid belt, each event, each time, as well as my life as a whole and the world at large, were *a priori* completed, even if the actual completion had not yet happened and even regardless of whether it was a "positive" or a "negative" event. Each thing, each qualitative moment rested *in itself* and therefore *rested*. The band

---

[16] Concerning the topic of slavery cf. Hillman, *op. cit.* (*Facing the Gods*) p. 6 and note 12 (p. 34).

[17] Heino Gehrts, "Beitrag zur Polytheismus-Diskussion," *GORGO 2/1979*, p. 62, who, on the other hand, emphasizes that the mandala can at the same time *also* represent the opposite, the standing eternity of the mono-God.

around each particular time or thing gave each event a measure and a boundary (*péras*) and caused it to carry its center of gravity, its meaning, in itself.

For this reason alone was it possible that the world could be experienced as being full of Gods and animated by mythical beings. Necessity binding man to each event was the factor that forced the image or face of each reality to the fore. Unconditionally surrendered to and thrown back upon whatever passed, archaic man could not take refuge in "explaining" events from external, i.e., former, causes, nor in hoping for better subsequent events. He had to behold the imaginal depth, the inner essence of each event—the God in it. If Okeanos was unable to come to the assembly of the Gods because he had the task of holding the world together, we now understand that he truly could not come: because his staying where he was was *what made the appearance of the Gods in the world possible in the first place*. As the band girt around the world and holding us inescapably in each event, Okeanos grants that kind of embeddedness in Being and that devotion to each moment for which alone man's being-in-the-world (and the world itself) can be of a mythical, poetical constitution. Okeanos can never appear *in* what only through him *is* 'world,' the (beautifully, perfectly ordered) 'kosmos.' If he appeared as something *in* the world, the assembled Gods would immediately be voided inasmuch as then our glance, released from its bond, would flit from one event to the other and we could no longer experience the divine depth of a single one.

The serpent named Okeanos or Chronos who surrounds us on all sides is the image and the guarantee for the *psychological* existence of man. As Jung has stressed again and again, we are enveloped by psyche on all sides, and it is the nature of psyche to be what surrounds us. This same idea is also found in antiquity. When Pythagoras was asked what the serpent Chronos was, he answered that it was the *psyché* of the universe (Onians).

The Orphic Dionysos had the epithet Lyseus (the 'Looser'), for he was supposed to loosen, for those to be initiated by certain rites, the cord of the 'cares hard to bear.' However, the kind of deliverance brought by Dionysos still remained tied in the mythical world surrounded by the serpent; it was merely an incidental deliverance of each individual initiate, without changing the world at large in its ontological constitution. Total deliverance from the serpent was brought only by Christ. He is the absolute Lyseus who tackles the problem once and for all and fundamentally, for Being as such. "And the God of peace shall bruise Satan under your feet shortly" (Rom. 16:20), Satan, who, as we know, is "the old serpent" (Rev. 20:2). Christ has cut any compelling bond, "blotting out the handwriting of ordinances that was against us ... nailing it to his cross" (Col. 2:14). The beam of the cross even bursts the utmost bond of life as a whole, death: "that through death he might destroy him that had the power of death, that is, the devil; and deliver them who through fear of death were all their lifetime subject to bondage" (Heb. 2:14f.). Christian man essentially is delivered man.

Unless we interpret this Christian event of deliverance again in terms of its Christian understanding, this deliverance must be viewed as a trauma, a wounding of Being. The beam of Golgotha has been driven into the joint where the serpent bites its tail, and thus the compelling bond around Being has been burst. The circle of Father Okeanos was broken apart, the closed circle of Time was straightened out into a line stretching in both directions into infinity. Since then, time is linear *Heilsgeschichte* (the history of the world interpreted as showing forth the workings of God's grace). Now it is possible to speculate with Jaspers about "The Origin and Goal of History" and with Teilhard de Chardin about an evolution from "point Alpha" to "point Omega" and to break out of the compelling ring of each present into the future (hope for the beyond, utopias, Ernst Bloch) or into the past (historicism, restoration, conservation, nostalgia). Now there is an exit, and the idea of a "*Huit clos*" or "No Exit" becomes equivalent to hell (Sartre), which incidentally once more substantiates the truth of the earlier experience, even if only through the hostile medium of the modern longing for freedom from every bond, for hell is nothing but the demonized underworld and thus still reflects the finite nature of man.

Of course, deliverance through Christ was at first still bound to what in Christian terminology is called "faith"; redemption was thus a certain psychic state of man. History shows that the Christian world did not and probably could not rest content with deliverance as a psychic state and thus subject to contingent, empirical factors in the lives of individuals; for faith was always threatened by doubt and indifference. Deliverance, however, had to become an *absolute certainty* and, beyond being a personal experience, also a "cosmic" reality. For "if Christ be not risen, then is our preaching in vain, and your faith is also vain. ... If in this life only we have hope in Christ, we are of all men most miserable" (1 Cor. 15:14, 19). Thus, there was a strong inner pressure from within Christianity itself to transform deliverance from a mere ontic condition of each person into an ontological mode of Being, a mode truly prevailing even if the individual was not personally in the state of faith and firmly founded in it. The Christian truth had to be reified, turned into a "physical" truth. It, the deliverance from every bond, had to be itself liberated from its own being bound by the vicissitudes of time. After the Middle Ages established man firmly in faith as a subjective condition, the soul of Western man was put into a position to also translate the objective nature of the world and of man into the ontological state of deliverance. This has been the task of the early modern age, at the end of which, that is, today, an additional step in the historical development becomes visible: the seeping down of the now ontologized and reified redemption into the personal psyche of the individual. For most of the so-called "psychological problems," most neuroses turning up in the consulting room of the analyst, can in their deeper content be understood as Christianity having withdrawn from the world into the personal psyche: modern psychology as sunken Christianity.

The devout man of the Middle Ages essentially lived in a world that still corresponded to the pre-Christian existence-in-Necessity (which now in Christian parlance might be translated as "sickness unto death," existence in sin) and by no means expressed literal deliverance. The medieval *ordo* was still encircled and held together by a primal ocean. Man still lived devoted to each present, and each individual activity, such as that of the craftsman, carried its meaning in itself. Faith merely had exchanged the former polytheistic Gods for the One God of Christianity, but it had by and large left the ontological state of the world as it had always been.

But how was deliverance from Okeanos, from the uroboric serpent, from Time (Chronos; the Christian *saeculum*) to become an objective ontological reality, if existence had indeed been surrounded by the World Encircler? How could the primal stream enclosing the world be removed? Certainly, through Christ the serpent had long been overcome. But only *for* the psychic condition of *each* believer, whereas the world (including the world of the believer himself) remained held together by Necessity, with the only difference being that this Necessity was now given Christian names such as God's Providence. The task thus still remained to be fulfilled, and it was an enormous task: how could that reality, the very meaning and essence of which it was to be absolutely inescapable because it surrounded human existence on all sides, be removed precisely by him who was encircled by this inescapable force? How could man, as it were, pull himself out of a swamp by his own hair? The stream of events flowing around human existence as such could not truly be gotten rid of, compelling Necessity could not really be removed: it could only be incorporated, *interiorized*. The manifestation of the event of this ontological incorporation of Okeanos by man was Harvey's invention of the circulation of blood. The pulsating stream of life, the ever circling origin of all spontaneity was now located in man himself. He was no longer exposed to Okeanos and the inescapability of Being; he carried them in his body, and only to the extent that he carried them in himself were the head and tail of the serpent coiled around the world torn apart and was the world freed to be absolutely open, without limits and measure.

Thus, in a certain way Illich is right after all in stating that the idea of a stuff circulating in itself had been completely unknown to the ancients. If by stuff one means the visible and tangible, then the water of Okeanos was no stuff. For Okeanos was, as we heard from Kerényi, "not an ordinary stream," that is, not a phenomenon *in* the world like the other streams, not an object of a possible (empirical) perception. Wherever you would go in the visible world, you would never come across Okeanos as a river lying before your eyes, because such going inevitably would take place within the world enclosed by him so that everything that you could come across would *a priori* have been encircled by him. But Okeanos is the outermost border between world and non-world. As such, he has, even as a stuff (water or solid band: serpent, mountain-range), an imaginal nature, and it was only as imaginal stream or rather as the stream of the imaginal that he was the continuous source of all the visible waters in the world. The reason why the invention of the circulation of blood is radically novel is that now circulation is attributed to something *in* the world, an ontic, empirical-factual stuff, which was also the birth of the idea of a "stuff" proper. The circulation of blood is truly "material" because it has its ontological foundation and its truth exclusively in its literal, physical, and manifest existence, whereas for the mythological mind even the visible rivers, indeed all things in the world, were not *merely* physical stuff, since they originated, and thus had their truth in, the stream of the imaginal that was expressly called the "generation of all." Therefore, the inversion of Being that occurred with the shift from Okeanos to the circulating blood also means a fundamental removal of man and the world from the ontological element of the imaginal and their transposition into the medium of ontic, literal materiality.

It seems that the archetypal idea of Okeanos—or whatever name we want to give to the inexorable stream of events—proves to be an inescapable reality even at the time of our deliverance from it. For this deliverance did not really free us from the bond of Okeanos; we might even say that it burdened us with it in a much more oppressing fashion inasmuch as it now is, instead of an imaginal reality, a literal (medical) reality and as it is "stuffed" into the narrow confines of the personal existence of each of us. It is questionable whether the inside of us is a better place than is the outermost border of the earth. If Okeanos is now in us, is this not as if we had swallowed something too big and undigestable? For now we occasionally have to suffer from its compelling force very literally in our own bodies (heart attacks, circulatory collapse, hardening of the arteries, not to mention the purely psychological "problems" that we now have to wrestle with within ourselves—the space contained in the skin—whereas formerly, their equivalents could avail themselves of the wide expanse of the entire mythical world).

The invention of the circulation of blood rendered Christ into an *ontological* reality and thus made the unleashing of Being initiated by Christ definitive. The handwriting written by fate through any event has been blotted out. No matter what a person has done, his deed no longer represents a compelling obligation for him: Christ is the guarantee of the ultimate deliverance from all our actions and fates. Christ is *the* alternative, i.e., the fundamental availability of a (maybe not always empirical, but metaphysical) way out of the binding necessity of what passed. The essential confinement in finite, earthly existence has been lifted, man is no longer a "servant" of and in "bondage" to death as the inexorable border around our lives; he is absolutely "free from the law of sin and death" (Rom. 8:2). This is why Paul does not have to shake the foundations of slavery as a social institution, because this is a trifle compared to the world-shaking metaphysical deliverance he is concerned with. If Paul speaks of man "according to the flesh" and "according to the law of sin," he does not refer, on the ontic level, to obvious evildoers and slovens. He much more radically and comprehensively aims for the ontological state of those whose condition it is to be bound by the inexorable band of each real situation. It is a total attack against man's original embeddedness in Being.

As soon as deliverance ceased being merely a psychological state of man (faith) and turned into an ontological reality, the band around the earth was burst asunder even in the ontological constitution of empirical reality, so that the cosmos opened up into an infinity of worlds (Giordano Bruno), reality became a realm of unlimited possibilities, and all things of this earth were delivered over to man's will without restraint. The things and moments that formerly had firmly been enclosed in their *eachness* (by virtue of which they each carried their own center of gravity and value, in the last analysis, their God, in themselves), were now, ontologically speaking, equalitarian pieces or parts of a homogenous space and a homogenous time.

The mythical, metaphysical reality of the Christ as the absolute deliverer having turned from an object of devotion into man's ontological constitution: this is what made the revolutionary and untamed upsurge of the modern age possible—the starting out of the explorers from Columbus to the astronauts; the spiraling development of the sciences; the limitless urge to go beyond the natural world of things with shape and contour into the boundlessness of the dimensions of astronomical magnitude and micro-physical minuteness; the unleashed longing for the optimal; and the endless craze for stimulation through ever new attractions and through experiences that might provide an answer to the question of the meaning of life. Deliverance from the serpent means the absolute unleashing of desire, of man's reaching out and striving. Only that kind of man whose nature is defined as having interiorized the primal stream from out there into himself does not know himself any longer to be contained in and bound to the world by an inextricable band, and conversely he no longer experiences the world as a binding obligation, but rather as essentially free prey to man's manipulation, indeed as inviting exploration and exploitation. Only man with blood circulation can and must start out in search of new continents or venture into outer space or into the realm of micro-physics. He alone must search for the meaning of life.

At the time at which Okeanos still held the world together, each thing was, as we pointed out, firmly enclosed and man was inescapably bound by each of his actions. This is why people of earlier ages could find fulfillment in kinds of manual work that we would consider intolerably monotonous, such as when African women grind their grains by hand for hours every day, or when in our culture logs were manually sawn into boards, or wool spun into yarn throughout the winter. Fulfillment was possible because these people were, by virtue of the ontological situation, devoted to each activity and did not, could not wish to get out of it, inasmuch as the band of the serpent tied them to and held them in whatever they did. Delivered man can no longer truly dwell in the moment. He must hasten onwards to other moments, to some kind of beyond which alone might give a meaning to a particular present. He needs machines to relieve him of all monotonous work in order for him to be freed for a higher life "in the Spirit" (Rom. 8:9): for planning, grand designs, control—perhaps also for educational and cultural activities, sports, entertainment, encounter groups or other psychological experiences. Paradoxically, even monotonous activities such as spinning or knitting can now be rediscovered—but only as pastimes affirming man's absolute freedom, that is, as the opposite of what they once were: necessary work.

The circle of man's economic intercourse with nature was also broken, that closed circle that according to Marx's analysis consisted in the fact that in earlier agricultural societies the exchange of goods more or less served the sole purpose of providing what was to be consumed, without producing any profit.[18] In the moment when, in the same ages that saw the beginnings of the journeys of discovery, of modern science, and the invention of blood circulation, money turned from a mere means of exchange into self-generating 'capital' in Marx's sense, an explosion happened and the economic growth spiral was set in motion. Since then we have a growth of needs for commodities as well as of industrial production to fill these needs, which ultimately

---

[18] Cf. David Holt, "Jung and Marx: alchemy, Christianity, and the work against nature, " in *Harvest 1975*, p. 50 f.

resulted in the reduction of things to the alienated goods of a throw-away society. Again we must say: Only the man of the blood circulation can be a capitalist.

Through the linear stretching of Time, human existence has been placed into the ontological mode of the comparative (in the linguistic sense): it is now subject to the idea of the 'better,' the more desirable. This idea and its absolute culmination in the idea of the 'best' ('optimal') could alone give rise to optimism and pessimism, which would have been impossible during the time of Ananke, since at that time everything was the way it was, and the flirtation with the idea of the better was *a priori* excluded by the unsurpassable border marked by the primal ocean between Being and Non-Being, reality and possibility. Man lived in the (linguistically speaking) 'positive form,' outside of or prior to any degree of comparison: in his reality, regardless of whether it was, as we today might say, 'positive' or 'negative.' The Teuton, we remember, allowed himself to be sold into slavery without antagonism once he had lost his freedom through dice. Modern man, by contrast, who on account of the circulation in himself is delivered from the binding stream around him, can never rest content in any situation; he must at once demand something better. Leibniz tried to rescue some kind of contentedness within the real world by his labored proof that this world was "the best of all possible worlds" and that we live in "the optimum." But as soon as this proof no longer finds credence, the untamed desire for the better must upsurge and drive the one into the country of unlimited possibilities, the other into revolutionary hopes for a better future and an ideal society, and the third into conservative hopes for a restoration of the good old days or, in the case of the pessimistic variant, into resignation, cynicism, or suicide.

Even though people still buy wedding rings when they marry, man today nevertheless is, even in marriage, essentially delivered man (delivered also from the bond of marriage), i.e., he is *a priori* divorced. As the one who is delivered from the ring of Necessity, the demand for the "optimal" spouse is indispensable to him or her. He or she must always hope to be able to reform the other: marriage as a kind of reformatory for one's spouse. There simply has to be a time—this is the hope out of which the married person lives—when the other will finally come to his or her senses and change for the better, change into the ideal spouse that one has sought in him or her all along. Countless fights arise because one wants to have his or her spouse *better* than he or she actually is. Delivered man cannot rest content with the way his spouse really is, and cannot see that each human being is, as it were, a hopeless case. He cannot admit that marriage means to be inescapably bound to a life with the other person as he or she really is (no exit) and to have the task of getting along with him or her for better or worse; even to come to learn to like his or her faults, to love him or her with all his or her faults. To be essentially 'hopeless': this is the very meaning of marriage. But this is something delivered man cannot by any means accept, because deliverance means to be in thrall to hope. It is an especially striking example of the dissociation in Christian consciousness that the doctrine of the Catholic church insists on the indissolubility of marriage and prohibits divorce without realizing that it is *her own truth*—the deliverance of man—that alone forces many married people onto the road leading to divorce. Christian truth is indivisible. If man in the Christian world is delivered, then this does not apply only to the subjective "Sunday creed," but also objectively to everything in all of life that would represent a compelling obligation.

Only with the invention of blood circulation do inner and outer worlds begin to separate. At the time when man was inescapably encircled by Okeanos, his existence was essentially moored *in* the world and thus he necessarily would look at events occurring in the world from within, with an "inner" perspective, and see them in their imaginal depth: as image and God. It was his embeddedness that made the world (and everything in it) brighten up with a mythical light, for the psychological or poetic nature of the world is nothing but the correlate of man's rootedness in his reality. Mythical imagination is not a psychological property of man, which might or might not be employed; it is an ontological state, a fundamental way man is positioned in the cosmos: being inescapably surrounded by the serpent *psyché*. Circulation of the blood, on the other hand, means that now the border between life and non-life, between the essential and the non-essential falls into the empirical world itself: what is outside of it is the cold, dead "external world," whereas true life is surrounded by it as the "interior," the "inner world." It is thanks to circulation that modern man turned into a "subject" who has the things of this world as his "objects" inevitably outside of and opposite himself. "Inside" and "outside" are split apart only by the *incorporated* border stream of Being; exteriorization or alienation is borne only from the interiorization of Okeanos.

In accordance with our habitual parlance, I have spoken of the subject having the object opposite himself. But actually it is not an opposition that we are dealing with here. As man now has circulation in himself and is no longer moored *in* whatever happens to pass, he is now free totally to surround the phenomena of the world himself. Works of art, e.g., have become "objects" by being placed in a museum showcase so that we can walk around them and view them from all sides, whereas originally they would, as altarpiece, mask, or statue of a God, have "assaulted" man with their demand for devotedness, in which sense they would have surrounded man ontologically on all sides. The things studied by the sciences are "objects" because, having become mute and outlawed, they can be turned and twisted at the scientist's pleasure so that the scientific glance surrounds them completely. Every theory of knowledge has, simply by virtue of the question it asks and not only because it would give a comforting answer, the psychological task of enabling modern man ever newly and in principle to satisfy himself as to his ability to encircle each and every thing. Deliverance from embeddedness in Being is complete only if man himself has become the Thing-and-World-Encircler. And only as the World Encircler is he truly "subject." Thus, the subject is not so much opposite but, much rather, fundamentally *above* whatever he looks at as his object, in just about the same way that the Creator God is above his work, having a complete overview of it and penetrating with his glance into the very heart of things.

Erich Neumann's psychology, too, serves the purpose of once and for all interiorizing what originally was the World Encircler. Neumann turns the uroboros, who once was the very circle of Times, into a mere phase in a person's psychological evolution, a phase that we as adults have long overcome, even if perhaps we should now and then regress to it. Whereas the circle of Times, as the serpent biting its tail, was beginning *and end* in one, it now is only the starting point from which the line of development extends to the stage of the solar consciousness of the hero: the circle is reduced to a point on the straight line and is thus incorporated by the line. Formerly, the beginning was precisely not a point *from* which something started; it was what kept everything that it was the beginning of inexorably encircled and thus *shut in*: Okeanos, the "generation of all." All dynamics and all development of an initiated event remained enclosed by and under the rule of its beginning (that is why the Greek *arché* means "beginning" as well as "rule"): all streams, springs, wells continuously arise from the primal stream surrounding everything. And the heroes of myth (Herakles, Theseus, Siegfried, etc.) as mythological figures perform their deeds *within* the world enclosed by the uroboros, whereas for Neumann heroic consciousness is characterized precisely by having stepped out of the uroboric. Neumann deprives that which would relentlessly encircle us of the inescapability of its encircling us. But as soon as the Okeanos serpent is no longer inescapable and does not enclose us *until the end*; as soon as Okeanos, too, can come to the assembly of the Gods as just one among them because he has become dispensable, the uroboros will have ceased being a uroboros. The instrument for rendering the reigning serpent encircling us powerless is here the idea of development, for it reduces the mythological insight into man's ontological constitution to the idea of one specific ontic condition, correlated to a particular evolutionary phase in the life of empirical man: a fall out of psychology into biology, from the realm of the imaginal into the question of the literal child, the literal mother and the literal evolution from the embryo onwards.

From the perspective of evolutionary thinking, archaic man must appear primitive, which, even if we are expressly assured that this word is not to be understood as a derogatory term, nevertheless does mean as much as "still without ego," "with *undeveloped* ego," "representing an earlier stage." I would like to set another understanding against this view: the primitive as that kind of man who is embedded in Necessity, inexorably devoted to his real present, who has not escaped from Being into deliverance. The temporal interpretation of the primitive in the sense of "early stage" etc. only serves the purpose of rendering the compelling time serpent impotent.

The man of blood circulation is called upon to be a self-contained whole, a "personality," an "individual." The "personality" is nothing but the concrete way man represents himself—to others and before himself—as the "*Grosse Runde*" (Neumann), as a closed circle. We might say that it is to William Harvey (this name taken only as a cipher) that we owe the entire humanistic, educational idealism of a

Herder, Goethe, Schiller, Humboldt, the urge to develop one's personality or one's self, furthermore the need to put into effect the idea that I as individual am an inner infinity and carry the entire world in myself (the World Encircler in psychological guise). We also owe to him the compulsion to be free (freedom of thought, emancipation, liberation, free development of the personality, freedom from work: vacation, weekends, and leisure time). Modern man *must* be free, because only to the extent that he is free in various respects is deliverance from the compelling *telos* of Okeanos made true. Without blood circulation, the idea of the genius would also be unthinkable, for at the times of Okeanos, people *were* not geniuses, but a relentless *daimon* or *genius* dwelled in them as in all of nature.

But modern man, having turned into a personality, is, by virtue of the circle that he himself now is, not only free, but also enclosed in himself and decidedly impenetrable, unaffectable. It is not only through arteriosclerosis that a hardening occurs; modern man is *a priori* hardened on the ontological level, inaccessible to the imaginal depth of events. For the circle is the perfect, the unassailable figure. Nothing can penetrate the armour of the hard circular shell. Monads, as Leibniz rightly stated, have no windows. They are closed, once and for all. This cannot be undone by "sensitivity training," by trying to learn to feel and to be open to emotional experiences. Emotional experiences are precisely what only that kind of man can have who is conceived as holistic personality and thus *a priori* locked into himself. As individuals and subjectivities we are fundamentally, namely ontologically, removed from that existential locus at which we could be reached and affected. Whatever happens to us, however emotionally upset we might be, it is never *more* than an ontic state of emotionality occurring on ontologically armoured man. Only as long as man had his ontological essence in being encircled by relentless Necessity and thus in being embedded in the world could he be reached and struck by the essence of events, because only then was he unconditionally exposed to what happened and as such vulnerable. Just as the world became free prey to man's manipulation as soon as uroboric Okeanos was bent apart, so, conversely, was the inner substance of man *a priori* permeable for the imaginal depth of events and the demands that they made on him, as long as man had not turned into a self-contained, enclosed circle. Reichian therapy of the character armour, too, is of no avail, happening long after the fact and not reaching down to the root of the matter. Indeed, it attempts to fixate the problem by trying to get precisely the *interiorized* Okeanos into renewed and increased flux.

Okeanos was, as we said, pure streaming. Since man no longer is *in* the circulating stream of Time, but carries the stream of life in himself, the pulse of life is now dependent on him, on each individual human being. It is man who now, with his own effort and will-power, has to keep Time moving. He must be its motor, because he now exists as the very circle of Time. Is it astonishing that modern man is plagued by haste and stress, is compelled to perform, must do physical exercises, and prove to himself his youthfulness again and again as long as he lives, until a circulatory failure or heart attack may, after all, put an inexorable end to him, delivered man? Is it astonishing that he who carries the border stream between Being and Non-Being personally in himself is plagued by neuroses—neuroses whose nature it is to be a kind of compromise formation between some compelling and obsessive force and the indispensable striving for freedom from any imposed *telos*, freedom from any fateful obligation binding my nature and life?

CHAPTER THIRTEEN

The Lesson of the Mask

A widespread phenomenon in what one might call "archaic" cultures was the ritualistic dances of dancers wearing masks. Rituals can be understood as the way a people, tribe, or community openly in behavioral acts plays or acts out particular aspects of the inner logic of human existence as such—the logic of being a human being—in order to give this hidden logic an explicit place in their lives and also periodically to consciously affirm and honor it. For humans it is obviously not enough to be *de facto* governed by the inherent logic of their existence, as seems to be sufficient for animals. Humans in addition have to display and articulate what by nature informs their existence. The articulated logic of humanness in its complexity is the "soul" of human existence, and the human "soul," conversely, has to be comprehended as logical life. I speak of logical *life* because the logic of human existence has to be distinguished from what is known under the name of formal and mathematical logic, which are abstract *instruments* of processing thoughts, whereas the logic that psychology is concerned with is the logic of the real. In later stages of consciousness and cultural development, the need to articulate the logic of being persisted, but it took other forms, no longer predominantly that of rituals, but, e.g., of religious doctrines and, later, of classical metaphysics.

All doctrinal statements have become *a priori* suspicious for us as probably being ideological; in any case, as explicit assertions they tend immediately to evoke questions about their truth or illusoriness, inciting us to take a stand pro or contra. Ancient rituals, by contrast, have the advantage that we can look at them as the innocent, unreflected self-display of the soul's logical life, and, *qua* display, as what makes the hidden logic *visible* for us. We merely have to look closely, and see what they show. It is in this spirit that I turn to the phenomenon of the masked dance. In the space of this paper, it is impossible to pay attention to the local particulars and details that distinguish in empirical reality the various dances of different peoples, at different times, and for different festivals. I will confine myself to an analysis of the essential features of a kind of "ideal type" of masked dance.

The dancer, who in everyday civil life is an ordinary member of the community familiar to everyone, first of all puts on a mask, the mask of some spirit, demon, or god. He thus shows himself as being different from himself. The need to wear the mask expresses the implicit notion that he is not exclusively himself, is not confined to and within his own empirical reality and personal identity. He is more. He is also what he is definitely not. Thus, by putting on the mask, the dancer sets himself up as, enacts, and thereby *becomes*, the "psychological difference," the difference between himself as ordinary human (all-too-human) person and his other; between himself as an individual of the species *homo sapiens* and himself as soul, spirit, or divinity. He is both at once; in other words, he is the unity of his identity with himself and his difference from himself.

What is on either side of this difference is fundamentally different. The two sides are not of equal kind and status. The mask is hollow, and as such is meant to be quasi-immaterial. The fact that this hollow object is not in fact totally immaterial is, as it were, no more than a necessary evil. Ultimately, the mask is, is intended to be, mere appearance, image, show effect. It has no full-fledged body, no substance and life of its own. It is a "nothing," a representation of something unreal, merely ideal. All substance and life are on the side of the human being as animal organism. The psychological difference as displayed by the masked dancer is thus also the difference and tension between the real and the ideal.

By wearing the mask the human dancer carries his soul or spirit aspect in front of him. It is "out there," up front, at the surface, totally manifest, for everyone to see. Conversely, as human person, as ego or consciousness, he steps back, disappears behind the mask. The real human being is reduced to the status of an instrument, a mere support for the "unreal" image shown by the mask that is unable to stand on its own. The situation here is contrary to the way modern psychology imagines the relation of the human being and his soul. Here, the physical aspect or empirical reality of man is what is up front, whereas the psyche is thought to be hidden deep inside. The psyche now goes especially under the names of the subconscious, the unconscious, even the repressed. Thus, it is the opposite of what is openly displayed. What we today "display" is thought to be a façade, behind which the true self is hidden, ultimately inaccessible even to ourselves. This is why the psychoanalyst has to be a kind of detective, trying to get behind what for *us* is the mask. For Freud, the manifest is a cover camouflaging the latent. Although Jung did not see things exactly this way, he introduced, with explicit reference to the masks worn by the actors in antiquity, the Latin word *persona* as a psychological term denoting the functional complex that originated from an individual's adaptation to social reality and, comprising a set of habitual attitudes, forms an external personality that in routine situations both facilitates (to some extent almost "automates") his dealings with others and protects his true or innermost personality from having to enter the interaction and to become visible: a complete reversal with respect to the meaning of the mask in ritualistic societies.

There, the mask did not conceal and protect the true identity of the dancer. And the true identity was not what was behind the mask and deep inside the empirical person. The dancer as empirical personality had (to stick to our modern expression) his "true self" precisely in the external mask freely shown to the world, and this is why he had to step behind the mask in the first place, giving *it* priority and himself only serving it and disappearing behind it. The institution of the masks shows that the idea was that the true personality of man could *only* be "out there," in the display. But the fact that the mask showed a spirit or god also indicates that the true self was here not the individual's private self, not he himself, but what he was not. It was a concrete universal, the self of a community (or a group within the community).

The mask is a dead and man-made object. It needs the dance and the dancer's relentlessly giving himself over to it to come alive. The true self here is not a perpetual possession that the person carries within himself as his core. It is not simply there as a given, natural reality. And as spirit or god it is also not an eternal being that demands human devotion. No, it is in itself temporal, a momentary event. It has the character of a project: it has to be brought forth through human activity from time to time, in order to come into being in the first place. How can it be brought forth? Curiously enough, through the act of the empirical person's disappearing behind the mask. To the extent that the human person disappears, the (to begin with unreal) true self, i.e., the spirit or god, can manifest and become real (cf.: "He must increase, but I must decrease," John 3:30).

His disappearing, however, is self-contradictory. The person does not simply go away and be literally gone. On the contrary, as dancer he has to stay intensely present and put himself behind the mask with all his soul passion in order to bring it to life. How then does he nevertheless disappear? He disappears, as it were, "forward" *into* the logos or truth of the mask by dancing himself into ecstasy. Ecstasy is not an *Erlebnis* that he has, not his "high," not his intensely feeling himself. Here the dancer does not let out what had all along been repressed deep down inside. No, ecstacy is the move away from himself as subjectivity and into the "objective" meaning and spirit of the *mask*, a meaning or spirit that as long as the mask was only a dead thing was merely suggested by, and dormant in, it. *Qua* ecstasy, the dancer's disappearance is logical, not physical, also not emotional: it is a transport into another dimension or status, into another non-human personality, that of a demon or god.

Now we can understand how the empirical person's disappearance can be the appearance and coming to life of the god of the mask. Human being and mask exchange their natures, so to speak. By wholeheartedly, *à corps perdu*, giving himself over to the dead mask that he is wearing and logically entering it to the point of disappearing in it (ecstasy), the logos of the mask comes alive in him, in his body, his dancing, and *as* the nature spirit or god that it represents. It is the moment of the dancer's *theosis*. He has *become* the god.

Psychology is full of warnings against inflation by powerful archetypal images or ideas, and full of the fear of psychosis. Why does our dancer, who clearly has identified with the deity, not show any sign of being psychotic or inflated? Because in his dancing he relentlessly releases himself to the logos of the mask. He uncompromisingly, even recklessly towards himself, abandons himself into what he is not. He *does not hold on to his personal identity*. Therefore there *is* nothing and nobody that could become inflated. Indeed, *nothing* is being held back or held on to in this ritualistic dance, not the identity of the dancer, but also not the image of the god with whom he merges. It is all movement, all given over to the flow of time and thus also to its coming-to-be and passing-away. The experience of the god is not protracted beyond its time, so that it would coagulate into, e.g., a dogma of an atemporal godhead. The dance, whose obvious purpose is to bring about the ecstatic identity of the dancer with the deity and thus also the deity's manifest presence for the onlookers, is from the outset heading for its own end. The dancer dances not only into his ecstatic oneness with the god, but also into his own exhaustion, and thereby even into the self-exhaustion of the image and presence of the god as well as of the soul's longing for merging with him. At the end he could truly say, "*tetélestai*" ("It is finished," John 19:30). In the end, the dancer, lying totally exhausted and sweaty on the ground, has obviously returned full-circle to his creatureliness.

So we could say that the ritual dance is the display of the full dialectical logic of human existence *displayed* in the medium of time, of temporal movement. In itself this logic is the (not physical, but logical) movement from animal organism to divinity, from earth to heaven, from empirical reality to ideality *and back*—however the up and down movements here, in contrast to their ritual display there, occur not consecutively, but both simultaneously. As such the dance could also be said to be "psychological difference" comprehended dynamically, as logical *life* or dialectical *movement*.

By ritually acting out the logic of being human in the medium of time and in sensuous experience, archaic societies at the same time opened up for themselves a logical space, an open expanse into which "the soul" could roam and release itself into its other. They paved, and kept open, the routes along which the soul's logical life could move. Thus, they attended, we might say, to the upkeep of a "logical infrastructure" for themselves.

Very far removed from such societies, we today do not have an equivalent for the dance of the masks. Even more, it also seems that there is no open expanse into which "the soul" could release itself, no logical infrastructure publicly established and kept up. We seem to be locked into ourselves. Indeed, the notion of the "personality" *is* the self-enclosure of man, his enclosure in his identity. Today the mask invites us to look not "forward" into its spirit, but behind it, in a search for a hidden *inner* truth. Jung, to be sure, believed he had discovered that the inside is a whole other world of cosmic dimensions, but it is becoming more and more apparent that the openness of this world resembles pretty much that of cyberspace, in other words, the absolute *confinement* (positivization) of the very notion of openness. We are indeed in danger of inflation, because when overcome by archetypal images, *we* have to hold on to our identity. Although there are "mind-expanding" drugs, they lead only to intensive sensations and heightened emotional states in the loneliness of one's private subjectivity, but do not open up the logic of human existence, least of all for a public, for the community as a whole. As "hallucinogenic" drugs, they at best produce hallucinations, not the real presence of a truth. And in contrast to the ancient rituals, the drug experience does not have the moment of (logical) exhaustion that would reward the person with the feeling of a deep and lasting "enough" (satisfaction, fulfillment). It, rather, produces addiction, an endless craving for more and more. In the drug named "ecstasy," even the notion and phenomenon of ecstasy have become positivized, locked into the personality.

Index

A

"actual conflict" 104–106, 116
  theory of neurosis 104n
Adler, Alfred 2, 63, 160, 193
advent 204, 208, 215, 231
  Christian 204
  true 204
Aktualkonflikt 104n
Albert, H. 55
alchemy 36, 53, 144, 167, 169, 216, 222
analysis 9, 42, 55–61, 64, 66, 158, 187
  euhemeristic 54
  interminable 41, 57, 58
  Jungian 158, 224
  personal 186, 187
"Analysis Terminable and Interminable" (Freud) 58
anima 39, 54, 99, 100, 103, 112–115, 145, 148, 149, 183, 217
anima mundi 84
Answer to Job (Jung) 20, 181
anti-Semitism 191, 192, 194
anxiety 109, 115
applicatio 135, 140, 150
archetype(s) 7, 11, 14, 21, 25–35, 37, 46, 47, 54, 55, 62, 77, 78, 90, 91, 105, 122–128, 130–133, 135, 141–144, 148, 149, 152, 154, 177, 187, 218
  doctrine of 122
  father 22

hero 35, 36
  mother 22
  quasi-personal 141
  Self 181, 182
  theory of 11, 63, 90, 122, 123, 126, 132, 142–144, 217, 218
  uroboros 31
Archimedean point 2, 4, 5, 168
Aus der Erfahrung des Denkens (Heidegger) 179
authentic communication 139, 140

B

Barlach, Ernst 20
Baucis 197–202, 205, 206, 208, 209, 216
beauty 143, 145, 201
Berry, Patricia 50
bi-personal field 97n, 100, 101
Black, David 165, 167
blindness 193, 211–214
Bloch, Ernst 213, 244
blood circulation 15, 233–236, 246, 247, 249, 250, 251, 253, 254
Briefe (Jung) 192
Bröcker, Walter 133

C

Carus, Carl Gustav 144
castration 20, 166
  complex 25
  threat 24
Child: Structure and Dynamics of the

Nascent Personality, The (Neumann) 30–31
Christ 179–182, 188, 244, 245, 247, 248
Christianity 56, 57, 108, 204, 221, 223, 230, 245
  secularized 107
circle of Times 242, 252
circulation 233, 234, 236, 246, 250–252
circulation of the blood—*See* blood circulation
Cocks, Geoffrey 192, 194
collective unconscious 21, 29, 36, 54, 77, 78, 112, 128, 141, 144, 164, 165, 220
complex(es) 25, 34, 43, 80, 103, 109
  archetypal 239
  castration 25
  ego 90, 91, 96
  Oedipus 31, 56, 220, 221
  of reality 238
complexio oppositorum 36
coniunctio 62, 113
coniunctio oppositorum 166
consciousness 4, 7, 9, 15, 21, 22, 27, 29, 31–33, 36, 37, 39, 43, 44, 59–62, 64, 66, 72, 73, 80, 84–86, 91, 103, 104, 113, 141, 148, 153, 173–178, 182–185, 189, 193, 215, 220–223, 225, 226, 228–230, 257, 258
  archetypal structure of 104
  Christian 251
  development of 20, 21
  habitual 175
  heroic 253
  higher 175
  history of 21
  human 178
  individual 33
  knowing 177
  masculine 22
  matriarchal 22
  modern 176
  myth of 173
  mythic 176
  natural 175, 176, 229
  objective 230
  origin of 21
  patriarchal 22, 23
  patterns of 21
  personal 65
  positivistic 156
  psychological 9
  revolution of 175, 176
  solar 252
  stages of 22, 27
  structure of 110
  subjective 230
  uroboric 62
cosmogony 89, 176
counter-transference 9, 157, 162
creativity 38, 92, 157
Creuzer, Georg Friedrich 144
culture(s) 22, 24, 25, 64, 173, 187, 195, 228–230, 239, 249
  archaic 257
  primitive 22
  ritualistic 228, 229, 240
  scientific 228, 229
  technological 228

D

de Chardin, Teilhard 244
defense mechanism 49, 51, 60, 72, 155
deliverance 243–245, 247, 248, 251–254
Depth Psychology and a New Ethic (Neumann) 44
Descartes, René 80, 152

dialectic(s) 15, 42, 66, 178, 184
dialectical movement 183, 184, 261
dialectical relationship 139, 182
Dionysos 243
displacement 51, 57
dissociation 5, 47, 48, 60, 62, 79, 251
divine child 28, 140, 145
dream(s) 65, 73, 87, 90, 91, 105, 114, 123, 136, 137, 141, 142, 148, 150
  archetypal 48
  images 73, 90, 93, 105, 138, 141, 142
  interpretation 73, 105
dualism 34, 35

E

ego 15, 35, 37, 38, 46–48, 61, 63, 65, 72, 86, 88, 90, 91, 95, 96, 112, 113, 135, 141, 156, 165, 184, 187, 213, 217, 258
  death of 184
  development 47, 96, 112
  habitual 66
  heroic 35, 48
  historical 38
  stages of 47
  strength 96
ego complex 90, 91, 96
ego functions 112, 184
ego-consciousness 21, 47, 65, 96, 198, 214
ego-functions 47
ego-mentality 48
ego-personality 94, 111, 112, 138, 139, 184, 185
ego-psychology 47, 95, 112, 141, 187
ego-self axis 38, 96
ego-self paradox 35, 65

ego-self unity 37
ego-strengthening 47
Einheitswirklichkeit 33–36, 60
Eliade, Mircea 24, 30
empiricism 23, 51, 64, 104, 127, 143, 150, 186, 224
Enlightenment 69, 70, 84
Entwicklungsgeschichte 20, 29
evolution 23–29, 37, 38

F

fairy tales 75, 77
faith 27, 34, 86, 98–100, 129–131, 148, 194, 198, 244, 245, 248
  personal 228
  psychological 128–133, 148, 193, 194
  unscientific 225
fantasy 31, 32, 36, 38, 44, 45, 66, 72, 75, 76, 80, 90, 98, 105, 126, 133, 135, 147–149, 156, 168, 216, 218
  archetypal 25, 26, 32, 54, 73, 95
  as *prima materia* 99
  delusional 126
  developmental 108
  Ego-Self 35
  empiricist 104
  eschatological 47
  Faust's 214
  figure 217
  Freudian 31
  genetic 37
  geometric 75, 77, 80, 85
  images 79, 98, 217
  infantile 45
  mechanistic/biological 29
  medical 109
  mythic 26, 28, 30
  neurotic 48
  of genesis 27, 29, 36

of nature 99
of phylogeny 26
of physics 98, 99
of unity and opposites 35
root 98–100
science 147
spatial 36
uroboric 31
fascism 191, 192
Faust 62, 91, 197–199, 206–216, 218
Faust II (Goethe) 197, 215
Faust (Goethe)198, 199, 205–207, 216
freedom 242, 244, 249, 250, 254, 255
Freud, Sigmund 2, 24, 26, 30, 31, 38, 41, 43–45, 51, 54–63, 92, 100, 106, 116, 139, 140, 150, 152, 160, 171, 192, 193, 195, 213, 215, 220, 234, 259
Fromm, Erich 145
Future of an Illusion, The (Freud) 51

G

Gadamer, Hans-Georg 135, 136, 139, 143
Gebser, Jean 30
Gehrts, Heino 228
God(s) 28, 29, 37, 45, 71, 91, 98, 100, 166, 178, 202, 204–206, 208, 217, 218, 226, 227, 234, 243–245, 251, 252
  absent 99
  death of 229
Goethe, Johann Wolfgang 36, 75, 197–199, 205, 207, 208, 211–213, 215–217, 254
Goodheart, William 97, 99, 100
Gorgon 91
Götzendämmerung (Nietzsche) 8
Great Mother 23, 28, 38, 39, 115, 145, 174, 217

Grinnell, Robert 132
Grubrich-Simitis, Ilse 192, 194
guest 142, 148, 200–204, 206, 208, 209, 216, 218
  divine 204
  literal 216
  strange 218n
  true 206

H

H$_2$O and the Waters of Forgetfulness (Illich) 233
Harvey, William 15, 233, 234, 236, 238, 246, 253
Hegel, G. W. F. 6, 16, 69, 172, 222, 224, 225
Heidegger, Martin 16, 76n, 93n, 111, 135n, 179, 191, 224
Heilsgeschichte 244
Herclitus 240
hero 21, 22, 47, 48
Hillman, James 7, 11, 23, 31, 57, 58, 94, 97, 104, 181, 220
historian(s) 14, 23, 27, 28, 192, 221
history 13, 14, 20–30, 37, 38, 53, 149, 187, 194, 195, 209n, 221, 222, 226, 228, 233, 244
  collective 221
  cultural 20–24
  cyclical idea of 240
  empirical 21, 25, 27, 30
  intellectual 24
  of consciousness 21
  of ego-consciousness 21
  of the soul 198, 238
  personalistic 25
Homer 133, 235, 239
Hornung, Erik 235, 239
hospitality 197, 199, 201–203, 205, 206, 209, 218
humanness 179, 187, 257

empirical 95n
Husserl, Edmund 227

I

id 45, 61, 113, 213
identity 13, 155, 159, 160, 163–167,
    180
  formal-logical 165
  internal 12
  Jungian 154–158, 160, 163–165,
    170
  of identity and non-identity 169
  of psychology 81, 169
  personal 258, 261
  positive 165
  professional 154
  relation 165–168
  split 159
  style(s) of 156, 157
  true 159, 162–165, 259
identity styles/structures
  apologetic 159
  heretical 157
  missionary 158, 167
  orthodox 157
  polemical 159–160
Illich, Ivan 233, 234, 246
image(s) 15, 28, 31, 35, 45, 72, 75,
    76, 78, 85, 87, 90–93, 95, 96,
    106, 115, 125, 130, 133, 142,
    143, 145–147, 151, 152, 156,
    167, 169, 174, 176, 177, 179,
    180–182, 188, 202, 203, 205,
    207–209, 216, 227, 231, 238,
    239, 241–243, 251, 258, 261
  alchemical 185
  archetypal 21, 25, 32, 33, 43, 54,
    90, 96, 124, 143, 181, 260, 262
  divine 176
  dream 73, 90, 93, 105, 138, 141,
    142

fantasy 79, 98, 217
  inner 78
  lyrical 93
  mental 143
  mythic 31, 32, 181
  mythical 20
  mythological 21, 173, 188
  negative 46
  poetic 85, 95
  positive 46
  primordial 28, 54, 128, 143, 152
  psychic 130, 141, 143
  static 188
  unreal 259
Immersion in the Bath 5, 185, 186
immersion of psychology 6
individuation 37, 56, 65, 79, 91,
    93–96, 103, 107, 112, 113, 122,
    154, 158, 185–187, 217, 224
infinite regress 97, 100
infinity 12, 14–16, 59, 164, 166,
    176, 244, 248
inflation 187, 198, 260, 262
inhospitality 197, 205, 209
initiation 24, 56, 61, 63, 66, 95, 134
inner infinity 164–166, 169, 254
inner space 84, 94
interiority 5, 10, 70, 111, 222, 227
  true 94
interiorization 50, 77, 237, 238, 252
intersubjectivity 151, 161
introspection 15, 60, 61, 63, 66, 77,
    79

J

Jaffé, Aniela 173
Jaspers, Karl 244
Jensen, Adolf 23
Jung, C. G. 5, 13, 19, 20, 28, 31,
    33, 34, 37, 41–47, 49–53, 58–
    60, 62–65, 69, 70, 76, 81, 83–

85, 90, 92–94, 96, 98, 99, 104–
    106, 108–113, 115, 116, 119–
    126, 128–152, 154–160, 164–
    167, 169–170, 171–182, 184–
    186, 188, 189, 191–195, 198,
    216–218, 220, 222–226, 230,
    242, 243, 259, 262
Jupiter 200, 201

K

Kant, Immanuel 64, 69, 100, 120,
    153, 185
Kerényi, Carl 235, 246
Kraus, Karl 44

L

Law of Contradiction 35
Leibniz, Gottfried Wilhelm 250, 254
libido 2, 34, 36
literalism 75, 194
    psychological 89
logic 6n, 184–186, 189, 224, 228–
    230, 257, 261, 262
    dialectical 261
    epistemological 99
    formal 6n, 163, 166
    Hegel's 224n
    hidden 257, 258
    mathematical 257
    objective 227
    of the real 257
    of the soul 187
    uroboric 3, 6, 7, 9, 15
logical life 13, 16, 257, 258, 261
logical movement 16, 184, 185, 189
love 145, 164, 181, 202, 203, 205,
    218n
    erotic 181
    sensuous 181

M

mandala 32, 92, 125, 140, 188, 242
Mann, Thomas 29
Mann, Ulrich 15
Marx, Karl 26, 207n, 223, 249
Mattoon, Mary Ann 193
meaning 175, 176, 177
    divine 177
    Jung's idea of 175
mediation 9, 65, 66
Memories, Dreams, Reflections
    (Jung) 198
Menschheit in der Person 185, 187
Mensching, Gustav 23
Mercury 200, 201
Metamorphoses (Ovid) 199
metaphysics 74, 257
Miller, David 166, 237
mirroring 64, 81, 207
modernism 215, 221
monism 34, 36
movement 80, 82, 88, 89, 93, 94
    backward 82
    derived 93, 94
    dynamic 87
    inner 88
    internal 80, 93
    of psychology 93
    of the soul 83
    ontic/literalistic 89
    ontological/psychological 89, 93
    original 93
    projective 79
    psychological 93, 95
    static 87
    throwing 87, 88
mundus imaginalis 29, 36
mysterium coniunctionis 9, 33, 140
myth(s) 13, 20, 21, 22, 25–29, 31,
    35, 38, 90, 96, 141, 172–175,
    177, 179, 201, 203, 253

Christian 172, 205
cosmogonic 176
creation 20, 22, 26
Great Mother/Hero 28, 38, 39
hero 20, 26, 35, 36
involuntary 26
loss of 173, 175, 179
of consciousness 173
of genesis 27
of meaning 173
Philemon 205, 215
stages of 21
sublated 172
transformation 21, 22
transpersonal 30
mythology 15, 21, 31, 53, 54, 111,
    141, 167, 171, 173, 176, 177,
    189, 197, 208, 222
Greek 123
Indian 237

N

Nachsommer (Indian Summer)
    (Stifter) 93
nature 38, 98–101, 179, 249, 254
necessity 99, 240–243, 246, 247,
    253, 254
existence in 245
psychological 241
ring of 250
negation 206, 209, 225
of the negative 44–51
negativity 13, 16
neo-Platonism 143, 144, 215
Neue Sachlichkeit (New Objectiv-
    ity) 86
Neumann, Erich 8–9, 16, 19–25,
    27, 29–31, 33–39, 44, 92, 106,
    113, 252, 253
neurosis 9, 43, 44, 46, 47, 51, 52,
    55–58, 60, 62, 66, 101, 104,

105, 109, 173, 220, 245, 255
Nibelungenlied 82
Nietzsche, Friedrich 8, 66, 96, 125,
    163, 223, 224, 226
nihilism 225, 226, 229, 231
non-ego 112, 166
non-identity 163, 167, 169, 170
nostalgia 228, 244
not-self 182, 189

O

objective psyche 61, 79, 141, 157,
    165, 169, 238
objectivity 79, 84, 127, 141, 169,
    217
psychological 217
scientific 52
Oedipus complex 31, 56, 220, 221
Oedipus myth 20, 116
Okeanos 15, 32, 235–239, 241–247,
    249, 251–255
Old Wise Man 28, 113, 145, 188,
    217
"On Reduction" (Berry) 50
"On the Nature of the Psyche"
    (Jung) 2
Onians, Richard Broxton 239, 242,
    243
ontogeny 24, 30, 32
ontology 13, 35, 36, 39, 97, 99, 144,
    217, 218
opposite(s) 9, 10, 13, 33–36, 75,
    163, 180, 182, 184
deadlock of 66
fantasy of 35
mutual exclusion of 35
principle of 34
problem of 34, 36
psychic 9, 16, 180, 185
reconciliation of 163
tension of 34

undialectical 14, 225
union of 12, 13, 179, 180, 182–184, 187–189
union of separation and union of 16
unity of 9
unity of unity and opposition of 183, 184
Origins and History of Consciousness, The (Neumann) 20, 24, 25, 30
Other 13, 182, 183, 215
Otto, Rudolf 23
Ovid 199, 215, 217

P

Paracelsus 88
pathology 11, 43, 45, 66, 116, 136, 138, 148—*See also* psychopathology
personal equation 2, 86, 116, 154–158, 160, 163
personalism 51–55
personality 29, 49, 50, 58, 61, 73, 85, 94, 95n, 112, 114, 140, 141, 149, 154, 160, 186, 193, 253, 254, 259, 262
    and soul 186
    cult 165
    empirical 55, 166, 259
    external 259
    holistic 254
    human 141
    mana 187
    total 153, 215
    true 259
    unconscious 214
personification 114, 115, 156, 181
Philemon 197–209, 214–218
philosopher's stone 157, 167
phylogeny 21, 24–27, 32, 37
physics 2, 41, 74–76, 78–81, 83, 85–

90, 95, 98–101, 114, 120, 131, 136, 153, 168, 169, 221, 249
    classical 81n
    mathematical 98
    nuclear 81n
Plato 30, 145, 148, 234, 236
Platonic Form(s) 124, 167
Platonic school 124
Platonism 143, 221, 224
Plotinus 208
Portmann, Adolf 27, 28, 32
positivism 4, 209
positivity 6, 7, 10, 12, 156, 166, 170
prima materia 10, 32, 99, 100—*See also* prime matter
primal horde 24, 30, 32, 38
primal scream 48, 49, 61, 112
primal stream 235, 237, 238, 241, 245, 248, 253
prime matter 126, 150—*See also prima materia*
projection(s) 10, 26, 51, 60, 70–73, 77–79, 81–86, 89, 91, 96, 180, 181, 182
    negative 72
    positive 72
psyche 3, 5, 33, 34, 43, 48, 51, 52, 57, 59, 62, 72–74, 80, 83, 85, 100, 101, 161, 169, 221, 222, 259
    autonomous 97, 99–101
    autonomy of 10
    objective 220
    personal 245
    transpersonal 65
psychic content 73, 181
psychic energy 149
psychoanalysis 30, 31, 34, 43–45, 54, 116, 159, 195, 213, 220, 221, 224

psychological difference 11, 87, 91, 95, 111, 112, 114, 115, 117, 141, 258, 261
psychological equation 154, 235
Psychological Types (Jung) 1
psychology 3–6, 9, 10, 12–16, 22, 23, 27, 31, 32, 35, 39, 41, 43–53, 55–67, 69, 70–84, 86–96, 97, 99–101, 103–105, 108–114, 116, 121, 122, 133, 134, 136, 137, 146–149, 152, 161–163, 167–169, 173, 179, 183, 184, 186, 219–225, 229, 230, 253, 257, 260
    academic 30
    analytical 1, 19, 34, 39, 54, 56, 64, 77, 104, 112, 120, 220
    archetypal 1, 7, 11, 25, 29, 30, 31, 39, 104, 105, 220
    as theory 88
    autonomy of 63
    classical 63
    complex 1
    conventional 77, 82, 89, 94, 95, 111
    critical 1, 7, 8, 9, 13, 58, 59
    depth 41, 44, 45, 46, 48, 59, 62, 87, 115, 152, 193, 220
    ego—*See* ego-psychology
    ego-self-axis 39
    empirical 52, 114, 119
    empiricism of 51
    Germanic 192
    humanistic 111
    implicit 230
    Inner Space of 84, 94
    isolated 52
    Jungian 3, 7, 34, 111, 115, 116, 119–121, 124, 132n, 143–150, 152, 155, 156, 158–160, 165, 167, 170

    medical 46, 57
    modern 1, 245, 259
    Neumann's 16, 35
    objective 57, 113, 137–141, 145
    of blame 97
    of development 31
    of Jung's personality 149
    of the Self 178, 183, 185
    origin of 70, 83, 96
    originary 83
    personalistic 7, 15, 54, 56, 62, 114, 115, 137–141, 162, 186, 220
    physicalized 74n
    political 193
    psychological 87
    real 81, 88, 89, 114, 166
    scientific 52
    Self 187, 188
    spirit of 91
    standard 162
    sublated scientific 3
    theoretical 49, 141
    therapeutic 44, 57, 221
    transcendental-dialectical 64
    transpersonal 113
    true 9, 66, 93, 115, 169, 170
psychopathology 46, 109, 116, 133–137—*See also* pathology
psychotherapy 42, 43, 45, 48, 49, 56–59, 61, 62, 66, 75, 77, 78, 106, 110, 114, 134, 137, 139, 153, 194, 224
    medical 69
    personalistic 61, 141
puer aeternus 145
Pythagoras 243

R

Radin, Paul 23
reality 6, 52, 54, 73, 78, 79, 85, 86,

91, 95, 108, 109, 113, 115, 116,
    129, 131, 134, 135, 144, 147,
    148, 152, 177, 184, 198, 200,
    201, 206, 229, 238, 240, 241,
    243, 246–248, 250, 251
archetypal 181
autonomous 78, 98, 100, 101
binding 241
cosmic 237, 245
distortion of 78, 85, 86
dominant 185
earthly 201
empirical 25, 31, 37, 39, 180, 187,
    248, 258, 259, 261
essential 133
everyday 201
external 85
factual 32, 33
Faustian 207
full 47
imaginal 247
independent 43, 133
inner 79
intellectual 224
literal 33, 247
logically higher 172
metaphysical 248
natural 260
negated 172
numinous 130
objective 5, 200, 217, 227, 245
objective psychic 140
of dreamer 114
of the psyche 217
of the soul 141, 198, 217
ontological 245, 247, 248
ordinary 184
outer 80
phenomenal 174
physical 73, 79, 198, 227
practical 180

present 11, 94, 240
psychic 56, 79, 83, 130, 132–134,
    140–142, 145, 181
psychological 2, 7, 78, 132n, 136,
    137, 148, 149, 184, 198
quasi-empirical 227
real 79
reflected 6
scientific view of 85
social 259
soul as a 114
subjective 162
sublated 172
ultimate 186
worldly 201
reality principle 78, 85
reductionism 51–55
regression 45
religion(s) 14, 15, 23, 24, 56, 95,
    108, 121, 132, 195, 219, 220,
    223–231
    death of 226
    factual 108
    Greek 181
    high 228
    intolerant 108
    literal 228
    redemptive 56, 57
    sublated 15, 225
repression 45, 47, 58, 59, 66, 109
res cogitans 80
res extensa 80
ritual cultures 240
ritual(s) 56, 59, 85, 177, 189, 218,
    241, 257, 258, 261, 262
Rorschach test 156, 167–169
rupture 14, 226, 227, 229

S

Sartre, Jean Paul 244
Schelling, Friedrich Wilhelm

Joseph 144
Schiller, Friedrich 35, 36, 140, 254
Schlegel, Leonhard 34
science(s) 3, 24, 26, 28, 56, 59, 65,
    70, 74, 78, 80, 87, 90, 98–100,
    136, 146n, 147, 153, 160, 161,
    167–169, 220–225, 230, 248,
    252
    anthropological 221
    empirical 11, 29, 120, 146–150,
    160
    human 220, 224
    modern 98
    natural 2, 3, 22, 115, 119, 120,
    121, 125, 136, 144, 147, 152,
    225
    sublated 3, 15, 225
sciences
    human 225
scientific method 99
Sedlmayr, Hans 38
self-definition 161, 185
self-identity 164, 165
self-reflection 3–6, 9, 65
Self/self 12, 13, 35, 37, 38, 65, 66,
    95, 165, 171, 172, 177–189
    alien 66
    true 259, 260
Seneca 239
serpent 236–246, 248, 249, 253
    Kundalini 82
    Midgard 239
    uroboric 245
shadow 45, 47, 51, 69, 73, 84, 145,
    148, 183
shamanism 22, 228, 229
Socrates 50
solar penis/phallus 122, 125, 127–
    135, 137–139, 142, 148, 151
soul 3, 6, 10, 13, 26, 32, 38, 39, 43,
    51, 52, 64–66, 73, 74, 76–78,
    81–86, 90, 92, 96, 100, 104,
    109–111, 114, 115, 130, 133–
    135, 138, 141, 142, 145, 148,
    151, 156, 166, 181, 184, 186,
    187, 194, 198, 217, 234, 238,
    245, 257–259, 261
    and personality 186
    autonomy of 111
    autonomy of the 117
    loss of 111, 161
    reality of the 115
    self-reflective character of 6
    theory of 90
soul-making 7, 62, 67, 136, 161
Spinoza 98
Stifter, Adalbert 93
subjectivity 52, 60, 61, 138, 141,
    160, 169, 174, 176, 182, 189,
    260, 262
    objective 61
sublation 176
    dialectical 225
Successful Repression, The 56

T

Tacitus 242
theory 3, 4, 6, 9, 24, 31, 32, 43–45,
    47–49, 54–56, 58, 59, 61, 66,
    70, 78, 82, 87, 88–90, 92, 104,
    108, 116, 122, 134, 144, 146–
    148, 161, 162, 218, 222, 224,
    238
    dead 84
    empiricist 146
    genesis as 27
    genetic 36, 37
    impersonal 56
    Jungian 46, 166
    libido 34
    of archetypes 11, 122, 123, 126,
    132, 142–144, 217, 218

of knowledge 252
of psychology 9
of science 144, 146
of the collective unconscious 220
of the Self 171, 179
of the soul 90
psychological 5, 44, 45, 49, 59, 60,
    96, 107, 141, 217, 218
psychology as 9, 137
scientific 12, 75, 120, 132, 144
therapy 43, 48, 55–58, 60, 63, 64,
    73, 88, 107, 113, 138–141, 166,
    221
and theory 60, 66, 70, 137, 161
and transference 161, 162
dialectic understanding of 42
group 42, 49
individual 42
of neurosis 173
of psychology 57
practical 141
primal scream 112
Reichian 254
third person in 42
Three Faces of God (Miller) 166
time 234, 239–245, 248, 250, 255,
    261
time serpent 253
transcendence 8, 16
transference 9, 42, 49, 55–57, 60, 62,
    64, 81n, 97n, 161–164
transference neurosis 55, 62
trinity 125, 166, 188
truth 28, 86, 127, 138, 145, 226,
    227, 230
absolute 27, 86
empirical 28
psychological 28, 133, 145
scientific 28
Tylor, Edward B. 23

U

unconscious 1, 36, 52, 65, 70, 72,
    73, 78, 96, 150, 155, 156, 164,
    166, 169, 221, 235, 259
Aryan vs. Jewish 192
creative 92
Jung's confrontation with 137
personal 112
private 112
prophet of 120, 121
unconsciousness 21, 39, 43, 59
mutual 42
underworld 111, 152, 165, 236,
    244
unity 35
unus mundus 33, 92
uroboros 22, 31, 32, 60, 62, 63,
    252, 253
Ursprung und Gegenwart (Gebser)
    30
Ursprung/Ur-Sprung 83, 89, 96
Ursprungsgeschichte 21, 24, 26, 27,
    30, 35, 37
Usener, Hermann Carl 202
utopia 85, 204, 212, 214, 244
concrete 213

V

Virgil 152
Voltaire 223
von Flüe, Niklas 147
von Franz, Marie-Louise 33

W

water 233, 246
Weltanschauung 36, 43, 74n, 215,
    225
Weltbesitz 209
wholeness 48–53, 60, 65, 78, 91,
    92, 113, 242

Wind, Edgar 53, 59
World Encircler 235, 239, 245, 252, 254
world parents, separation of 25, 35, 174

Z

Zarathustra 163, 164, 166
Zeno's Paradox 80